SIR JOHN BRUNNER, RADICAL PLUTOCRAT
1842–1919

CONFERENCE ON BRITISH STUDIES
BIOGRAPHICAL SERIES

Editor: PETER STANSKY
Consultant Editor: G. R. ELTON

Sir John Brunner by Augustus John, 1906

SIR JOHN BRUNNER
RADICAL PLUTOCRAT
1842–1919

STEPHEN E. KOSS
Barnard College, Columbia University

CAMBRIDGE
AT THE UNIVERSITY PRESS
1970

Published by the Syndics of the Cambridge University Press
Bentley House, 200 Euston Road, London N.W.1
American Branch: 32 East 57th Street, New York, N.Y.10022

Standard Book Number: 521 07906 3

Printed in Great Britain
at the University Printing House, Cambridge
(Brooke Crutchley, University Printer)

TO MY PARENTS

CONTENTS

PLATES

PREFACE

One may feel justly confident that Sir John Brunner would have been the last to mind the neglect his memory has suffered. Even at his most self-conscious, he was concerned not with posterity but with principles. Content to march behind others in the nineteenth-century army of progress, he sought neither office to increase his personal authority nor honors to immortalize his name. The popularity he enjoyed among the electors of Cheshire's Northwich division was most gratifying in that it gave him for twenty-five years a seat in Parliament, where he might strive to accomplish good. The wealth he attained as co-founder of Brunner, Mond and Company, which soon established itself as one of the world's leading producers of alkali, afforded him the means to promote the causes in which he believed. His ambition, to improve the world in which he lived before he left it to claim his reward in the next, perhaps makes him a difficult figure for the modern reader to comprehend; but it is an ambition that makes him all the more representative of the age to which he belonged and, therefore, all the more worthy of historical study.

The extent to which the concept and content of politics has changed since Brunner's day can be measured by the fact that a man regarded as the devil incarnate by many of his contemporaries should today run the risk of appearing the subject of hagiography. The propertied gentlemen upon whom he intruded in Cheshire society thought him a rude upstart, his Radical doctrines pernicious, and his chemical works a public nuisance. Those who sat across from him in the House of Commons—indeed, the more whiggish of his own colleagues—thought him too defiant of established interests, too eager to flout political conventions, and insensitive to the duties and glories of empire. In later years the more irrational of his opponents accused him of seeking private commercial gain at the expense of national prosperity and security, and there were even those who alleged that he had stealthily purchased control of the Liberal Party with a view to scrapping the British navy. Never one to suffer gladly either fools or Tories—the two were not to be confused, for Tories had a method to their madness—Brunner invited the abuse that his enemies obligingly showered upon him. In the face of presumption, he was insolent; in the face of privilege or monopoly, intemperate. That, after all, was the hallmark of the earnest Radical and the prerogative of the self-righteous. Although it might occasionally appear otherwise, he did not engage in conflict for the sake of conflict, and was never happier than when class and party differences were subordinated to moral considerations. He lived, however, at a time when partisan emotions ran high, and he responded accordingly. His constituents, many of them his employees, applauded him as much for his pugnacity as for his paternalism. Even among family and friends, he was affectionately known to practice an authoritarianism which, however benign, was as impossible to challenge as the dictionary with which he armed himself in after-dinner conversation. To be sure, his fiery temperament did not preclude a boisterous humor, nor his impatience many gentle kindnesses. That he should, however, appear in retrospect almost a saintly creature is as much a commentary upon our times as upon his own.

Brunner was among the last of a breed which by its faith, industry, and concern for justice had done much to create the texture of Victorian society. At any given moment, he could be depended upon to champion the most advanced cause, regardless of the cost to himself, his company, or his party. But his Radical politics, like his Unitarianism, lost its dynamism and much of its wider relevance with the passing decades. Reaching a climax in his prewar campaign for naval disarmament and improved Anglo-German relations, his experiences reflected increasingly the weakening of the tradition he embodied, the frustration— one might say the futility—of the independent backbencher, and, not least of all, the problems that brought his party to ruin.

There are certain lesser known historical figures—of whom Brunner, I believe, is one—who offer new perspective upon the issues and events of their lifetimes. Such biographical subjects pose special problems of research, which could not have been overcome in the present case without the cooperation of Sir

Felix Brunner. In addition to placing his family papers at my disposal, Sir Felix provided comments and suggestions that saved me from committing numerous errors of fact. All the while, he respected my right to exercise independent critical judgment. Although I do not presume that he will agree with all of my conclusions, I am confident that he will welcome the spirit in which they are made. I am also deeply indebted to another of Sir John's grandsons, Mr J. B. Gold, who resourcefully ferreted out information, introduced me to several of his cousins, and proved a delightful guide to his family history. Mr Hugo Brunner, a great-grandson, gave me the encouragement of his valued friendship and the benefit of his editorial experience.

Professor Robert K. Webb of Columbia University added to the immeasurable debt of gratitude I owe him by criticizing each chapter, often more than once, and by allowing me to draw freely upon the lectures on English Unitarianism that he delivered at the Victorian Studies Centre of the University of Leicester in 1967. Since my student days, I have never ceased to marvel at the vigilant eye that he brings to bear upon a manuscript. Nor have I ever ceased to appreciate the influence he has exerted upon me as a teacher and writer of history.

Mr W. J. Reader lightened my task by providing me with copies of draft chapters from his forthcoming history of Imperial Chemical Industries. With Miss Elspeth Jervie, his knowledgeable research assistant, he did his best to help me master the commercial arrangements and technical processes in which Brunner was engaged. I am grateful to both of them for reviewing the manuscript, which, I hope, proved a useful complement to their own research.

Others, too, gave generously of their assistance. Professor Peter Stansky of Stanford University, a most thoughtful editor, offered stimulating criticism that helped me to focus my ideas. Mr D. G. O. Ayerst kindly gave me a glimpse of the material from which he is fashioning his eagerly awaited history of the *Manchester Guardian.* Dr Peter Clarke of University College, London, supplied me with references from his exhaustive research into Liberal Party organization in the north-west. Mr

Neville Stanton allowed me to consult the records of the Lanca-shire, Cheshire, and Northwestern Liberal Federation. Mr Wynne Jones, assistant manager of the *Chester Chronicle*, opened archives to me. Mr Geoffrey Moore, editor of the *Northwich Chronicle*, extended courtesies that made my brief visit to Northwich and Winnington a memorable one, and introduced me to Mr A. S. Irvine of the Mond Division, ICI, who has been a fund of infor-mation. Among the many librarians upon whom I relied I must make special mention of Miss D. Tindall of the Reform Club, Mr G. Awdry of the National Liberal Club, and Mr M. R. Per-kin, curator of special collections at the university library, Liver-pool. I have enumerated in my bibliography those institutions and individuals who gave me the privilege of access to private papers in their possession; those who permitted me to quote un-published materials for which they own copyright have received my private thanks.

I enjoyed an interview with Mrs Hilda Ransom, who, in 1914, became the last of Sir John's private secretaries and the first woman to serve in that capacity. Although members of the family warned her to beware his temper, she retains many fond memories, which she graciously shared with me.

The Augustus John portrait, presented in 1906 to the Univer-sity Club, Liverpool, by Sir John's fellow members, is reproduced by arrangement with the Club. Like so many of John's subjects, Brunner was not flattered by his likeness, which, he protested, made him appear too full in the waistcoat. But, more than any of the other portraits of him that survive, it captures the intense gaze that invariably impressed those who watched him in debate. Other plates in the book were provided by the Brunner family and by the Information Services Department of Mond Division, ICI Ltd.

Acknowledgment is also due, and gladly made, to the American Philosophical Society for assisting my research with a grant from its Penrose Fund.

Lastly, I must thank my wife, who miraculously found time from family routines to prepare the manuscript for publication, and for whom no published words of gratitude could possibly be adequate.   STEPHEN E. KOSS

CHAPTER I

A NONCONFORMIST YOUTH[1]

Sir John Tomlinson Brunner, who left his mark not only on the landscape but also on the folklore of Cheshire, merits no less prominent a place in the economic and political history of the British nation. Others might be more readily identified with the history of the Liberal Party, but few better personified the sources of its impetus and inspiration. Industrial magnate, politician, philanthropist, he was the very stuff of Liberalism, which was for him more an ethic than a party allegiance. His business career, among the most remarkable of his time, was distinguished by the consistent application of Liberal principles, as he understood them, to problems of labor and commerce. His parliamentary career, which spanned the years from the party's split over Home Rule in 1886 to its ultimate fissure under the impact of the first world war, keenly reflected the shifting content of Liberalism, its achievements and frustrations.

When Brunner died in 1919, H. W. Massingham paid tribute to him in the *Nation* as 'one of the Conscript Fathers of Liberalism', who, before the outbreak of war, had 'aimed at being, and in some degree was, a leader of its medium thought'.[2] His Liberalism, observed a correspondent for the *Manchester Guardian*, was 'expansive, courageous, militant against evil, and eager for experiment and action'.[3] Lord Bryce, an ally in countless battles, wrote that his friend's 'uprightness, his candour, his geniality and his unfailing public spirit inspired confidence in all who knew him'. He could think of no one who 'was more popular in the

---

[1] Material for this chapter has been drawn, except where otherwise indicated, from the following sources, all among the Brunner Papers: a set of brief autobiographical memoranda that Sir John dictated late in life; a series of letterbooks into which he or his secretaries pressed his correspondence; and a typescript of his inaugural address at the University of Liverpool, written in 1909 and from all indications never delivered. The letterbooks pose a particular problem, for the addressees are often as obscure as the penmanship for the early years. I have therefore identified in footnotes to this chapter only printed sources, letters to and from well-known individuals, and items from other manuscript collections.

[2] July 5, 1919.   [3] July 2, 1919.

House of Commons on both sides, for though he was a "good party man," he never allowed partisanship to lead him into acrimony or ill will'.[1] But by far the best testimonial to the quality of Brunner's Liberalism came during his lifetime from the thousands of men at Brunner, Mond and Company, who recognized the confluence of their interests and his—what one historian has designated the 'political mutualism' that often emerged in such situations[2]—and accordingly gave him their enthusiastic support in his successive electoral campaigns. They knew him as a progressive employer who helped to pioneer the eight-hour day, ungrudgingly assumed responsibility for workmen's compensation, devised schemes for paid holidays and baby bonuses and, in short, achieved in his firm's relations between capital and labor the harmony for which he strove with equal ardor but less success in international affairs.

In politics and business, Brunner waged a double-edged crusade against poverty and privilege. His two careers cannot be compartmentalized, for each drew sustenance from the other, and both were governed by the same Liberal maxims of peace, retrenchment and reform. His Liberalism was completely spontaneous, a product of upbringing as much as enlightened self-interest. Service in Parliament exposed him to new currents of thought that helped to make him a more liberal employer; and his parliamentary Liberalism was, in turn, enriched by his experience as an entrepreneur. His interest in such causes as temperance and educational reform was fostered by a desire to make his countrymen more responsible as citizens, more productive as workers, and more virtuous as human beings. His efforts to promote disarmament and international cooperation were inspired no less by his nonconformist idealism than by his disdain, as a businessman, for wasteful expenditure.

When he was first elected to Parliament in 1885, *The Times* (to his unending delight) dubbed him the 'Chemical Croesus'. He revelled in his immense wealth, grateful for the opportunities for

[1] Bryce to J. F. L. Brunner, July 28, 1919, Brunner Papers (hereafter BP).
[2] J. Bartlet Brebner, 'Laissez Faire and State Intervention in Nineteenth-Century Britain', in R. L. Schuyler and H. Ausubel, eds., *The Making of English History* (New York, 1966), p. 508.

2

leadership and public service that it opened to him. 'Gentlemen, I am a rich man,' he remarked to the Northwich Liberals whose endorsement he sought for his first candidacy, 'and it is possibly because I am a rich man that I am standing here. Otherwise I would not be here, being a man with nine children.'[1] In an age when elected office carried no salary, his success as co-founder of the largest British alkali works gave him ample means to undertake a political career; certainly it permitted him to be a generous patron of party projects. In his quarter century in the Commons, not only his wealth but also the force of his personality won for him an influence in party councils that far exceeded his reputation. Adding to his stature was the high esteem in which he was held by scores of Liberal backbenchers who shared his background and convictions, and among whom he became in time an elder statesman. J. A. Spender, the veteran Liberal journalist, ranked him 'as one of the *viri pietate graves* who stand aloof from office but have a great influence over private members and are always consulted by their leaders when parliamentary weather is unsettled'. 'When Brunner shook his head,' Spender declared, 'the Whips began to run about and it was recognized that the leaders were in danger of touching, perhaps unconsciously and unintentionally, one of the sensitive nerve centres that are just below the surface in the Liberal physiology.'[2] In private as well as public life, Brunner was the quintessence of the nonconformist Radical, a mainstay of the nineteenth-century Liberal order whose gradual decline deprived Liberalism of a large measure of its social relevance and popular appeal.

Like many prominent Liberals of his generation he was of alien extraction, though not himself an alien. Like countless others he was a self-made man, intensely proud of the fact, whose roots were in the industrial north. His father, after whom he was named, came to England from Switzerland in 1832 to join Dr Carl Voelker, a fellow Swiss, who kept a school at Everton, then a prosperous suburb of Liverpool. The eldest of six children, he had been intended by John's grandfather, a dyer by trade, to enter

[1] Speech at Leftwich, April 11, 1885, *Northwich and Winsford Chronicle*, April 18, 1885.
[2] J. A. Spender, *Sir Robert Hudson, A Memoir* (London, 1930), pp. 123–4.

the Lutheran ministry. Probably he had all along doubted his call, for in 1826, on a passport application, he described himself as '*un homme de lettres*'. After years of preparation, he found himself unable to take ordination and, acutely aware of his father's disappointment, left his homeland and renounced his patrimony. Soon after his arrival in England he became a Unitarian, which allowed him to reconcile his theological uncertainties with a strict Christian piety. The foremost figures in Unitarian thought and society prided themselves on advanced pedagogical views and emphasized the value of catechetical instruction to the young. Though Brunner never had a congregation, he was known to his students and neighbors as the Reverend, probably because it was common in his day for Unitarian schoolmasters to be ministers who ran schools in order to disseminate ideas as well as to supplement their meager incomes.

In 1835 the first John Brunner terminated his informal partnership with Voelker and, at thirty-five years of age, began his own school and family. He married Margaret Catherine Curphey, born in 1814 at Ballydroma on the Isle of Man, and moved to a large, old-fashioned building in Netherfield Road, Everton, known as St George's House. 'It is my house,' John Brunner could recall his father remonstrating proudly, 'not St George's.' There he founded a school that he maintained until his retirement in 1863, and there John, his parents' fourth child and second son, was born on February 8, 1842.

John had only dim memories of his mother, who died five years after he was born, but he enjoyed a warm companionship with his father, whom he eulogized as 'the gentlest of men, never willing to believe evil of others, always ready to impute to them good motives... He was the truest Christian I have ever known.' His father's scholastic attainments, particularly his linguistic talents, were a source of pride and amazement to his children. He taught his pupils at St George's House mathematics, astronomy, anatomy, and geology, as well as German, French, English, Latin, Greek, and Hebrew. John remembered with affection a family outing in North Wales one Sunday shortly after his mother died, when his father was accosted by

4

a tall bearded stranger who turned out to be a Polish Jew. He...told him that he had come to Wales to study Welsh—his seventeenth language. They spoke at first in English, then my father addressed him in German and then in response to a demand from us conversed with the Jew in French and then in Italian, following with Latin and Greek and with classical Hebrew. The Jew thoroughly appreciated the fun and smiled broadly. We children stood round and clapped our hands and applauded vociferously and then we were all utterly cast down when the Jew spoke in a Slavonic language.

As an educator, the elder Brunner was guided by the precepts of Jean Heinrich Pestalozzi (1746–1827), precepts that later influenced John's campaigns for educational and penitentiary reform. There were marked similarities, personal and professional, between the elder Brunner and Pestalozzi, though it is doubtful that they ever met. Both Protestants from Zurich, they were equally dedicated to the mingling of children from different economic backgrounds, to a nonsectarian approach to education, and to the inculcation of moral standards that would assist the natural development of each student. And, like Pestalozzi, John's father spent most of his career on the brink of bankruptcy, more concerned with training minds than collecting fees. His school, like Voelker's, was conducted along Pestalozzian lines:

The means employed for the development of the moral faculties are religious and moral instruction, and the attention which is paid to the direction of the feelings and affections, and to the conduct of the pupils; and the endeavour on the part of their masters to implant by precept and example, in the heart of their pupils, a veneration for what is holy, a love towards every thing that is good, and an aversion to all that is evil. The treatment of the pupils is marked by patience and parental kindness, severe language and punishment being never resorted to but in extreme cases.[1]

To be sure, Pestalozzian theory and Unitarian practice reinforced each other, and there were other Unitarian schools—including Dr Lant Carpenter's at Bristol and the school attached to Upper Chapel, Sheffield—that drew their inspiration from Locke or Priestley with much the same effect.

In deference to what Pestalozzi called 'the essential needs of childhood', Brunner and Voelker postponed the study of

[1] 'Plan for the Education & Instruction of the Pupils Under Mr Chas Voelker's Care at St Domingo House, Everton, near Liverpool' (BP).

classical languages by their pupils and devoted the preliminary years to 'such branches of education as are adapted to their age', the reading and writing of English, arithmetic, and the sciences. No less daring were their attempts, also reminiscent of Pestalozzi, to provide religious instruction that would propagate values without imposing dogma. An exclusively secular education would have failed in its primary task, but equally distasteful was the imposition of a religious uniformity or the mindless memorization of texts that, more often than not, passed for religious training. At each level, the pupils were offered instruction in a different aspect of the history and ideas of Christianity. At San Domingo House, Voelker's establishment, and afterwards at Brunner's own school, the curriculum was typically Unitarian, wide in intellectual breadth, and coupling a strong interest in the natural sciences with an emphasis upon morality.

As an immigrant and an educational reformer, the elder Brunner found particularly vexing the sectarian disputes that rent English society. His attempts to achieve a fervent yet tolerant Christianity were applauded by James Martineau, the eminent Unitarian divine, whom he met soon after his arrival in England. 'I deeply sympathise with your sentiments respecting the state of religion in this country', Martineau wrote to him in 1834,

and with the difficulties in which, in common with all enlightened and conscientious instructors, you have found yourself involved by it. I can never advert to the subject without melancholy; nor cease to sigh for a time, which our boasted Reformation ought not to have been so long in introducing, when entire freedom of thought may prevail in union with deep religious sentiment, and a morality may be adopted by society, friendly alike to the intellect, the benevolence and the devotion, of mankind. Few things will contribute more to this happy end, than such instructions as, it is evident, you impart to your pupils,—instructions which impart ideas and awaken feelings, instead of the dead language of creeds, and the senseless prejudices of faction.[1]

The next generation of nonconformists, enjoying the fruits of the 1867 franchise reform, sought the solution to this problem not in

[1] Martineau to John Brunner, December 12, 1834 (BP). It is worth mention that Martineau, then minister of Paradise Street Chapel, Liverpool, wrote this letter at a critical moment in his career, when he broke with the Priestleyan tradition.

apply himself to it unless there was a commercial inducement, as when he taught himself enough Spanish from a Spanish diction- ary to prepare a customs declaration and thereby impress his first employer. In 1911 he confessed to J. L. Hammond, whom he had introduced to political society as his private secretary and whose scholarship he found 'a matter for envy', that he had 'hardly read anything for forty years'.[1]

Although it has been suggested that John and his younger brother were 'pitchforked out to work as clerks in Liverpool' after the family funds had been lavished upon the firstborn,[2] it was in fact John who took the decision to leave school at an early age. 'Wishing to be a man and not to remain a pupil for what seemed to me an eternity', he plumped for a career in business as soon as the opportunity arose. He detected a note of disappoint- ment in the voice of his father, who nonetheless knew better than to oppose him. Edward Estell, a family friend and the proprietor of a shipping firm, agreed to take John into his office and house- hold at Orange Court, Castle Street, Liverpool. It was a trial arrangement for a year, with the salary to be determined by the boy's performance. John began in August 1857 with unbounded enthusiasm, and promptly forgot all he had learned of Latin and Greek.

No one could have been more convinced of his importance than John Brunner, fifteen years old and a wage-earner. He had only pity for his older brother, Henry, who had gone to live with rela- tives in Zurich, where he was studying physics at the Polytechnic. That seemed to John an infinite postponement of manhood. Al- ways cocksure of himself, he had yet to acquire the talent for gentle self-mockery with which he would instantly disarm his antagonists. But it did not take long, he later recalled, to have 'the conceit taken out of me'. The clerks at the Liverpool customs house, more amused than irritated by his swagger, allowed him to overpay on the duty for a shipment of wine, and waited for him to return, suitably humbled, to claim his refund.

John soon discovered that the shipping trade was neither as

[1] December 3, 1911, Hammond Papers (Bodleian Library, Oxford).
[2] J. M. Cohen, *The Life of Ludwig Mond* (London, 1956), p. 76.

lucrative nor as exciting as he had imagined. The work proved tedious, and he began to wonder whether he had chosen the right path to commercial success. Looking back, he concluded that his years would have been better spent learning 'the law regarding Bills of Lading and Charter Parties, Marine Insurance and the way in which goods and passengers are carried about the world, rather than the mere mechanical making out of Bills of Lading and presenting them at the office of the shipping company'. Long hours were unavoidable, and Estell apologized to his friend when John was detained one December evening '(much to the discredit of the parties concerned) until past twelve o'clock, waiting for bills of lading which had to be sent by a steamer to sail at seven the next morning'.

Like most Liverpool houses, Estell's was dependent upon the American trade, which grew increasingly unstable with the approach of the Civil War. In John's first year, ending in August 1858, business 'proved so disastrous to all concerned in mercantile affairs' that Estell found himself unable to 'remunerate him so liberally as my inclination would dictate'. John received five pounds in recognition of his 'services and good conduct', and was offered an arrangement for three years at a progressive salary of fifteen, twenty, and thirty pounds per annum. With the outbreak of hostilities across the Atlantic in April 1861, the commercial life of Liverpool ground to a virtual standstill. Each morning, John recalled, he and the other clerks at Estell's 'came down, got out our blotting paper and our pens, and put them down very neatly on the desk, and there they remained for the rest of the day'. For the next six months, until he left the firm, he and his fellows would leave the office for beer at eleven each morning, in no hurry to return to their empty ledgerbooks. In early May he approached Estell and asked whether he should 'seek another situation after Midsummer'. Estell, who had 'for some time felt rather anxious on this point', assured John's father:

It has always been my desire to retain him in my service, and I had hoped to have been able to offer him terms, on the expiration of his present engagement, which would induce him to remain. But the lamentable state of affairs in the United States for many months past, has so prostrated our business, that, as he has probably made you aware, there has been much more leisure in the office than is desirable or advantageous for the young men engaged. The prospects of any change for the better have recently, unhappily, become more doubtful than ever. And now, therefore, that he himself has put the question, I feel that I ought not to do otherwise than at once to leave him free to take the course which that question suggests.

I need not say that it will give me great pleasure to render him any assistance in my power in finding other employment. He has done his duty faithfully towards me. I have the highest opinion of his ability and integrity, and most cordially wish him every success in his future career.

John made the most of his remaining months at Estell's, working diligently at his bookkeeping and perfecting his Spanish. In October his older brother, now technical manager at Hutchinson and Sons, chemical manufacturers at Widnes, arranged an interview for him with Richard Powell, general manager of that firm, who turned out to have been a pupil at St George's House before John was born, and who greeted him with the remark: 'I didn't know there was such an animal as you, but your father's son is sure to be a decent fellow, so you shall have a job if I can give you one.' The next step was for John to meet John Hutchinson, who asked a few abrupt questions, nodded his head, and said 'forty shillings', the amount John would be paid a week. There was no allowance for expenses and, under the law of that day, he was compelled to pay tax on his annual income of £104. Still, these were difficult times and he was grateful for the opportunity. He took lodgings at Widnes and, nineteen years of age, began his long association with the alkali trade.

Widnes, then known to its old-timers as Widnes Dock, was situated on the Mersey a few miles to the south-east of Liverpool. It had been rapidly transformed by the forces of industrialism from a marshy hamlet, boasting little more than a limestone quarry, into a thriving chemical manufacturing center, replete with the miseries of early industrial life. A traveller could recognize Widnes, Sir John Brunner told the House of Commons in 1899, 'not so much by sight as by smell. One knows when one is passing Widnes in the dark, when going north, a little past Runcorn Bridge.'[1] The smell was not simply the result of the

[1] *Parliamentary Debates*, 4th ser., LXVI, cols. 532 ff. (February 10, 1899).

13

nature of local industry, for Widnes was a classic example of a town developed without planning, restrictions, or consideration for human values. The *Warrington Guardian* looked disapprovingly upon its neighbor as a 'locality...where everyone appears to be able to do that which is right in his own eyes...If this state of things is allowed to continue we should not be surprised to find Widnes decimated.' Not until June 1865 did reformers succeed in creating a local board of health to grapple with such serious problems as congestion, sanitation, and water and air pollution; at long last a public sewer was provided for the town's 10,000 inhabitants.[1] Yet precisely these haphazard conditions had helped to attract to the vicinity chemical manufacturers like Hutchinson, William Gossage, and James Muspratt, who sought to avoid the local authorities and strong landed interests that were the bane of the chemical trade elsewhere. Other inducements were an abundant labor supply (much of it Irish), the proximity of the Cheshire saltfields and the Lancashire coal deposits, and the convenience of cheap transport—rail and water—that would facilitate the shipment of products and, no less important, the disposal of waste materials.

In his dozen years at Hutchinson's, John rose rapidly from clerk to office manager to general cashier. At any point his duties were hard to define, and in his later years he was a kind of general factotum who ran the office, kept check on accounts, and superintended personnel. His attitude toward John Hutchinson, head of the firm, remained subservient; on one occasion he humbly apologized for delaying the delivery of a letter to Richard Powell:

I stayed on my way to the office to get something to eat, and consequently did not arrive there till quarter past five o'clock, when I found that Mr. Powell had already left for Appleton.

My lunch should have been put off if I had thought you wished the letter delivered more promptly.

In March of 1866 Hutchinson died of tuberculosis, and the firm was managed—not very effectively, John thought—by Powell.

[1] See George E. Diggle, *A History of Widnes* (Widnes, 1961), p. 32; also S. G. Checkland, *The Rise of Industrial Society in England, 1815–1885* (New York, 1966), pp. 170–1.

Chertsey, was due to the fact that his wife's Liverpool physician had prescribed the milder air of Surrey.

From his earliest days at Widnes, John understood the rudiments of credit finance and knew how to get the maximum working value from the assets he possessed. In 1868 he insured his life for £500 and promptly pledged the policy as collateral for business ventures. Sixty-five years later, when he bought Silverlands, he insisted upon a heavy mortgage, seeing no reason to tie up capital that might yield a higher return if invested elsewhere. More than shrewdness, this was a typical reflex on the part of nineteenth-century industrialists, men of fairly limited resources, who pledged their last penny and more to their enterprises and who were responsible not only for their own solvency and reputation, but also for that of the friends and family they had persuaded to invest.

By the late 'sixties, John had increased his resources, his contacts, and his ambitions. He thus had all the makings of a successful entrepreneur, save the right opportunity. Clearly he was on the look-out for one and stood in financial readiness. At this juncture he met Ludwig Mond, with whom his name and fortune were to be linked.

Mond was born at Cassel in 1839 to a Jewish family with a history of persecution in Germany and with well-placed connections in England; his uncle, Philip Goldschmidt, later became Lord Mayor of Manchester. His education at Heidelberg was financed by another uncle, a chemist at Cologne, whose daughter he married. After completing his studies he worked for a short time at Utrecht, where he found the people 'as monotonous as their surroundings, and as boring and still as their swamps'.[1] His mother, who took encouragement from the success story of Disraeli—already Chancellor of the Exchequer—urged him to try his luck in England, where he arrived in time to attend the second Crystal Palace Exhibition in 1862. He made little headway in his attempts to market the patent he held for extracting nitric and nitrous acid from sulphur until he approached John Hutchinson, who took him on as a salaried research scientist on whose discoveries Hutchinson's would have first option.

[1] Cohen, p. 66.

19

Though the English he had learned as a German schoolboy stood Mond in good stead, he was most comfortable in the company of those who could speak his native tongue.[1] Among his first close friends was Henry Brunner, with whom he could communicate not only in German but also in chemical theory. On first sight Henry appeared as 'cold and silent' as the burghers of Utrecht, but Mond soon warmed up to him. Henry arranged temporary lodgings for him at the Mersey Inn, formerly the old Snig Pie Inn, and introduced him to his brother John, five years Mond's junior. Mond was happy for a time at Widnes, especially after John helped him find more quiet rooms at the house of the Appleton postmaster, but his prospects were poor and he was eager to marry his cousin, Frida Lowenthal, to whom he had been engaged for two years. Before the family would give its consent to the match, he would have to show that he could maintain his wife in proper style. In 1864 he left to manage the construction and operation of a Leblanc soda works at Utrecht, keeping up a correspondence with Hutchinson in the hope that his terms would be met.

Precisely at the moment that Mond seems to have given up all hope of coming back to England, Henry Brunner became works manager at Hutchinson's and invited Mond to return to supervise the installation of machinery and the inauguration of his sulphur-recovery process. Mond arrived in February 1867, leaving behind his newly acquired wife, who followed soon afterward. They settled at The Hollies, a house at Farnworth, a bit past Appleton on the road from Widnes. Mond had not yet decided whether to remain permanently, but waited to see how many firms would adopt his process and how much they would pay. There remained the distinct possibility, indeed his wife favored it, that he would return to the Continent. Not until 1871, which his biographer has singled out as 'a crucial year' in his career,[2] did he make up his mind to settle in England, accepting John Brunner's invitation to pool their resources and embark on a commercial venture of their own.

---

[1] John recalled that Mond 'could hardly speak English' when they met, but there are ample indications that this was not the case. Rather, it seems, Mond was inclined to lapse into German in the Brunners' company.   [2] Cohen, pp. 77, 126–7.

During the three years he had been away from Widnes, Mond received long intimate letters from John containing welcome words of encouragement and keeping him abreast of developments at the works. After his return, they resumed their friendship. The Brunners were among the few in the neighborhood who penetrated Mond's exterior, which had recently grown more forbidding as a result of damage inflicted upon his left eye by caustic soda. They invited him frequently for dinner and he in turn was 'exuberantly hospitable' to them. On evenings the two men would take long walks in the hills behind Widnes to discuss their personal problems and the events of the day. Mond would give flight to 'the sweet torments of imagination', while John would lecture him on 'the dangers of unbridled dreams'.[1] Though he was no match for Mond in scientific knowledge, the necessarian doctrines of Brunner's Unitarian upbringing had inspired a metaphysical belief in science and an enthusiasm for technological innovation. Mond's marriage for a time brought the men closer, as Frida Mond took a kindlier view of Salome Brunner than of other ladies in the neighborhood. At first she came to Appleton after dinner to watch Salome bathe her baby, and in October 1868 Salome was a great help when the Monds' second son, Alfred, was born. The Brunners were 'such dear, simple, good people', Frida wrote in gratitude.[2]

For intellectual stimulation, which was hard to come by at Widnes, Brunner and Mond helped to found the Qu'est-ce-que-c'est Club in January 1870.[3] There were nineteen monthly meetings before other affairs distracted the seven members and the club was disbanded. Other participants were Henry Brunner, Eustace Carey, who became secretary of the United Alkali Company, James L. Muspratt, later a lawyer at Flint, Walter Watts, a chemist at Hutchinson's, and James Raven, headmaster of the Farnworth grammar school. The last two were Tories, genially tolerated by the others. They met one evening a month 'to propound and discuss the definitions of various words', and, for

[1] Hector Bolitho, *Alfred Mond, first Lord Melchett* (New York, 1933), pp. 26–7.
[2] *Ibid.* p. 23.
[3] This paragraph is based upon the copy of the minute book that survives among the Brunner Papers.

reasons best known to themselves, each identified himself by a motto; John's was 'Onward and Upward' and Mond's was 'Unverzagt' (undaunted). The chairman, who lent his house for the meeting, was allowed to select the words for that night's agenda. 'Should disagreement or doubt arise as to the ordinary meaning or grammatical construction of any word, reference shall be made to a standard dictionary, which shall be final.' Debate was to cease at 10.30, leaving half an hour for refreshment and social intercourse before the meeting was adjourned at eleven. Collectively the members pondered the subtleties of 'beauty' ('Onward and Upward' thought it was the 'quality in persons and things which gives pleasure to the higher senses'), 'art' ('Onward and Upward': 'work expressive of beauty'), 'vulgarity', 'religion', 'morality', 'madness', and other suitable abstractions, concluding on the evening of March 27, 1871, with a vigorous debate on 'hypocrisy'.

It would be difficult to imagine two men more dissimilar in background, taste, and temperament than the cultivated son of a German Jew, self-consciously a Continental, and the plain-spoken son of a Swiss immigrant, self-consciously a first-generation Englishman. Even the radicalism that they both professed proved, as we shall see, antipathetical. Yet Brunner and Mond were able to understand and respect each other and to recognize, almost instinctively, what was unique in the other. It is idle to speculate on which was the dominant partner, for Mond could no more have realized his dreams without Brunner's resourceful management than Brunner without Mond's technical skills. Their talents and energies were different but complementary, one bringing to the partnership a genius for theory, the other a command of practicalities. All they shared was their confidence in the future, and upon this they built their industrial empire.

study will concentrate upon John Brunner's role in these affairs, not simply to redress a balance, but to provide an index to the climate of investment and the rigors of management in this period.

Shortly after Mond's return from Brussels, Brunner resigned the secretaryship of the local branch of the National Education League: his 'engagements have of late been so onerous', he explained, and in any case he would soon be leaving Widnes. The matter that occupied so much of his time and virtually all his attention was the recruitment of investors. All Mond could put up was £1000, though he was prepared to pledge his patents as collateral. Brunner was able to raise four times that amount, the bulk of it from his stepmother and mother-in-law. It was common for the savings of family and acquaintances to be the principal source of risk capital in this period when an impersonal capital market was first extending its facilities.[1] According to Mond's calculation, however, they were still short some £7000 and, failing to enlist the Solvays, they sought a sleeping partner who would provide capital but leave control undisturbed in their hands. This proved a depressing business. They approached several likely candidates, all without success, and even considered placing a classified advertisement in *The Times*. By November Mond had pared his estimates, and he and Brunner were prepared to go it alone on a more modest scale. At this point they made contact with Charles M. Holland, a Manchester civil engineer whose father Brunner had met in Liverpool. Holland offered them £5000 at a rate of five per cent with a third of the firm's profits not exceeding a quarter of his investment. These were terms roughly comparable to those they had offered to other prospective investors and, their capital secure, Brunner and Mond proceeded with their plans.

For the site of their proposed works, Brunner and Mond, 'after protracted enquiry', decided upon Winsford, in the heart of the Cheshire saltlands; here brine came in unlimited supply, and limestone and ammonia, the other basic materials, could be easily

[1] William Ashworth, *An Economic History of England, 1870–1939* (London, 1960), pp. 178–9.

brought by rail or by the River Weaver, which connected by canal with the Mersey. The tract of land that they found 'most suitable (as offering the securest foundation for the heavy and valuable plant)'[1] belonged to Lord Delamere, the head of a local family that had last distinguished itself at the time of the Glorious Revolution. His lordship was not prepared to incur the disapprobation of his neighbors by allowing a chemical works (no less!) to blight an area that was still the retreat of country gentlemen. The partners recovered from their disappointment and quickly settled upon another site down the river near Northwich. This second piece of property belonged to Lord Stanley of Alderley, who had long since given up residence and now allowed brine to be pumped there. This meant that a railway siding and docks were already to be found on the premises. Notoriously short of funds, Lord Stanley had two years earlier put the estate of some 600 acres up for auction, but there had been no bidders. Winnington Hall, the mansion that stood on the property, had in recent decades been leased as a ladies' finishing school. Sir Charles Hallé had visited to give recitals, and John Ruskin, who lectured there on art, had celebrated its architectural graces.

Brunner and Mond applied for a ninety-nine-year lease on the property around Winnington Hall, not including the house, for which they saw no use. For this, they were prepared to pay as much as £20,000.[2] After their rebuff from Lord Delamere, they took pains to extol the virtues of the undertaking. It would 'ultimately be of enormous value to the neighbourhood', Brunner assured Lord Stanley's agent. 'You are aware that it is the use of Sulphur in this manufacture that does all the mischief connected therewith, and as I am not going to use Sulphur, but Ammonia, you will no doubt easily credit my assertion that my works will do much less mischief to vegetation than a Saltworks.'[3] Lord Stanley, eager to divest himself of the holding, needed no per-

[1] Brunner to George Garfit, June 8, 1872 (Letterbook).
[2] Edward Milner advised Brunner to bid £15,000 for the property, and told him that 'there were three Dowager Ladies Stanley each drawing a large jointure out of the estates and that Ld. Stanley wants money to carry himself till one of their lives falls in...' Brunner to Mond, July 30, 1872 (Letterbook).
[3] Brunner to Robert Sampson, June 26, 1872 (Letterbook).

suasion, though he insisted upon selling the manor house and adjoining woodlands along with the riverside property. The partners consoled themselves that the timber in the park and the lead in the old roof might fetch a good price, and, in addition, they planned to raise a hefty mortgage on the land. Rather than waste precious time they agreed, relieved to pay no more than £16,108 for the entire parcel.

Winnington Hall was essentially a Tudor house onto which a more fashionable Georgian wing, variously attributed to Adam and Wyatt, had been clumsily grafted. Its hybrid nature seemed to reflect perfectly the Brunner–Mond partnership. Though the partners' first impulse was to level the old hall, they came to see the usefulness of living together in close proximity to the works. Mond and his family moved into the newer wing in the early summer of 1873 and, six months later, the Brunners came to live in the old hall. The Tudor section was not without a charm of its own, though extensive alterations and repairs were necessary to render it habitable. The stucco facing was peeled away to reveal a black-and-white timbered framing. Comfortably installed, Brunner had his initial carved into the base of the oak stairway that separated his section of the house from that which the Monds occupied.[1] Soon every building on the property was put to use, the cow shed, the poultry house, the stables, and even the harness room that accommodated a double desk and was made to serve as the head office. The works as they expanded wound round Winnington Hall, and Frida Mond kept the windows closed to keep out the ammonia fumes. The curtains were never drawn, however, for her husband found the view intensely satisfying, if rather less than idyllic.

The year 1874 brought unmitigated private misfortune and professional distress for Brunner. At a time when his attention was urgently needed elsewhere, he was left a widower with six young children. Entrusting them to the care of his in-laws, which caused him great pain, he moved temporarily into the Mond household, hoping each month that the old hall would be ready

[1] A. S. Irvine has written a charming history of Winnington Hall that was privately printed by the Imperial Chemical Industries Ltd. (Alkali Division) in 1951.

for occupancy by the beginning of the next. 'Brunner has lived with us for six months', Mond wrote to his parents in February, 'and is a complete member of our family, and at present he lives with us for the greater part of the week. As soon as his house is ready, one hopes in four weeks, he will move in with his six children and be our only and next neighbour...'[1] Business affairs were no less gloomy and, even with Ernest Solvay's active assistance, it took nine months longer to put the plant in operation than had been hoped. The first soda ash was produced that summer and sold at a loss of five pounds a ton. 'Everything that could break down did break down, and everything that could burst did burst,' Brunner later recalled of these chaotic months.[2] One by one, these problems were ironed out, and by autumn he could proudly report that the works had begun to 'look the very picture of prosperity, very dirty and very full of stuff'.[3]

For the time being, however, prosperity was more apparent than real. Credit was scarce and the alkali market at home and abroad remained depressed. To meet his payroll, Brunner resorted to loans from Joseph Crosfield, a local soap manufacturer who later became the first chairman of Brunner, Mond.[4] At the close of 1874, when he drew up his accounts for the first complete calendar year, he and Mond discovered that their working capital was exhausted. The next year showed a modest profit of £2400, but they were 'compelled to lock up' three quarters of this sum 'in extensions'[5] to the plant. Brunner crossed the Atlantic the following summer to drum up business in America, where he found the heat oppressive, society 'indescribably dull', and sales 'miserable'.[6] Unable to repay his in-laws the money they had advanced him, he nursed vain hopes that there would be 'an improved market' before the end of 1877.[7] But the market failed to oblige him and remained, the following February, 'in an awful state'. He complained that 'prices are lower by far than I have ever known

[1] February 16, 1874, ICI Archives.   [2] Watts, *The First Fifty Years*, p. 27.
[3] Brunner to Holland, October 24, 1874 (Letterbook).
[4] Musson, p. 73.   [5] Brunner to Mond, March 27, 1876 (Letterbook).
[6] Mond to Holland, June 15, 1876 (Letterbook); Brunner to William Davies, August 16, 1876 (Letterbook).
[7] Brunner to Edward Nettlefold, January 8, 1877 (Letterbook).

of a boiler explosion with his own bed linen. But once, coming to the rescue of a man who lay motionless after a fall from a scaffold and finding that he was not hurt, Mond ordered him to his feet and back to work.[1]

By 1885 Mond, then in his forty-sixth year, was already regarded by his subordinates as the 'Old Man'. A. W. Tangye, whom he hired that year for a pound a week and who became a director of the company in 1919, never forgot their first encounter:

He was only some 5 feet 8 in height and stooped forward slightly, a rather fearsome figure, [with] magnificently developed chest and arms.

He was just in from a tour of the Works, in a long black overcoat and wearing a black shapeless hat with a broad brim, both hat and coat covered with white dust.

From under the brim of this hat a much tortured and disfigured left eye (damaged with caustic in a Dutch works) first met me, and then a heavily bearded face with a powerful racial nose. His moustache and beard were rough black hair, rather aggressive, and he was smoking a black cigar. The right eye was very powerful and searching. The whole head seemed very powerful in proportion to the body.[2]

Unlike Tangye, who came to idolize Mond, most of those with whom he came into contact continued to be unnerved by his appearance and frightened by his tempestuous outbursts. At his most accommodating, Mond was often curt and abrasive; at his most democratic he was strangely dictatorial. 'Don't call me Sir,' he rebuked one of his laborers, 'I am not a gentleman, I am a workman.'[3]

By contrast, Brunner practiced his paternalism with a lighter hand and a friendlier disposition. His staff was devoted to him, and he returned their loyalty handsomely.[4] He applied himself to any office chore, and the story goes that he once sat up through the night trying in vain to help a book-keeper find a twopenny discrepancy. A great believer in communal festivities, he mingled

---

[1] Bolitho, p. 26.

[2] Tangye's diary, ICI Archives. A fictional portrait of Mond was provided by Ethel Brunner, Brunner's daughter-in-law, in her novel, *Celia's Fantastic Voyage* (London, 1924?). Tangye considered it 'an extremely clever sketch of Ludwig Mond in later life...'   [3] Bolitho, p. 32.

[4] In later years Thomas Forgan, who had served him from the beginning, received £500 a year from Brunner, and assurances his family would be remembered in Brunner's will. Forgan to Brunner, July 8, 1909, BP.

freely at company outings. At one such occasion, late in the 'nineties, the local press described him 'attired modestly and looking cool as an obelisk', with 'a word of encouragement here, a little playful banter there, and a cheerful smile for all'. A cyclist, hired to entertain the crowd, 'called out in stentorian tones, "Sit down! the spectators can't see,"' and Brunner, to the delight of his employees, 'was one of the first to squat on the grass... Then the great chemical manufacturer saw the joke, and he laughed heartily. He had bowed to superior rank, for he was not an official.'[1]

At a time when the average large-scale employer regarded labor, like raw materials, as a factor in production and little more, Brunner, Mond and Company took into account the welfare and dignity of their men. Various benefits and facilities were made available that will be discussed presently. These, in large part, were Brunner's inspiration, a product of his religious heritage. Like so many progressive employers of Victorian England—the names of Rowntree, Cadbury, Courtauld and Wedgwood come most quickly to mind—he stood apart from traditional society because of religious differences or foreign antecedents. This vantage point afforded a sensitive appreciation of social inequities, which these individuals attempted to rectify through company welfare schemes and, as a rule, through the Liberal Party.

This distinction held particularly true among the industrial titans of Cheshire. W. H. Lever (later Viscount Leverhulme), the soap manufacturer at Port Sunlight, was a Congregationalist, and the Brocklehurst family, makers of silks at Macclesfield, were Unitarians; both distinguished themselves as benefactors of their workpeople, and both played an active role in Liberal politics. Long known as the 'seed plot of gentility', Cheshire was galvanized in the second half of the nineteenth century by men of this stamp who generally arrived after the railways and canals had opened the resources of the Weaver valley. Coming from Manchester, Liverpool and farther afield, they were as motley as the area they transformed with their works. In their train came great numbers of laborers who converged upon the factory towns that

[1] Undated cutting, *Northwich Chronicle*, BP.

clustered along the Weaver and the south bank of the Mersey. At the same time other towns developed to house the overflow from Merseyside and south-east Lancashire. The population of the county soared from 192,000 at the start of the century to 664,000 in 1881. These new arrivals, predominantly Protestant nonconformists (many of them Welsh), and Roman Catholics (most of them Irish), gave new life to the struggle against the authority of the traditional landed classes and the monopoly of the established Church. An overhaul of local government and its transfer to new hands was not long in coming, and the immediate beneficiaries were the manufacturers who inherited the mantle of social leadership and public service. The shift of political influence and control, a crucial theme in Brunner's career, was of course a long and intricate process. Such men had previously enjoyed local office only if they assumed the trappings of the landed gentry. Brunner was testimony to the fact that this prerequisite no longer held.

Notwithstanding the often fierce antagonism that was generated between the Cheshire manufacturers, overwhelmingly nonconformist in religion and Liberal in political affiliation, and the landed interests, almost exclusively Anglican and Conservative, there were certain attitudes they held in common. According to J. M. Lee, in his impressive survey of social and institutional change in the county, the relationship between employer and employee tended to bear a striking resemblance to that between landlord and tenant. Indeed, Lee was moved to remark, 'It is sometimes hard to see a difference between the concern of the Duke of Westminster for his tenants and that of W. H. Lever for his workmen.'[1] The managerial structure of these firms was also conducive to a paternalistic approach, in that their respective founders left a strong imprint upon them and retained a close interest in them; and in some cases—Brocklehurst's silk firm, for example—they did not become limited companies until relatively late. All of these factors in one measure or another combined to create a more salutary employer–employee relationship than that which prevailed in neighboring counties.

[1] J. M. Lee, *Social Leaders and Public Persons* (Oxford, 1963), pp. 33–4.

John Brunner, who served longer and more prominently in the House of Commons than either Lever or W. B. Brocklehurst, was, like them and countless others, a successful industrialist whose 'entry into politics appeared to be a natural extension of his managerial activities'.[1] The first step for such an individual was to become involved in local politics, in most cases the County Council, but in his case the Quarter Sessions. The second was to obtain election to Parliament, usually for the constituency in which his works were located. It was a short and logical step from being the guardian of a community and the patron of its public projects to being its member of Parliament, serving the same basic interests in a wider arena. The causes that Brunner supported in the House, and the issues that most concerned him, clearly reflected his personal and professional experience. At the same time he personified the new Cheshire, its vitality, and its diverse and humble origins. When he first stood for Parliament, a heckler called him a foreigner, and he replied by reciting his pedigree: 'My father was a Swiss, my mother was a Manx-woman, I was born in Liverpool, my nurse was Welsh: is that Cheshire enough for you?'

Just as Mond looked upon business partly as an opportunity to increase the fund of human knowledge, so Brunner looked upon it as an agency to realize and develop human potential. The employer, as Brunner saw him, was the custodian of moral and material well-being among his men, and by far the most effective instrument in the community for social betterment. For this reason he opposed parliamentary legislation that would make government an intermediary between labor and capital, warning that this would inhibit the creative employer at the same time that it would drive a wedge between him and his employees. This was no cynical espousal of *laissez-faire* arguments, but rather the expression of a strongly held belief that management must assume the full burden of its responsibilities. '... The best employers', his eldest son later stated, 'are in advance of the law' and require no coercion. 'In other words', he explained, 'the require-

---

[1] *Ibid.* p. 33; also p. 91. Brunner's two surviving sons served as county councillors, John for the Sandbach division (1894–5) and Roscoe for Northwich (1907–18).

ments of the law do not represent the maximum but an average,'[1] and this was to be deplored.

How well did Brunner measure up to the rigorous standards he professed? This can best be gauged in the context of his parliamentary career and must therefore await more detailed analysis. But it can be safely said that the wide range of industrial problems that engaged him in the House were those he had attempted to combat in and around his Cheshire works. His economic background provided him with a quick frame of reference and a testing-ground for his ideas; it did not override moral considerations, nor did it dictate the way he voted.

For himself as well as others, Brunner was a firm believer in the Victorian gospel of work, which he advocated with all the fervor of a Samuel Smiles. Like so many of his contemporaries, he regarded perseverance and application as the hallmark of respectability, the key to a useful existence, and the fulfillment of a debt to God and a duty to society. 'Work,' Dr Arnold enjoined his children. 'Not work at this or that—but, Work.'[2]

As a citizen, Brunner saw work as the basis of an ordered community; as a man of business, he saw it as a means of production; as a Christian, he saw it as a gift he possessed to bestow upon others for their improvement in this world and their salvation in the next. In each of these capacities he found cause to deprecate the existing penitentiary system, 'with its long sentences, its degradation, and its absence of work... Most of those who are in prison', he contended, 'went there because they did not like work, and the prison rules taught them to hate it.'[3] Even when it did not enforce idleness, prison deprived a man of his self-respect and sense of purpose. Brunner was scandalized when a worker at his plant 'who was drunk and riotous' was given the excessive sentence of two months hard labor for assaulting a foreman.[4] He was even more incensed by the severity of the law in the case of

[1] J. F. L. Brunner, 'Industrial Politics', in *The Policy of Social Reform in England* (Brussels, 1913), p. 70.
[2] Thomas Arnold the Younger, *Passages in a Wandering Life* (London, 1900), p. vi. See the illuminating discussion on 'the glorification of work' in Walter E. Houghton, *The Victorian Frame of Mind* (New Haven, 1963), pp. 242 ff.
[3] *Parliamentary Debates*, 3rd ser., CCCXIX, col. 1501 (August 22, 1887); CCCXXVII, col. 483 (June 18, 1888). [4] Brunner to Mond, September 27, 1883 (Letterbook).

youthful offenders, and, perhaps with his father's Pestalozzian principles in mind, he campaigned for greater leniency. 'I am grieved that you should consider it necessary to prosecute a lad of 15 for stealing,' he told a company official. 'It will ruin the boy's life, and I believe the shame of the discovery is just as deterrent in its effects upon the staff as the committal of the boy to a Reformatory.'[1]

The place for young people was not the reformatory but the schoolhouse, and Brunner did all he could to bring and keep them there. The founding and endowment of schools was for him more than a philanthropic exercise, it was a commitment to a vision of society. He found special need for such activity in Cheshire, which had been 'unfortunately content to loiter for generations' on the road to educational improvement, and where there was 'consequently no room. . . for the counsels of a spurious economy or of a grudging spirit'.[2] To compensate, the company built a school at Winnington in 1886, and Brunner, on his own, built others at Barnton and Northwich, where he also provided a new building for the pre-existing grammar school. Architecturally, these schools were among the most up-to-date in the country, and academically they excelled, collecting more than their share of merit grants. Free libraries were another of his passions, and institutions of higher learning did not escape his bounty. He was a prominent patron of both Unitarian College, Manchester, for which he served briefly as president, and Liverpool University. It was a standing rule between him and Mond that each would keep his charities separate from the other and from the company. He reported with 'regret' to the Reverend Charles Beard that Mond did not 'feel called upon' to join him in support of Liverpool University College, chartered in 1903 as Liverpool University, but that he nonetheless felt it 'incumbent on me to help if I can'. The difficulties he cited provide some idea of the extent of his benefactions and the spirit in which they were made: 'Having recently pledged myself for over 3000 for the local Grammar School, and a proposed Free Library, the question for me is one of time.

1 Brunner to Milner, August 30, 1886, ICI Archives.
2 Sir John Brunner and J. L. Hammond, *Public Education in Cheshire in 1896* (Manchester, 1896), p. 22.

Kindly say when the *cash* will be wanted, and I will say promptly what I can do.'[1]

Naturally the company made good use of the expanded facilities in the neighborhood. In 1886 it was decided that boys under fourteen years of age would be required to attend evening continuation classes until they reached the age of seventeen; in 1894 this was extended until the age of nineteen and it was also laid down that passing the sixth standard was the prerequisite to employment. Apprentices were required to attend these classes until they turned twenty-one. In all cases the company bore the five-shilling fees of those students who produced a certificate of regular attendance, and added to this half a crown as a further inducement. The system aroused considerable interest, and Brunner travelled widely to explain its workings. *The Times,* among those impressed, urged 'the Government, the railway companies, and other large employers of young lads' to follow the Brunner, Mond example.[2]

Though many employers continued to look suspiciously upon the education of workmen as a needless expense and a potential threat to their authority, Brunner considered the experiment well worth the effort and investment. He discerned a marked improvement in his young employees, who retained more of what they had learned in their early schooling and who acquired valuable skills and greater efficiency. Education as he saw it was designed to impart moral values as well as technical training, and here too he was not disappointed.[3] He therefore agitated for parliamentary legislation to duplicate on a national scale what he had achieved in his community. The Bill he proposed in 1906[4] enjoyed the

[1] Brunner to Beard, January 11, 1884 (Letterbook).

[2] September 24, 1904; Brunner found these words 'very gratifying', and replied in a letter to the editor on October 6; see also Sir Alfred Mond's speech, May 30, 1911, in A. Mond, *Questions of Today and Tomorrow* (London, 1912), pp. 298–9.

[3] See *Parliamentary Debates,* 4th ser., CLX, cols. 1401–3 (July 16, 1906).

[4] Bill No. 220 (printed May 21, 1906) 'to amend the Education Acts, 1870 to 1903'; it provided 'that local authorities may fix thirteen as the minimum age for total exemption from attendance at a public elementary school if they frame byelaws for the attendance of children so exempted at some recognised continuation school for at least three evenings a week until they attain the age of sixteen years'. Separate provision was made for rural districts, and it was proposed that the Board of Education would contribute toward the maintenance of continuation schools.

proclaimed support of Ramsay MacDonald, Sir William Anson, and C. F. G. Masterman, each a progressive of a different political stripe; yet it was dropped after its first reading, the victim of an over-crowded agenda. It was not in fact until H. A. L. Fisher's Education Act of 1918 that Parliament took significant steps in this direction.

In other areas too the company stood far in advance of the norm. A scheme was instituted in 1884 that gave a week's paid holiday to all men who had missed no more than ten days, except for sickness, the previous year. In the first year only forty-two per cent qualified, but the number steadily increased and, correspondingly, the number of lost workdays declined. In 1902 it became company policy to give double pay for the holiday week to enable the men and their families to enjoy a change of scenery. In addition, Brunner pointed out no less proudly, the experiment achieved a notable improvement in the habits of workmen that extended into their home lives. 'I have watched the improvement,' he declared in his inaugural address as pro-chancellor of Liverpool University.

I have seen how since 1873 the wives and the children are better fed and better dressed and better mannered, and I am almost ready to say without any suspicion of irreverence, 'Lord, now lettest Thou Thy servant depart in peace', considering that I have introduced by this simple method of reward...happiness and comfort into four thousand households.[1]

A variety of recreational facilities was made available at the company's expense, beginning with the formation of a workmen's club at Northwich in 1877. Members paid monthly dues of a shilling, or 2s. 6d. a quarter, but anyone could enter on payment of a penny and 'feel as free as gentlemen members of any Pall-Mall Club'. The attractions included 'a skittle-alley and a sporting ground, both *free*, a billiard table...and a bagatelle table..., a reading room well supplied, and a beginning of a library, which we hold *in trust* for a possible future free public library'. Tobacco was sold, but not 'intoxicants'. Brunner ascribed the success of the venture to the fact that the management had scrupulously 'avoided any appearance of *patronage*' and had kept clerical and

[1] Typescript, BP.

squirearchical influences at bay. It was a place for workmen to relax among themselves in a healthy atmosphere. There was one 'little scandal' when gambling was reported on the premises, but the company's solicitors 'spoke up for us very well indeed, and we have lived it down I think. . . '[1]

Working hours posed a problem that could not be solved by good intentions or private generosity. Because the alkali manufacturing process was continual, the company had little room for creative maneuver, and reform was slow and tentative. Again, Brunner, Mond compared favorably with other large employers, particularly with its rivals in the chemical trade, but this was small consolation for the shiftmen, well over a thousand in number, who were 'engaged. . . in the "process" which goes on day and night throughout the year'. Before November 1889, Brunner explained, these men had

worked in two shifts (from 7 a.m. to 6 p.m.; 6 p.m. to 7 a.m.). To prevent the continuance of the same men at either day work or night work, a double shift was worked at the end of the week. This, of course, meant that once a fortnight each man engaged in the 'process' had to work for about 24 hours at a stretch.[2]

When operations had first begun at Winnington shiftmen worked an average of eighty-four hours a week. Day workers, fewer in number, worked a six-and-a-half-day week for a total of fifty-six and a half hours. The works were kept going on Sunday despite Brunner's social and theological misgivings. 'There was not an alkali works in the world in which work was not done on Sunday,' he told a political meeting in 1885, for this was a trade 'in which Sunday work was absolutely necessary'. He confessed, however, that 'more work [was] done in Winnington than necessary', assuring his audience that 'for years he had done his best to limit that' and that his efforts would not abate.[3]

[1] Brunner to the secretary, Workingmen's Club and Institute Union, August 15, 1877; also Brunner to ?, July 6, 1878 (Letterbook).
[2] See Brunner's letter to the editor of *The Times*, February 7, 1895, in which he recounted at length the results of this experiment and appealed for 'legislative control over the hours worked in industries in which work people are necessarily employed seven days a week'.
[3] Speech at Weaverham, November 10, 1885, *Northwich and Winsford Chronicle*, November 14, 1885.

In 1889 the worst abuses were rectified when the shift was reduced from twelve to eight hours. There was a reduction in pay of ten per cent 'as a precautionary guarantee against the too heavy loss which might have resulted', but within a year it was apparent that the directors' fears on this score had been unfounded. Full pay was restored, and the men received for eight hours the amount they had formerly received for twelve. Though the number of workmen had increased by thirty-five per cent, production costs per ton quickly declined to their previous level. Brunner attributed this not to any innovations in technique, but 'to an increase in the energy, power, skill, and attention—in a word, to the increased efficiency of the men themselves', who came to the job healthier and more relaxed. This system continued in operation, under careful scrutiny, for five years, when it was decided to reduce further the work week to forty-eight hours for those who fell into the category of tradesmen and to forty-nine and a half hours for laborers, again without loss of pay. On both occasions reductions came only after extensive study had revealed that productivity and profits would not suffer. And Brunner, Mond could well afford the experiment. This, after all, was a period in which the company rapidly expanded and dividends rocketed as high as seventy-five per cent; it was only fitting that a share of the prosperity should be passed on to the worker. 'My trouble', Brunner wrote to his banker in 1909, 'is that the men who make the profits get too little and the shareholders too much.'[1] This was a sentiment that few industrial magnates felt, and still fewer acted upon until legislation left them no choice.

It can therefore be said that, with regard to welfare benefits, Brunner, Mond and Company anticipated national policy and practice. And Brunner's subsequent activities made clear that this was, for the most part, his work. W. E. Gladstone applauded him for setting an example 'very well calculated to encourage others to go and do likewise. It is this wise and humane temper of employers', he added, 'which we must count upon as a main factor in the adjustments necessary from time to time between

[1] Brunner to Mr Whalley [?], general manager, Parr's Bank, December 21, 1909 (copy), BP.

a School, with little or no guarantee as to the fitness of the Master. The Act should have required a certain amount of *attainments* before a child became a full timer.[1]

Mundella was a natural ally for Brunner. The son of an Italian immigrant and a prosperous hosiery manufacturer at Leicester, he practiced as an employer the reforms he preached as a parliamentarian. All he lacked to complete the comparison was a nonconformist background; but Mundella, educated at an Anglican school, compensated with the declaration: 'Creeds and Catechisms were my especial abomination, and even the beautiful collects of the Church of England were imposed on me so often that they became distasteful.'[2]

Throughout the decade Brunner widened his circle of political acquaintances and increased his memberships. Like most youthful Radicals of the 'seventies, he moved haltingly into the orbit of Gladstonian Liberalism. He attended meetings of the Liverpool Cobden Club and its dinners were the highlight of his social calendar. Nor did he neglect the public and social life of the Northwich area. Soon after his arrival, he volunteered to manage the British School in Witton Street, Northwich, and served successively on the local board, the board of guardians, and the local sanitary authority.[3] This activity, coupled with the fact that he was a leading employer in the area, entitled him to a voice when the political map of Cheshire was redesigned in 1885, according to the provisions of the Redistribution Act of that year.

The parliamentary representation of the county had been doubled from two to four members at the time of the Reform Act of 1832, and further increased to six by the Reform Act of 1867; but on both occasions the constituencies had been drawn, as in the remote past, according to the ancient hundreds of the shire. The

---

[1] Brunner to Mundella, July 29, 1872, Mundella Papers (University Library, Sheffield). There is no mention in the *Transactions of the National Association for the Promotion of Social Science* of the presentation of a paper by Brunner at its celebrated Congress at Manchester in October 1866. It remains possible, however, that he delivered his remarks the previous month, as he told Mundella, to a subsidiary group.

[2] Armytage, p. 16.

[3] This information, which appeared in an obituary notice in the *Chester Guardian*, has unfortunately proved impossible to corroborate. The Brunner (Central) Library, Northwich, has no record of the British School, and the records of the local board, which ceased to exist with the formation of the urban district in 1894, have not been preserved.

Act of 1885, which divided the counties and larger boroughs into single-member constituencies or divisions, marked a departure in principle as well as practice. As R. K. Webb has lucidly explained:

Roughly approximating the old Chartist ideal of equal electoral districts, the act broke up the historical constituencies, extinguishing the peculiar prestige that had always attached to county members, and making a member not so much the representative of the whole constituency as the delegate of the majority who returned him.[1]

The redistribution of parliamentary seats was part and parcel of a reform scheme produced by a compromise between the parties. Lord Salisbury, the Conservative leader, grudgingly assented to a franchise reform despite his party's fears that it would open the floodgates to a Radical victory in the approaching general election; in return, he received from Gladstone a Redistribution Act, designed to mitigate the effects of democracy. Nonetheless the combined legislation of 1884–5 effected a revolution in the relationship between the parties in the country if not between them in the Commons. One can see this most clearly in Cheshire and, particularly, in Brunner's career.

The Conservative landholders, who had hitherto dominated Cheshire politics, looked to the Act of 1885 to strengthen them against the nascent forces that contested their authority. In the respected opinion of Lord Egerton of Tatton, who led the party in the county, this could best be accomplished by isolating the pockets of industrialism as separate constituencies, insuring Tory control of the outlying areas. 'It will be fatal to our interests', he warned Sir Stafford Northcote, Conservative leader in the lower house, 'if some of the towns above 10,000 are not taken out of my old constituency of Mid-Cheshire.' He suggested the creation of one constituency containing Northwich and the salt towns along the Weaver, a second containing Crewe, Nantwich and Sandbach, and a third containing Macclesfield and Congleton.[2]

---

[1] *Modern England* (New York, 1968), p. 401.

[2] Christ Church, Oxford, Salisbury Papers, cited in Lee, *Social Leaders*, p. 38. D. C. Moore cites as a vital factor behind the 1832 Reform Act and other nineteenth-century electoral reforms the determination by 'reformers' to halt the penetration of urban radicalism into the counties. 'Social Structure, Political Structure, and Public Opinion in Mid-Victorian England', in Robert Robson, ed., *Ideas and Institutions of Victorian Britain* (London, 1967), pp. 20–57.

John T. Brunner in 1885

The Liberal leaders were quick to recognize the merits of such a scheme, which would accord them an advantage in those constituencies liberated from aristocratic influence. A Liberal blueprint for redistribution, attributed to Brunner and bearing the imprint of his style, arrived at conclusions basically the same as Lord Egerton's.[1] The eventual arrangement, therefore, had its benefits for both sides and carried as much bipartisan support as could have been expected. Eight divisions were created, of which three were industrial in character (Northwich, Crewe and Macclesfield), two suburban (Altrincham and Wirral), and two agricultural (Eddisbury and Knutsford); the eighth, Hyde, was a cotton manufacturing center that did not conform to the pattern. The Conservatives more or less wrote off the first group, stood at least an equal chance of winning Altrincham and Wirral, and held Eddisbury and Knutsford secure in their grasp.

In size and social composition, the Northwich division seemed tailored to Brunner's specifications. In 1881, at the time of the last census, its population was 57,607, of whom some 10,000 were now eligible to vote. Many of the electors were newly enfranchised, and a majority were, like Brunner, comparative newcomers to the county. It is therefore not the least surprising that he quickly achieved political pre-eminence, eventually converting the constituency into his own domain. With the assistance of Algernon Fletcher, soon to become his agent, Brunner persuaded the authorities to name the division after Northwich rather than another of the towns within its boundaries. He was also instrumental in the formation of a Liberal Three Hundred and, most fittingly, when this body assembled in April 1885 at the old Drill Hall, Northwich, its first order of business was his adoption as the party's candidate in the next general election.

Not by any means was Brunner unprepared for the invitation. He had contemplated the prospect of a parliamentary career since at least the previous spring, when he was approached to succeed the Liberal member for Warrington who was ailing. 'We shall see what comes of it,' he had told Mond, alerting him to the situation.

[1] Gough Adds. Cheshire 8° 54 e/5 (Bodleian Library, Oxford).

'It would suit my views admirably.'[1] While he waited he received word that he had been named a member of the bench for Quarter Sessions.

Nothing had developed at Warrington, possibly because alternatives soon presented themselves nearer at hand. The promulgation of the Redistribution Bill gave new hope to Cheshire Radicalism by promising to break the hegemony of the Tory squirearchy. Brunner, determined to seize the opportunity when it came, readied himself by acquiring a private secretary. The pains he took attested to the seriousness of his intentions. Seeking someone young, earnest and steadfastly Liberal, he canvassed fellows of various Oxford and Cambridge colleges for names of likely individuals. He carefully checked the references of each candidate and, when the field was at last narrowed, conducted extensive interviews. One young man who came highly recommended by the senior fellow at Trinity College, Cambridge, seemed to him 'much more a man of the world than a politician'; another, from Queen's College, Oxford, appeared deficient in 'energy'; and a third, from Brasenose College, Oxford, despite a reputation as 'a good speaker and lawn tennis player', failed to impress his prospective employer.

His eventual choice—a singularly happy one—was Thomas Edward Ellis, a recent graduate of New College, Oxford, who struck him as 'very well suited'. Ellis, then in his twenty-sixth year, was a red-headed Welshman who, with only a third in Mods, was more or less resigned to earning his living as a tutor to sons of Welsh gentry. He was described by R. W. Hudson, an acquaintance of Brunner's at Bangor, as 'a lively, quick, clever fellow,...[and] just the sort of man who would enjoy being absorbed in ephemeral, popular topics of the day'.[2] It took considerable effort for Brunner to track him down to an address near Cardiff, where he was temporarily engaged. Though he found the offer 'a tempting one', Ellis regretfully declined, citing the commitments he had made through the following summer. Still, he confessed, he would like 'to have worked, as a private secre-

[1] Brunner to Mond, April 27, 1884 (Letterbook).
[2] Hudson to Brunner, May 8, 1885, BP.

tary, to turn the candidate into a member, and to keep him so'.[1]
A few days later Ellis wrote again, explaining that he had been
'haunted' by the proposal, and asking whether August 'would be
absolutely too late for me to begin operations...'[2] Luckily the
general election did not come until autumn, and Brunner was able
to wait nearly ten months for Ellis to join him.

By appointing Ellis his private secretary, Brunner launched
what is generally conceded to have been one of the most brilliant
careers in late-Victorian politics; without question it was one of
the most tragic. Elected member for Merionethshire in 1886,
Ellis rose to become chief Liberal whip within eight years. He was
regarded by many as a more imposing parliamentary figure than
David Lloyd George, his young compatriot who soon followed
him into the House and to whom he was inevitably compared.
His career, expected by some to culminate in the premiership, was
cut short by death when he was forty years of age. Throughout,
Brunner encouraged him in his ambitions and sustained him
financially. Until 1892, when he was appointed second whip,
Ellis continued to draw a salary as Brunner's private secretary. It
was of course unusual for one member of Parliament to serve
another, but by this time Ellis's duties were virtually non-existent.
In effect this was Brunner's tactful way of subsidizing the political
career of a gifted young man who could not otherwise have
afforded one.

To Ellis, as to the nine Brunner children, Brunner was 'the
Pater'; and Brunner in turn treated Ellis like a son. Ellis took
readily to the Brunner household, where he was a good companion to the three boys, not many years his junior, and an object
of fascination to the six girls who, rather daringly, were inclined
to lapse from 'Mr Ellis' to 'Tom'. Hilda Brunner proclaimed
herself his 'loving protectress', and all of her sisters fawned upon
him and were equally solicitous of his health. As long as he lived,
Ellis went at Brunner's expense on lengthy sea voyages to recuper-
ate from attacks of typhoid. And it was while he was Brunner's
guest at Cannes in 1899 that he died, leaving a wife of ten months
who was carrying his child.

[1] Ellis to Brunner, April 27, 1885, BP.   [2] Ellis to Brunner, April 30, 1885, BP.

Despite his key role in creating the constituency at Northwich and a local Liberal association of which he was chairman, Brunner's adoption as its first Liberal candidate was not assured. His rival, a formidable one, was Robert Verdin, the older of two brothers who held substantial salt interests in the area. The contenders confronted each other publicly on April 11, 1885, at a meeting of the Liberal Three Hundred at Leftwich. Both made energetic bids for the meeting's endorsement and, defying hecklers, entertained questions from the floor. At the end of a fairly rancorous session, even by Cheshire standards, Brunner was selected by a vote of 166 to 130.[1]

Brunner's speech, which carried the day, was a candid and systematic exposition of his Radical philosophy; as such, it illuminates the issues that most concerned the society from which he drew his support. Disclaiming any intention to cause 'injury to the interests of religion' and social harmony, he vowed his determination to 'persuade my fellow countrymen that this country will be far more Christian when the Church is disestablished than it is to-day'. When the cheers had subsided, he condemned the prevailing system that on the one hand made it 'an extremely difficult, indeed almost an impossible thing, for a poor man to get into the House of Commons', and on the other perpetuated 'the right claimed by the son of a peer to make the laws for us'. If elected, he promised to work for a thorough-going reform of the law of landed property, now 'maintained almost solely for the benefit...of a few wealthy families', and for the proposals of Henry Broadhurst ('an old friend of mine') to end the 'evil' of short leases. At this early date he declared his support of Irish Home Rule, though his few references to the subject revealed that his ideas remained indeterminate.

It is noteworthy that the reforms he advocated were at the expense not only of the traditional landed classes, whose privileges were undoubtedly most egregious, but also of the class to which he belonged. '...Being a Nonconformist', he explained, he had never 'claimed for myself an unjust privilege', for he was

---

[1] The following paragraphs are based principally upon accounts in the *Northwich and Winsford Chronicle*, April 18, 1885, and the *Liverpool Echo*, April 13, 1885.

brought up to believe 'that an unjust privilege does not go well with Christianity'. He pledged his efforts to amend the Employers' Liability Act of 1880 'so that no wealthy employer or any great corporation or railway company shall be in the position to compel a man to contract himself out of that Act'. Furthermore, knowing full well the cost to his own firm, he promised to press for legislation to indemnify property owners for damage caused by the pumping of brine.

Verdin followed Brunner to the rostrum and promptly struck a personal note. He opened by reminding the assembled delegates that he 'did not come before you as a man that has only been in the neighbourhood for a few years, but as one who has spent 40 or 50 years in this place'. Regarding the issues of the day, he was far less vigorous. He expressed support for disestablishment in both Wales and Scotland, but argued that disestablishment in England lay beyond the realm of 'practical politics'. On the land question, he suggested only technical reforms in the systems of entail and primogeniture. He favored 'compulsory, free, national education until children are 14 years of age or have passed the sixth standard', but admitted 'I can't go much further than this. Both trade and farming', he explained, 'have to contribute their money to the taxes of this country; and many taxpayers consider that they are burdened heavily enough already.' As a salt manufacturer, he could attest to the burdens of the county rates, and on these grounds he refused to endorse proposals to provide compensation for victims of subsidence, though he saw no harm in referring the matter to a Royal Commission.

Verdin's address was hardly one to inspire enthusiasm; nor was his attitude toward his rival. Whereas Brunner declared that 'to the chosen man of that day, he would devote all the time and energy he had', Verdin refused to reciprocate with comparable assurances. When the votes were counted, Verdin refused to shake the hand of the man who had defeated him and accused Brunner of rigging the election by filling the hall with his henchmen. According to all accounts, the meeting ended in confusion, and various correspondents who wrote to congratulate Brunner on his victory scored Verdin's 'vulgar', 'low', and 'mean' attacks in the final moments. Within a week, Verdin's reasons for denying his support to Brunner had become evident. On April 18, at a meeting at Northwich, his younger brother, William Henry, was unanimously chosen to stand in the Conservative interest. Robert Verdin remained aloof from the ensuing campaign; but his brother's acceptance speech was strongly reminiscent of his own remarks the previous week at Leftwich. Brunner's Conservative opponent promised, if elected, 'to promote...the interests of the salt trade of the district, and to advocate the remission of taxation which presses heavily upon farmers. In regard to compensation to property owners for subsidence by pumping brine, he said he would advocate the appointment of a Royal Commission of Inquiry.'[1]

The two competing candidates promptly initiated their campaigns, anticipating momentarily a general election that was not called until late autumn. From the outset Brunner proclaimed himself not simply a Liberal, but a follower of Joseph Chamberlain, which was tantamount in some quarters to identifying himself as the devil's disciple. Like many younger Liberals, he had come to despair of Gladstone for encumbering himself with Whig colleagues and Whig policies, and he looked to Chamberlain to lead the party more dynamically in pursuit of social ideals. His affinity for Chamberlain is not hard to understand: members of the same generation, they shared the same religious and social background, and struggled in their respective communities against the same privileges and prejudices. Moreover, they were distantly related by marriage. Brunner had for many years corresponded with Chamberlain on matters of mutual interest—proposals for legislation regarding patents and forms of industrial regulation—and had worked with him in the National Education League. This devotion to Chamberlain was not so strange as it came to appear a few years later, when the high priest of Radicalism proved an apostate to the creed.

Radicalism, as Brunner conceived of it and as he practiced it all his life, was a complex phenomenon, in many ways more an attitude than a movement. It was a tradition that had its counterparts

[1] *The Times*, April 20, 1885.

elsewhere, but it ran particularly strong in nineteenth-century England, where industrialism and democracy had proceeded furthest and where theories of progress held greatest sway. As both a political force and a social ethic, Radicalism lost its strength at the time of the first world war, with the disappearance of the psychological and material conditions that had fostered and sustained it.

A significant ingredient in English thought and society for more than a century, the Radical tradition was too varied in its origins and methods to escape the pitfalls of paradox. It was, at any one time, internationalist and fiercely parochial, individualistic and collectivist, secular and deeply religious. And it possessed a conservative strain which should not be discounted. Lord Lytton, before he repudiated his youthful Radicalism for Disraelian imperialism, justly observed that 'the unparliamentary Radicals, who are labouring to keep alive a sentient soul in English society, are infinitely more conservative in the only worthy sense than the so-called Conservative Party, which can see nothing better to do than to serve as an awkward squad in the great Philistine Army...'[1] One can trace many of the theories of Radicalism—and several of its contradictions—to the eighteenth-century enlightenment, but that can easily be carried too far. Rather its roots are to be found in the peculiarly English conditions to which it was a response, though there were links through certain individuals—Morley in particular—with the Continental tradition. The internationalism that was so prominent a feature of English Radicalism owed far less to eighteenth-century philosophic humanism than to the dictates of an expanding industrial economy.

Radicalism reflected, too, the self-confidence of the English middle classes, their aspirations, and their growing influence upon institutions and behavior. It was their instrument to obtain a political and social status commensurate with their economic power, and to free themselves from a humiliating subservience to traditional authorities, squirearchical and ecclesiastical. Imbued

[1] Lytton to Morley, March 16, 1871, cited in S. E. Koss, *John Morley at the India Office, 1905–1910* (New Haven, 1969), p. 174n.

with a strong nonconformity, Radicalism had its own ethic of public service and social utility. While Radicals tended to distrust interference on the part of a state dominated by privileged amateurs, their aim was rarely categorical *laissez-faire*; as the century wore on, it became evident that they welcomed state action undertaken in a professional spirit and subject to popular controls.

A sense of grievance was never far beneath the Radical surface, and it expressed itself in geographical as well as personal terms. One found intense Radical activity along the so-called Celtic fringe, where regional or national sentiments were frustrated and where, in most cases, an alien church was maintained. But the real center of Radicalism lay in the thriving manufacturing districts of the north and midlands, where men of commercial wealth were perpetually irritated by demonstrations that political control continued to reside in the south and social influence upon the landed estates. Men of this stamp, Brunner included, were not only outraged by this tacit denial of their contribution to national life, but also frightened by its wider implications. Secure in the belief that the age of industrialism had superseded the age of militarism, and that Free Trade would induce international cooperation, they saw the constant need to protect and consolidate their gains. Only by exerting a just influence upon British affairs could they insure prosperity for themselves and their country, and, more important, harmony among men and nations.

The Liberal press in the area was pleased with Brunner's candidacy, and letters poured in from well-wishers. There was no response, however, from Ludwig Mond, who did not begrudge his partner a political career, but could not go very far in support of it. Mond had come far since the day in 1868 when he travelled out of his way to hear Gladstone address a South Lancashire campaign meeting. The breach was soon to be widened by the Liberal Party's commitment to Irish Home Rule, a cause of which he roundly disapproved. Even the eventual adoption of his son, Alfred, as a Liberal candidate failed to bring him back to the party fold. Mond declined to endorse Brunner by appearing on his election platform; and politics, one of the consuming interests of their youth, became a topic they thought best not to discuss.

O'Farrell Cox of Chester to stand in their interest.[1] But Parnell, seeking an accommodation with one or another of the English parties, vetoed that proposal. Instead the Irish leader, throwing his support to Conservative candidates, dispatched Dr Bernard O'Connor to Northwich to advise his followers to vote for Verdin and against Brunner.

Parnell's misguided strategy has been credited with the defeat of as many as forty Liberal members who might have been expected to deliver their votes for Home Rule in the next Parliament. Yet it backfired completely at Northwich, where personal loyalties transcended ethnic lines. Brunner, who employed many Irish workmen, was known to be sympathetic to Irish demands and to the maintenance of Roman Catholic schools. Moreover, the Irish Catholic voter had little reason to be impressed with Verdin, who chose as his spokesman an Anglican clergyman of Irish birth distinctly unfavorable to the Irish cause. Edward Hill, president of the Runcorn branch of the Irish National League, confirmed reports that 'the Irish leaders' had sent directives to support Verdin; but he assured Brunner that 'the Irishmen of Runcorn will not on this occasion at least vote for a Tory'.[2] When Parnell's emissary arrived at Northwich to bring his recalcitrant compatriots to heel, his cab was surrounded by Irishmen, who barred the entrance to his hotel and threatened to throw him from the window.[3]

Brunner fared less well at the hand of other sections of the community. As one of the largest employers in the constituency, he was fair game for a good deal of working-class heckling, much of it innocent enough. One 'jolly faced fellow' followed him from meeting to meeting to ask 'with a twinkle in his eye' for a job at Brunner, Mond. On a considerable number of occasions, his speeches were punctuated by catcalls from men 'whose native wit had evidently been quickened by deep draughts of beer'. But it was in the rural villages of the division that he could depend upon the worst reception. It was evident 'that a strong opposition had been carefully organised' before he appeared at Great

---

[1] *The Times*, September 23, 1885. [2] Hill to Brunner, October 2, 1885, BP.
[3] Autobiographical notebook, BP.

Budworth on November 6; and during the meeting, hecklers—reportedly agricultural laborers—constantly interrupted him with their taunts and by 'troop[ing] out, presumably to wet their whistles'.[1]

By far the most strenuous opposition Brunner encountered came from Anglican clergymen. His persistent call for disestablishment and his casual remark that the clergy were 'robbing the poor' brought a flurry of letters of remonstrance and denunciations from several pulpits. At first he replied publicly and privately to his 'divine slanderers', but eventually he lost patience and instructed his secretary 'not to gratify...[their] vanity by entering into correspondence'.[2] To one constituent, who had inquired politely about his political philosophy, Brunner attempted to set the matter straight:

It is of course impossible to put into the limits of notepaper a full statement of the case, but as J. S. Mill held that it is a good mental discipline from time to time to attempt the impossible, and [as] I am an admirer of his, I will try. *Firstly*, I should hold strongly that self-sacrifice is the very essence of Christ's teaching and that the Church of England in maintaining the privilege incident to the establishment denies Him. *Secondly*, that the portion of the Tithes due to the poor has long been withheld from them, and that it ought to be restored. *Thirdly*, that the Tithes—through no fault of the clergy except in so far as they acquiesce in the injustice—...and the Tithe Commutation Rent [are] in a modified degree a charge upon industry and never upon wealth. Witness the fact that deer and a deer park were never and are not now subject to the charge while the farmers' sheep and the cottagers' poultry were taxed.[3]

How did Brunner intend to remedy the situation? For one thing he trusted that a majority of Churchmen would eventually 'come round to my way of thinking and decide that in voluntarily giving up the privileges they...enjoy, they will be acting in full accordance with their Master's behests'.[4] Yet he realized it was 'probably Quixotic to hope for unanimity amongst Churchmen on this question at any rate in our time', and for this reason parliamentary action would ultimately be required. Still, he agreed

1 *Northwich and Winsford Chronicle*, September 26 and Nobember 7, 1885.
2 Note from Brunner to Ellis on letter from the Rev. W. Preston, October 5, 1885, BP.
3 Brunner to Mr Bennett, October 12 [1885] (copy), BP.
4 Brunner to the Rev. J. H. Cooper, October 14 [1885] (copy), BP.

with Gladstone 'that this question is not one for which the Liberal Party ought to ask for a decision at this election', and he affirmed that, like his leader, he was 'content to await the ripening of public opinion'.[1]

Despite his warm words for Gladstone, even going so far as to defend Gladstonian policy in Egypt and the Sudan, Brunner left no doubt that he remained a Chamberlain man. The platform he expounded came straight from Chamberlain's 'unauthorized programme', and his rhetoric straight from the Birmingham caucus. In a key address at Northwich on September 28, he advocated reforms in local government, control of the liquor traffic, 'freedom of the schools', and 'free trade in land'. Like Chamberlain, whom he commended to his audience, he realized that Liberalism's hopes in the current election lay with those who were voting for the first time:

For many a long year have the faithful Liberals of Cheshire fought an up-hill fight against landlord domination and Toryism. Again and again have their gallant attempts to storm the Tory citadel been repulsed. But the democracy of Cheshire is now enfranchised, and the Liberals are facing the future with a fuller faith and a larger hope.[2]

His proposal to abolish school fees evoked the logical question where the necessary funds would come from, and Brunner echoed Chamberlain that, personally, he would 'cheerfully' pay an additional three farthings in the pound on his income tax for so worthy a purpose.[3] He wished it clearly understood that, notwithstanding his Radicalism, he could be as concerned for public welfare and as devoted to Christian tenets as an Englishman of any political denomination; and he boasted that in all the kingdom there was no more devoted monarchist than he.

Much of Brunner's electoral appeal was due to the fact that, unlike his opponent, he was not engaged in the salt trade and took a strong line on the question of compensation for victims of subsidence. There was no more palpable issue in the Northwich constituency, where the unregulated pumping of brine had brought about the collapse of buildings and indeed whole streets.

[1] Brunner to ?, November 4, 1885 (copy), BP.
[2] *Northwich and Winsford Chronicle*, October 3, 1885.
[3] Brunner to J. H. Cooke, October 9, 1885 (copy), BP.

Brunner demanded that the salt manufacturers, either independently or through the Salt Union, assume responsibility for this damage. Verdin, on the other hand, demurred, citing diverse legal and moral objections. The salt manufacturers, he argued from first-hand experience, could not afford to bear the costs of compensation, and he pointed to the fact that they paid a shilling to ship each ton of their product down the Weaver, while Brunner, Mond and Company shipped its alkali at only eight pence a ton. It was therefore Brunner, he insisted, who enjoyed privileges, and who should be made by increased rates to bear the brunt of compensation. Brunner easily disposed of that argument, disclaiming responsibility for the Weaver tolls, which had been fixed by the Weaver Trustees—a solidly Tory body—before he was born.

As the weeks passed, the level of the campaign descended. A leader in the local Liberal newspaper lamented the fact that Verdin chose to fill his speeches with 'nothing but remarks on Mr Brunner's personal character, his trade relations, his theological convictions, and other matters equally foreign to the issue before the constituency'.[1] To one degree or another, this was true of every election in which Brunner stood. Though his opponents differed considerably through the years in background and ability, they invariably challenged him to defend not only his political views but his company's record. With each campaign charges and innuendoes were revived about the exploitation of labor at Brunner, Mond, conditions at the works, and the extent of the firm's investment abroad. With Brunner's foreign name, a guttural inflection in his speech, and his German-Jewish partner, it was common for his national origins to be disputed and his patriotism impugned. On all of these scores, the 1885 campaign was particularly vicious. Verdin declared a churchwarden guilty of a 'moral offence' for supporting Brunner, and his charges of slave labor at Brunner, Mond were preposterous. Amusingly, his remarks rebounded against him when it was learned that his brother, Robert, held shares in the company.

Polling at Northwich, originally fixed for November 27, took place on Tuesday, December 1. It was one of the Cheshire con-

---

[1] *Northwich and Winsford Chronicle*, October 17, 1885.

tests that attracted least attention in the national press, but it was no less frenetic for that. In the closing days William Rathbone came to speak for Brunner, prefacing his visit with an affectionate letter to ask 'what merits in the son of my old friend it is desirable to bring into prominence'.[1] By this late date, a majority of constituencies had declared their polls, and the Liberal performance was not encouraging. Still Brunner nursed hopes of reversing the trend. On the 27th, Ellis jotted a hasty note to a Welsh friend: 'Electioneering like mad, think Brunner will win. Boroughs are disastrous. Just off to what will be a terribly stormy meeting.'[2]

The unruliness that had characterized the election came to a climax on polling day. Disruptions of the poll were a local tradition and, as the *Manchester Guardian* scornfully observed on December 2, 'the disreputable classes of Northwich seem[ed] determined to keep up their notoriety for rough play during election times'. According to a report that day in *The Times*, the violence was reciprocal. Voting

proceeded quietly until dusk, but there were unmistakable indications of coming disturbances and all the tradesmen put up their shutters. The central Conservative offices were first attacked. All the windows were smashed and several clerks narrowly escaped injury. The Conservative candidate had just left the building...Shortly after 7 o'clock the Riot Act was read...The police then made a determined charge with truncheons, and the streets being narrow and crooked, several deplorable accidents occurred. The Liberals indignantly denounced the action of the police as brutal, especially the case of an elderly man named Evans, whose head was cracked by a truncheon... The public library has been closed to guard against retaliation, the building being the gift of the Liberal candidate...The town bridge is specially guarded, men being overheard arranging to stop a brass band and to throw their instruments into the river.

Late that evening, the returning officer announced that Brunner had won with a healthy majority of 1028 votes. The ill feeling between parties and candidates was not dispelled, and Verdin, hearing the news, refused to extend his hand in congratulation.

The eight Cheshire divisions were split evenly between the Liberals and Conservatives, but the Conservatives outnumbered

[1] Rathbone to Brunner, November 20, 1885, BP.
[2] Ellis to D. R. Daniel, November 27, 1885 (postmark), Ellis Papers (National Library of Wales).

3-2

Liberals in the boroughs—Chester, Birkenhead and Stockport—three to one. In view of the 'unbroken Conservative traditions of the county', the *Manchester Guardian* was not entirely disappointed. But the outcome in the nation at large fell far below the expectations of most Liberals. Various correspondents to *The Times* suggested that the Radicals had frightened away voters with their revolutionary designs, but in truth Liberalism had drawn considerable strength in this contest from the Radical appeal to new voters. Recollections of the Sudan episode had worked against Gladstone, as had Parnell's directives. And certainly the disorganization of the Liberal leadership, reflecting deep ideological cleavages, had impaired the party's effectiveness. The Liberals emerged from the general election with a majority over the Conservatives of 86 seats; but the Irish Nationalists commanded precisely this number, making Parnell the fulcrum between the two English parties. Only the Liberals could form a majority Government, and this was possible only on the sufferance of Parnell.

Brunner's supporters were jubilant, and confident that a Radical age had dawned. 'No electoral triumph reflects more honour upon the new electors than that of Northwich,' declared the division's Liberal newspaper. 'The newly-enfranchised overcame theological hatred, insular prejudice, trade jealousies, and Parnellite dictation.'[1] But Joseph Chamberlain, in his letter of congratulation, put the matter in better perspective: 'I rejoice very much in your victory, which is the more gratifying because Cheshire has not done all that was expected of it. The Territorial influences that you have [had] to contend with are, however, very strong.'[2] The forces against Brunner had a resilience that was not to be underestimated; they drove him from his seat the following spring, and though he soon returned to Parliament, they continued for a quarter century to provide vigorous opposition to him. He achieved a victory in 1885 that allowed him to carry his battle to Westminster. But the war was only beginning and, meanwhile, the Liberal armies were in disarray.

[1] *Northwich and Winsford Chronicle*, December 5, 1885.
[2] Chamberlain to Brunner, December 5, 1885, BP.

CHAPTER 4

A BRIEF AND TROUBLED
PARLIAMENT

The Parliament to which John Brunner had been elected did not assemble at Westminster until after the new year. It opened with the Conservatives still in office, but on January 27 the Government was defeated on a relatively minor issue—Jesse Collings's amendment to an agrarian bill—and Lord Salisbury bowed to the inevitable and resigned. Within a week Gladstone, his intention to press for Home Rule by this time an open secret, had formed his third and shortest-lived ministry. It lasted until June, when another general election was called, and in its brief existence it changed the structure and spirit of British party politics.

Could there have been a more exciting session in which to make one's parliamentary debut? On both sides of the House the luminaries of late-Victorian politics stood at the height of their powers, and several of them—Parnell, John Bright, and Lord Randolph Churchill—would soon pass from the scene. Gladstone's retirement continued to be expected imminently, adding to the prevailing uncertainty and imparting all the more urgency to the Home Rule cause. The issues of the day lent themselves to brilliant oratory. The complex relationships between personalities and parties lent themselves to intrigue. And the allocation of seats in this Parliament—with the Liberals, badly divided, dependent upon Irish support for their slender majority—afforded a novice like Brunner the rare opportunity to cast a crucial vote. Exposed to such a situation, he quickly became a veteran parliamentarian.

'Mr Brunner', Ellis wrote to Edward Milner back at Northwich, 'was in the first batch of members. . .and got through the swearing very comfortably.'[1] But in an address to his constituents a few months later,[2] Brunner described his first day at Parliament as somewhat more of an ordeal. He arrived at Westminster on

---

[1] Ellis to Milner, January 15, 1886, ICI Archives.
[2] *Northwich and Winsford Chronicle*, April 24, 1886.

69

January 12, 'a sheep without a shepherd', and the first problem that confronted him was to decide which of the various doors to enter. This, he jested, posed a moral as well as a practical dilemma, for he had vowed to go to Parliament with 'a free right, and [to] ask nobody any questions'. After due deliberation, he compromised his principles and approached 'those appointed guardians of law and order, the "bobbies", and they...."moved me on". So, by slow degrees, I found where to hang my coat and where to deposit my hat.'

This second step, it seems, proved no less a hurdle for Brunner, who was admittedly more than a bit awed by his surroundings. He discovered that, for reasons no one could explain, 'the place for your coat and the place for your hat are a very long way apart'. The cloakroom was reached through three sets of doors, and around its walls were hooks, each labelled with a member's name. These were arranged in alphabetical order, and Brunner hung his coat, not far from the door, between those of R. P. Bruce and James Bryce. His fellow M.P.s, he recounted, noted a striking resemblance between him and Bryce, 'and I have been taken for Mr Bryce over and over again'. Luckily, they had substantially more in common than their bearded profiles, and it was easy for them to agree 'that neither of us will have any need to fear...[one] will do something that the other would not like to have attributed to him...'

Brunner continued to be amazed by the ancient traditions of the House, and particularly by the enthusiasm with which even the most outspoken Radicals submitted to them. 'I went one day to see the ceremony which is called the declaration of the Queen's consent to a Bill,' he told his enraptured audience.

The Speaker went in his usual dignified style to the House of Lords, preceded by the mace and followed by his trainbearer, and a very unruly and, as we should say in Lancashire, 'a thrutchin lot' of members. Arrived in the House of Lords, we stood in a place uncommonly like a sheep pen. Halfway down that noble building, which is one of the most beautiful rooms I have ever seen, there is a table with a clerk on each side, and almost at the far end there is the Lord Chancellor with a Peer on each side attired in scarlet robes lined and fringed with ermine. The Speaker of the House of Commons, the representative of the people of England, the representative of the majesty and the power of England, stands in the sheep pen, and these three men sitting far away in the distance with their hats on! I mean to protest, as long as I have breath, against that ignoble treatment of the representative of the people. These three figures, who hardly looked as if they were alive, lifted their hats exactly like waxwork. The clerks at the table went through a performance, it was not much more than a mummery, and we understood that the Queen had given her consent to the Bills passed by the House of Commons and the House of Lords.

Yet, incensed as he might have been by such elaborate rituals, he had to admit that he was not altogether immune from their appeal. As was the custom for new members, he left his card upon the Speaker, 'and in due course was invited to attend his *levée*'. His uniform for the occasion consisted of

a velvet cut-away coat, a splendid cocked hat, velvet continuations, and silk stockings, and the loveliest buckles on my shoes that you ever saw. That is not all. Such a sword! I really must have been, though I did not think so myself, perfectly beautiful.

More to his amusement than disappointment, he found himself at the *levée* 'a poor grub amongst a lot of brilliant butterflies', all dressed more splendidly than he. It was well worth the effort and expense to see L. L. Dillwyn, 'Radical amongst Radicals, [who] had blossomed out until it was almost impossible to identify [him as] the man who sat in the House of Commons with a shockingly bad hat'. Still, Brunner did not wish to leave his constituents with the impression that he did not respect the House or that he took lightly the duties they had entrusted to him. He closed by thanking them for their support and, above all else, for giving him the opportunity and privilege 'of sitting in the same House' as Gladstone, whom he expected to retire at the end of the present session.

Aside from a single interruption of thirteen months, Brunner sat for the Northwich division for the next twenty-five years. What sort of a parliamentarian did he make? The success of his career, as full as it was long, would be difficult to measure by conventional standards. His disappointments outnumbered his victories; his frustrations, his satisfactions. Yet his was always the gratification of fighting a worthwhile battle and fighting it well. For two-thirds of his tenure in the House, he experienced all the discomforts of the Opposition backbenches. He retired before Home Rule, the issue that had dominated his early career, was safe upon the statute book. And the outbreak of war in August 1914 put an abrupt end to more than a decade's efforts to achieve disarmament and international accord.

Despite the seniority that came to him in time, he never attained Cabinet rank. Not that he was material for Downing Street, but he would have made an admirable head of the Board of Trade, the Local Government Board, or the Board of Education. He was, however, too young and insufficiently known when the Liberals took office in 1886 and 1892, and too old to begin a ministerial career when they at last returned to power at the close of 1905. Nor was his career distinguished, in the Victorian manner, by lofty flights of oratory. In content and delivery, his parliamentary speeches rarely captured the flavor he projected at campaign hustings, where he was more in his element. Over the years his prepared addresses were comparatively few, and not nearly so effective as the spirited interjections for which he was better known. These verbal thrusts were intended to make a point and, more often than not, to provoke laughter at the expense of the Tories. They generally succeeded in both respects before the Speaker could rule him out of order.

Even staunch Tories found him difficult to resist. The *Liverpool Courier*, though it declined to go so far as to endorse his candidacy ('We lament his politics, but we appreciate his qualities'), paid him unusual tribute in 1905 for 'his English honesty and downright pugnacious determinism', and noted approvingly that he 'never loses a chance of cracking a joke. He will break off in the middle of the most serious oration to tell one, and positively refuse to continue his remarks until he has led the laughter with his own characteristic deep-chested roar.'[1] As one would expect, the Liberal *Daily News* spoke still more glowingly of his 'delightful' and 'fatherly humour'. Reporting his speech in the House on November 2, 1909, in support of the Lloyd George budget—his last and in every respect his most successful speech

[1] December 7, 1905.

in the chamber—it ascribed his effectiveness to moral earnestness: 'This heavily-bearded veteran of politics and industry, with the deep, dark eyes, the rich bass voice, and the clear, decisive, though benevolent style of speech, scored the success which always attends sincerity.' Yet this account did not ignore the 'happy wit' with which he punctuated his presentation, and his genial response when the Speaker once more 'gently' rebuked him for digressing from the subject.[1]

His digressions were nearly as predictable as the issues on which he chose to speak. They were anecdotal and invariably autobiographical. Sometimes they consisted of an amusing story he had heard from one of his children or from a colleague in the corridor, sometimes of a statistic he had obtained from his business, sometimes of a recollection from his boyhood. He never hesitated to allude to his achievement as an industrialist or, for that matter, to his immense wealth. After all, his commercial fortune was sufficiently well publicized for there to be no reason for him to deny his affluence. Besides, there was a delicious satisfaction to be obtained from displaying himself as a Radical plutocrat, whom age and material success had not rendered more conservative. Tongue in cheek, he professed not to 'speak...as the enemy of any man because he is wealthy', and he took the peals of laughter that greeted his remark as a welcome indication that 'my honourable friends here evidently believe in my sincerity upon that point'.[2]

Brunner faced the Northwich electorate a total of seven times, and he was successful all but the second. On at least two occasions his opponents were men of exceptional ability, but they stood little chance of dislodging him. After his first decade in the House it was evident that he could have his seat as long as he wanted it. It was rumored that the Conservatives, who grudgingly recognized this fact, offered not to oppose him in 1906 if he would reciprocate with a promise to withhold his support, financial and otherwise, from other Liberal candidates in the north-west; such a bargain was all the more unthinkable in Liberalism's long-

[1] November 3, 1909.
[2] *Parliamentary Debates*, 4th ser., LXVI, col. 535 (February 10, 1899).

awaited moment of triumph. The impregnability of his position was testimony to his high standing among his neighbors and to the effectiveness of the Liberal organization he had single-handedly created. These were assets that served him equally well in meeting challenges from a variety of directions.

Brunner's pre-eminence in Cheshire was assured by the defection of local Whig aristocrats from the Liberal Party. Chief among them was the first Duke of Westminster, raised from a marquisate in 1874, lord lieutenant of the county, and an extensive property-holder. The Duke, who sat in the Commons before his father's death in 1869, had been an implacable opponent of franchise reform; thereafter he grew increasingly unnerved by the drift toward Radicalism within his party. During the general election of 1885 he made known his sympathies by signing a manifesto that called upon Chester voters to reject any candidate who supported disestablishment. The significance of this move was not lost upon *The Times*, which observed that, 'with one exception, every Liberal candidate in Cheshire is in favour of the principle of religious equality...' If there remained any doubt of the Duke's intentions, he removed it a few days later by publishing a letter that asserted his neutrality in the contest at Chester, though 'I should have been in favour of a good [i.e. non-Radical] Liberal candidate'.[1]

The size and spirit of the Radical phalanx in the new House accelerated the Whig exodus. And Gladstone's appointment of Radicals in unprecedented number to his third Government confirmed Whig fears. Chamberlain once again sat in the Cabinet, though not for long, and the loss of Dilke was offset by the arrival of A. J. Mundella, Lord Herschell, Sir Henry Campbell-Bannerman, and John Morley. Gladstone welcomed this belated injection of young blood, but his Whig critics rightly interpreted the composition of the new Cabinet as a commitment to a host of far-reaching projects, most notably Home Rule. They had fought many battles beneath Gladstone's standard, but they were in no mood to fight others for principles that were anathema to them. The Duke of Westminster's response was typical. He refused to

1 *The Times*, November 6 and 11, 1885.

dignify the new ministry with his presence and announced his conversion to Liberal Unionism, a half-way house on the road to Conservatism.

Unlike those who refused to affiliate in any capacity with the new ministry, the most important being Lord Hartington, Chamberlain agreed—against his better judgment, he later made out—to take the Local Government Board, an office which his talents and reputation had long since outgrown. A more important assignment would have bound him too closely to the Government's Irish policy, from which he wished to maintain a distance. For nearly two months he exerted subtle pressures, waiting to see exactly how far Gladstone intended to proceed with Home Rule and on what terms. His questions were answered on March 26 with the promulgation of a bill to which he felt himself unable to assent. He resigned, taking with him Sir George Trevelyan, the secretary for Scotland. Though Chamberlain had refused to be a party to the sponsorship of such a measure, it remained for the time being entirely unclear what position he would adopt when the bill was put to the ultimate test of a third reading.

The new member for Northwich saw little reason to lament the departure of the Whigs, whose predominance in past Liberal Governments he had rightly regarded as a brake upon progress. In any event, he reasoned, a realignment of parties along more meaningful lines could not be long postponed. What distressed him was that many Radicals, and Chamberlain in particular, outdid the Whigs in their denunciations of Gladstonian policy. This was a situation for which he was not prepared, as indeed few politicians were. He had doubted for years whether the union between Whigs and Radicals would survive Gladstone's retirement; now, it seemed, such a union was being perpetuated with an anti-Gladstonian focus. This turnabout was painful to Brunner, who had made a conscientious effort to reconcile his devotion to Chamberlain with his allegiance to Gladstone's leadership. His predicament was shared by many Liberals, and in it one can see the forces that shattered Liberal unity.

Throughout these months Brunner never doubted the logic or the morality of conceding Home Rule to Ireland. Yet he was reluctant to accept the fact that his stand on this issue cut him off from Chamberlain, whose program in all other respects matched his own. Having arrived at Westminster a 'Chamberlain man', he hoped in vain that Chamberlain would do nothing to remove himself from the Liberal succession. As best he could, he attempted to keep a foot in each camp. He continued to take an active interest in the Allotments Association, founded by Chamberlain to promote the legislation of an Allotments and Small Holdings Bill.[1] And he was more than glad to respond to Chamberlain's appeal for subscriptions to help Jesse Collings, his trusty hench-man, defend his seat at Ipswich against charges of 'personal corruption'.[2] Brunner contributed fifty pounds on April 13, a week after the first reading of the Home Rule Bill; and the letter that accompanied his check made clear his desire to keep open the channels of communication: 'I am happy to believe that the second reading of the Bill is safe', he wrote to Chamberlain, 'and heartily trust that your opposition will be neither bitter nor vehement, so that...[with] as little difficult[y] as possible,... you...[will] resume your old place as one of the leaders of the united party, or better still to become the acknowledged leader.'[3] Chamberlain immediately wrote to acknowledge Brunner's gen-erosity and, still more, to correct the impression that his opposi-tion to Home Rule was strictly *pro forma*. 'I am sorry that you are going to vote for the Disruption Bill,' he told Brunner, making a sarcastic reference to the idea of breaking the Anglo-Irish Union. 'I think you will regret it before many years have passed. I fear that the Liberal Party will be disorganised for some time to come and that all progress will be stayed indefinitely.'[4]

Home Rule split the Liberal Party not only in Parliament, but also in the constituencies. The Northwich Liberal Association called for a special meeting of its general council at Runcorn on April 17, and summoned Brunner to justify his stand.[5] Before he spoke, various local leaders confided to him their grave reserva-

[1] Collings to Brunner, September 10, 1885, BP.
[2] Chamberlain to Brunner, March 24 and April 12, 1886, BP.
[3] Brunner to Chamberlain, April 13, 1886 (copy), BP.
[4] Chamberlain to Brunner, April 13, 1886, BP.
[5] *Northwich and Winsford Guardian*, April 21, 1886.

tions about Gladstone's Irish policy and reminded him of his campaign promises to defend the Chamberlain program. He thanked them for their opinions, but affirmed his intention to vote for the bill. It was not 'a perfect Bill', he admitted,

any more than I think the Land Purchase Bill a perfect Bill. With regard to the latter I have told you that I think the landlords are to get too much money. With regard to the Home Rule Bill, I don't like the exclusion of the Irish members from the Parliament of Westminster; and I agree with Mr Chamberlain in his reasons for disliking that exclusion, for I want the Parliament of Westminster to be the supreme, the Imperial Parliament. I agree with him, too, that it is a wrong thing to ask the Irish to pay money to us that we may spend it and that they should have no voice in the spending. I object, too, that when England shall get into trouble...and be compelled to go to war, that the Irish should...not be called upon to join us. It would place the Irish in a subordinate condition which I look upon as a position of degradation.

Notwithstanding these objections, Brunner declared his determination to 'keep my freedom' and to vote for Home Rule and Land Purchase, both measures that in his opinion contained 'a large balance of good'.

Brunner did not disguise from his constituents his concern at the disintegration of the Liberal Party, and he called the roll of politicians who had 'ratted'. He expressed relief that Lord Hartington was gone, and with him the Duke of Westminster. But there was no reason to celebrate the resignation of Trevelyan ('I trust that some day we shall be working side by side again') or Chamberlain, to whom he referred in affectionate and respectful terms. In private as well as public, he continued to ascribe Chamberlain's opposition to outraged principle rather than frustrated ambition. Yet it grew more questionable as the weeks passed whether this was indeed the case. Tom Ellis, who, more quickly than his employer, grew disenchanted with Chamberlain, described the situation on May 6 to a friend:

Chamberlain has been almost malignantly industrious in writing letters full of animosity against the G.O.M.—which as you may imagine is doing him no good. It was said openly in the Lobby just before Chamberlain's resignation that Chamberlain said he would 'sweep Gladstone out of public life'. He may ultimately but at present it is a mighty tough job![1]

[1] Ellis to Daniel, May 6, 1886, Daniel Papers (National Library of Wales).

Reginald Brett (later Lord Esher) provided a similar account to Lewis Harcourt, Sir William's son, on the 19th: 'Chamberlain hopes and expects to be Prime Minister in the next Parliament, but this John Morley and all C's friends see to be impossible *yet*.'[1] It cannot be denied that, however sincerely Chamberlain opposed Home Rule on public grounds, there were also strong personal grounds on which he acted. He had grown tired of waiting for Gladstone to step down, and with the introduction of Home Rule that prospect had become more remote than ever. Admittedly, he had been bruised by Gladstone's failure to consult with him on the matter, a tacit denial of his importance in party councils. And not least of all, he correctly perceived the lack of popular enthusiasm for Home Rule in the country, and had no wish to be tied to such an albatross for decades to come.

'Inside the House', Morley later recalled, 'subterranean activity was at its height all through the month of May...On the ministerial side men wavered and changed and changed again, from day to day and almost from hour to hour.'[2] On the 27th Gladstone summoned his followers by circular to a meeting at the Foreign Office, where he expounded for an hour upon the merits of Home Rule and the consequences of its possible rejection. He implored those who had doubts to give the bill their vote and to trust to its satisfactory amendment in committee. Many of his critics within the party had stayed away, and some who attended thought his arguments casuistical. Discussion was heated, and Brunner did the Prime Minister 'a personal service by bringing to a happy end the meeting...with a call for "Three Cheers for Mr Gladstone"'.[3]

The climax came in the early hours of June 8, when the Commons defeated the Home Rule Bill in its second reading by a margin of thirty votes. Until the last moment the 'subterranean activity' had continued, with frantic efforts to persuade dissentient Liberals to vote for the bill or, at very least, to abstain. But

---

[1] Lewis Harcourt's Journals, May 19, 1886, Harcourt Papers (Stanton Harcourt, Oxfordshire).
[2] Morley, *Life of Gladstone* (3 vols., London, 1903), III, 323.
[3] Brunner to Gladstone, October 4, 1886 (copy), BP; for the May 27 meeting, see Morley, III, 333–4.

ninety-three Liberals, led by Chamberlain, went into the Opposition lobby, thereby formalizing a situation that most observers had come to regard, happily or not, as a settled fact.

Under the circumstances, Gladstone could either resign, leaving Lord Salisbury to form a minority Government, or recommend a dissolution of Parliament and a new general election. Though his colleagues had mixed feelings on the matter, Gladstone favored the second course as both just and expedient. He was determined that on no account should the party appear to have lost heart on Home Rule. ' . . . A dissolution is formidable', he conceded, 'but resignation would mean for the present juncture abandonment of the cause.'[1] With moderate hopes of increasing their majority, the Liberals presented their case to the electorate in July. More specifically, they expected to impress the waverers in their ranks with the country's underlying sympathy for Ireland's ambitions. On both scores they were severely disappointed.

Only seven months after he had first obtained his seat, Brunner prepared to defend it. He had not expected his mandate to expire so quickly and himself to be faced so soon with the effort and expense of another election. Not that there existed any question of his intention either in his mind or in the minds of his followers. As soon as Parliament was dissolved, he announced that he would again stand for Northwich in the Liberal interest. *The Times*, reporting his statement, declared that it was 'generally understood' in the constituency that W. H. Verdin would again oppose him.[2] Brunner himself probably presumed that this would be the case. But the political situation had changed too drastically in the intervening months for a repetition of the previous contest.

In this election, unlike the last, the Irish Nationalists were enthusiastic allies of the Liberals. But the Liberals were grievously split, and a significant number—calling themselves Liberal Unionists—spurned Gladstone's leadership. The Conservatives effectively adjusted their strategy to these conditions. In constituencies where they were strong, they stood independently as before. But where they found that Liberals 'cannot be opposed

---

[1] *Ibid.* p. 341.　　　　[2] June 11, 1886.

with any chance of success', they threw their support to Liberal Unionists, through whom they worked to defeat Gladstonian candidates.[1]

Brunner's opponent in 1886 was not W. H. Verdin, but his brother, Robert, whom he had edged out for the Liberal nomination the previous year. Robert Verdin had professed his neutrality in the last general election, when his brother stood as a Conservative against Brunner. But his displeasure with recent trends in Liberal policy was well known, and had been heightened by Gladstone's espousal of Home Rule. As a Liberal Unionist, Robert Verdin sounded remarkably like his Conservative brother. Yet he made an undeniable appeal to many Liberals, who could not bring themselves to vote Conservative, but who nonetheless were confused or disheartened by the past session's events.

So far as Brunner was concerned, there was only one authentic Liberalism, the Gladstonian variety, and he was its accredited spokesman. The Liberal Council of the division agreed, and accorded him its unanimous endorsement on June 19. Moreover, he argued, there was only one true Unionism, not the 'union upon paper' that the Tories defended, but the union based upon mutual respect that Gladstone had proposed. 'You will be told you are to vote for union and not separation,' he told a 'Real Unionist' meeting at Northwich on June 23, and he urged his audience to beware of a union bound by chains. He had high praise for the Irish members, their sincerity and capabilities: 'These men are not as well dressed as the Tories. These men are like you and like me. They were not born with silver spoons in their mouths.' It was to social prejudice that he ascribed 'the largest part of the opposition' to Home Rule: it came 'from the "swells"—from the men of great rank, of great inheritance—... [who] are galled to the quick by the idea that they shall be governed by men of the people'.[2] This might have been an exaggerated account of the national situation, yet to a large extent it held true for the situation in Cheshire.

While Home Rule hardly introduced dissension into Cheshire

---

[1] *The Times*, June 14, 1886.
[2] *Northwich and Winsford Chronicle*, June 26, 1886.

politics and society, it unquestionably exacerbated tensions that had been gathering for decades. If nothing else, the Irish problem brought strong light to bear upon local issues:

It threatened the rights of property owners by bringing those of Irish land-lords into question; it proclaimed the right of the mass electorate to a popular franchise; it suggested an extension of the powers of the Church of Rome. On all these counts the landowners and businessmen of Cheshire, as elsewhere, tended to take the Unionist part.[1]

The Duke of Westminster had by this time divorced himself from the Gladstonians and had thrown his enormous influence to the Unionists. He acquired a controlling interest in the *Chester Courant*, converting it into a Unionist organ, and scrambled for shares in other journals. His activity precipitated a stampede into the Unionist camp on the part of the lesser gentry, and James Tomkinson, who was engaged in an unsuccessful attempt to win Eddisbury for the Liberals, described himself to Gladstone as the single member of the 'landed interest' in Cheshire who had not followed the Duke's lead.[2] Ducal influence was felt most acutely, however, in the borough of Chester, where Westminster main-tained his fief. Walter Foster, a Gladstonian Liberal who had sat for Chester in the previous Parliament, was denied the Duke's endorsement and was consequently unseated.

With time at a premium, campaigning began almost as soon as Parliament was dissolved and continued at a fevered pace. On June 19 Lord Spencer carried the Home Rule banner to Chester, and Brunner sat prominently upon the platform. In his remarks on this and subsequent occasions, he identified himself as a fervent Gladstonian and a confirmed Home Ruler. He nursed regrets that Chamberlain did not share his views, but it was in-conceivable to him that Chamberlain could very much longer perpetuate his improbable alliance with the privileged classes. He 'wished most heartily that they had him back again', he told a Northwich meeting later that day, 'and he would make great sacrifices to get him back again'. Yet to no extent would he blame

[1] Lee, *Social Leaders*, p. 37.
[2] Tomkinson to Gladstone, July 2, 1886, Gladstone Papers, British Museum, Add. MSS. 44498, fols. 114–15; see also Lee, pp. 36–7.

Gladstone for Chamberlain's alienation from the party, and he cited 'a private conversation last October' in which Chamberlain had assured him 'that he. . . never met a man more willing to hear the arguments of others' than the Grand Old Man.[1]

The essential task, as Brunner saw it, was to dispel popular misconceptions about the workings and intentions of Home Rule. But how was this to be done? The opposition preyed upon fears that loyal Irish Protestants would be placed at the mercy of treacherous Papists, that the Empire was being dismembered, and that massive Irish relief schemes would be financed out of the pockets of English taxpayers. Brunner did his best to refute such allegations, but even the eloquence of a Gladstone was powerless against them. Flanked by a local vicar, minister, and priest, he strenuously denied to an audience at Middlewich that Gladstone proposed to indemnify Irish landlords out of English funds to the sum of £150 million. To the contrary, he explained, the Liberals proposed to have the Government purchase land and to sell it directly to tenants: 'The experience of the past showed that while the Government had lost heavily by lending money to landlords, the money lent to tenants was returned with full interest, and almost to the uttermost farthing.'[2] Yet the subtleties of land purchase, like those of Home Rule, tended to elude his listeners, leaving the Unionists frightened and the Liberals doubtful.

It was customary for each candidate to publish an open letter to the electors of the division in the front-page classified columns of the local press; these duly appeared in the *Chronicle* on July 3. Verdin's address was indicative of the Unionist approach in that it avoided specifics and spoke in general terms about the vagaries of Gladstonian leadership, the potential evils of Home Rule, and the insidious threat to the Protestant faith. Brunner's address was more personal in tone: 'You took me into your service last December as an apprentice,' he reminded his constituents;

I wish to remain in that service as a journeyman. I ask no higher wages, but only a renewal of your confidence and a continuance of your kindness. . . Again, I say, that while holding myself at liberty to look beyond the pro-

[1] *Northwich and Winsford Chronicle*, June 26, 1886.
[2] *Chester Chronicle*, July 3, 1886.

gramme set forth by our venerated leader, Mr Gladstone, I vow myself now, . . . as heretofore, a warm supporter and a devoted follower of him who more than all living statesmen is entitled to our affection and our gratitude.

These humble pleadings were sufficient to win him the renewed endorsement of the *Chronicle*, whose leader concluded that 'it is impossible not to realize at once how unsubstantial and shadowy are the arguments of Mr Verdin, and how solid as to their foundations and firm as to their structure are those of his opponent'.[1]

Others were not so easily convinced, among them the industrial workers who competed for jobs with immigrant Irishmen. A rough campaign had been taken for granted, but the exploitation of the religious issue added appreciably to the violence and disruption. Each expression of support for Brunner received from the Irish voters, who were well organized, aroused more bitter antagonism on the part of those who professed to defend Church and Crown. On his way to a meeting one evening, he was attacked by hooligans who struck his groom, attempted to upset his carriage by frightening his horse, and pelted him with refuse; his wife, who accompanied him, was injured by an unidentified missile. Verdin promptly deplored the incident, for which he disclaimed any responsibility, but the Liberal press did not forgo the opportunity to proclaim that, 'even in their local contest, the Conservatives cannot forget their habits of coercion... Like their distinguished leaders in the country, they made mud flinging serve as a political argument.'[2]

The Northwich contest in 1886 was vastly more exciting in terms of issues than personalities. Aside from the modest assistance he received at the last minute from a few Radical M.P.s, all men of lesser stature, Brunner relied upon his own resources, local speaking talent, and, quite heavily, upon Ellis. The burdens of such concentrated activity took a toll upon him, and illness removed him from circulation during the crucial weekend before polling. By this time it was evident that things were going badly for the Liberals, and that at best he would be returned with a diminished majority. Under the circumstances, he would have gladly settled for that. In the polls that were already declared,

---

[1] July 3, 1886.   [2] *Ibid.* July 10, 1886.

beginning with Colchester on the first of the month, the voters had varied in their response to Home Rule between tempered indifference and outright hostility. Half-way through the election, prominent Liberals had begun to draft letters, diagnosing the party's ailments and prescribing remedies. Nor did prominent defectors lose any time gloating at the party's distress. 'The great mass of the working classes in the English constituencies', the Duke of Westminster wrote to Gladstone on July 13, 'have pronounced against your policy and...I find myself in cordial cooperation with them and with the aristocracy—a happy combination and one full of good augury for the future...'[1] That day, Northwich gave seeming confirmation to the Duke's view.

Henry Labouchere, in a letter to Herbert Gladstone on the 9th,[2] provided an astute analysis of the Liberal reverses that had taken place and that would claim Brunner's seat, among others, in the days ahead. 'We have not had speeches enough in the local meetings and lying has been triumphant,' he reported, basing this observation on the fact that 'every day I have had dozens of telegrams asking me to go down to this or that place, which I have been unable to do, as in winning my seat I entirely lost my voice, it being the unpleasant habit in Northampton to shout politics in the Market Place'. The Radical vote, sufficient to pull the party through the last election, had this time failed to turn out. This was not, he argued, out of loyalty to Chamberlain ('I do not think that he has influenced a dozen votes out of Birmingham'), but rather out of a disappointment that 'Justice to Ireland [was] not being accompanied by some radical sops for England'. In particular, Radical objections to the land purchase scheme would have to be overcome. Labouchere was confident that, given the right incentives, Radicals would flock back to the fold. The extent of the Liberal rout was not yet apparent to him. The party would recover by Easter, he was convinced, 'if only Mr G. will stand to his guns' and policy was clarified. 'So soon as the Radicals per-

[1] Westminster to Gladstone, July 13, 1886, Gladstone Papers, Add. MSS. 44337, fols. 385–6.
[2] Labouchere to Herbert Gladstone, July 9, 1886, Herbert (Viscount) Gladstone Papers, British Museum Add. MSS. 46016, fols. 93–9; this document appears as an appendix to M. J. Hurst, *Joseph Chamberlain and Liberal Reunion* (London, 1967).

ceive how near they have landed us with a Tory Govt. by their silly abstentions, and so soon as they are given a big Radical programme, they will awaken to their folly.'

But the Radical upsurge that Labouchere had predicted failed to materialize by the 13th, when the electors of Northwich had their turn to pass judgment upon the late Government's program. Brunner was defeated by 458 votes in a poll that was down sharply from the previous year's. The drop in the vote and the margin of his defeat pointed unmistakably to the fact that Liberal voters had stayed home. The *Northwich and Winsford Chronicle* considered the result 'surprising':

We did not expect a large majority [for Brunner]..., but we must confess that we did anticipate a moderate success. The declaration of the poll shows, however, that we, in common with the mass majority of the people who thought about the matter at all, greatly underrated the apathy that has temporarily benumbed the energies of the true Liberal party.[1]

Whether Brunner too was surprised is not known. But on the day that the ballots were counted and the tally announced, he laid a wager of '£10 to £5 that G[ladstone] does not get a majority' in the new Parliament.[2] Though the general election in fact continued, this was, as the terms suggested, indeed a safe bet.

The pattern of the Northwich poll repeated itself in the other divisions of the county. The Conservatives captured Hyde and Macclesfield from incumbent Liberals, strengthened their hold upon Eddisbury, and cut deeply into the Liberal majority at Crewe, the only seat they did not successfully contest. Northwich fell not to a Conservative, but to a Liberal Unionist. The outcome was not so gloomy everywhere in the country, but sufficiently so to deny the Gladstonian Liberals, even with Parnellite support, control of the new Parliament. The Home Rulers trailed the anti-Home Rulers—Conservatives and Liberal Unionists—by more than 100 seats, and both sections of the Liberal Party had lost heavily to the Conservatives. If the election had demonstrated the unpopularity of the Gladstonian program, it had at the same time revealed that Liberal Unionism posed no viable alternative.

[1] July 17, 1886.　　　[2] Appointment diary, July 14, 1886, BP.

With the declaration of Verdin's victory, one of the seventy-eight to the credit of the Liberal Unionists, Brunner addressed his friends and supporters from an upper-storey window along Witton Street. His audience was reported to be 'large' and 'enthusiastic', and except for applause his remarks were interrupted only once, when a butcher drove a cow through the crowd. Though he had been beaten, he declared that he remained 'too good a Liberal to lose pluck'. He appealed to his audience to give Verdin the chance to 'prove himself a Liberal', and he challenged his successor to give expression to the Liberal content of Liberal Unionism. 'If Mr. Verdin does not act as a Liberal', he warned, 'the next time, depend upon it, he will get no help from Liberals, and you will be certain to have a true Liberal in.'[1]

Though he conceded his own defeat, Brunner adamantly refused to concede that there existed any widespread Unionist sentiment among the electors of Northwich. Rather, he preferred to think, they had been confused by a choice between two Liberal candidates, the distinctions between whom had not been at all times clear. So far as he was concerned, the recent contest had settled nothing, for voters had given an uninformed vote on the basis of rumor and innuendo. Furthermore, he was convinced, 'a large number of men have not voted against me and for Mr. Verdin for political reasons at all', but because pressures had been applied to them by their landlords or employers. A Liberal acquaintance had reproached him for failing to exert comparable influence upon the men at Brunner, Mond and Company, who, in many instances, were known to have voted for Verdin. 'Gentlemen, would that be Liberal principles for an employer to cast a shadow upon a man who works for him?' Brunner asked, proud that his workers felt free to express their political beliefs and to dissent from him. His only regret was that others had not behaved so scrupulously, and in particular he condemned the Duke of Westminster, whose blatant interference had cost Foster his seat at Chester. Enumerating the Liberals who had gone down to defeat in nearby constituencies, he consoled himself 'that if I have failed, I have failed in good company'. And his personal

[1] *Northwich and Winsford Chronicle*, July 17, 1886.

disappointment was mitigated by the fact that Tom Ellis, more fortunate than he, had been returned for Merionethshire.[1]

He put down with utmost scorn speculation that, anticipating defeat, he had dispatched Ellis to Wales to obtain a seat and to keep it warm for him. For one thing, he had far too much respect for Ellis for such a stratagem; and, for another, he was too deeply committed to local issues. Not that he would have had the least difficulty winning the endorsement of a Liberal association elsewhere: a man of his means and experience rarely did. Francis Schnadhorst wrote on the 17th with heartfelt assurances he would

do anything I can to help you back to Parlt. It is probable that till things have settled down a little seats worth fighting will be scarce, but that won't last long and should a General Election take place again soon the openings will be numerous. The Unionists will find that the Tories won't want them and that the Liberal Assoc[iation]s won't have them.[2]

The life of a Parliament, especially one in which the Government enjoyed a healthy majority, could be an eternity for a man with political ambitions to sit upon the sidelines; for another try at Northwich he might have to wait as many as seven years. But if the idea of shopping for another constituency had entered his head, it did not long remain there. On the 24th he wrote an open letter to Edward H. Moss, president of the Northwich Liberal Association, vowing, like a jilted suitor, to remain ever faithful:

Seeing that my name as a politician has been mainly won through the kind and hearty support which has been accorded to me by my friends and neighbours, I feel that my reputation is as much theirs as it is mine.

Whenever therefore they have need of my services, those services shall be heartily and entirely at their disposal.[3]

The Association, meeting on October 2, responded with an address of 'unabated confidence' in him, making clear that he would be called upon to defend their interests when the opportunity came. Meanwhile, he assured them, they were fortunate to have at Westminster, Tom Ellis, who stood firm in his Liberalism and whose devotion to the Northwich constituency was not lessened by his election for another.[4]

[1] *Northwich Guardian*, July 24, 1886.   [2] Schnadhorst to Brunner, July 17, 1886, BP.
[3] Brunner to Moss, July 24, 1886 (printed copy), BP.
[4] *Northwich Guardian*, October 6, 1886.

The letters of commiseration he received in the wake of his defeat testified to the fact that on many levels Brunner had made his mark upon the party. Lord Wolmer (who became in 1895 the second Earl of Selborne) did not allow his recent repudiation of Liberalism to prevent him from writing to say how 'awfully sorry' he was 'to see you were beaten; but still more sorry to read of such a brutal attack being made on Mrs Brunner and yourself. Oh! When and how will this split be healed!!' he exclaimed. 'It all depends on the caprice of the G.O.M., and I must say I think his letters and telegrams are not reassuring as to his coolness and self-possession.'[1]

Brunner, who had not been detached from the parliamentary Liberal Party by choice, shared Wolmer's concern, but not his critical view of Gladstone. In adversity, he came more than ever to value the continued leadership of the Grand Old Man, who, more than their consciences, kept most Liberals from abandoning Home Rule. Even with Gladstone at the party's helm, justice for Ireland would be difficult to obtain; without him, it would be virtually impossible. Absent from the Commons, Brunner saw Gladstone from a new perspective, as a moral giant among politicians of inferior stature. 'I regretted my defeat here last July,' he wrote to his chief from Northwich on October 4, 'less for my own sake than for that of the great cause with which your name is so thoroughly and so worthily identified.'[2] Having been 'a devoted and hard-working follower', he wanted nothing more than to resume service at the earliest opportunity. There was of course no way for him to suspect how quickly his chance would come.

[1] Wolmer to Brunner, July 18, 1886, BP.
[2] Brunner to Gladstone, October 4, 1886 (copy), BP.

CHAPTER 5

THE NORTHWICH BY-ELECTION, 1887

With the passage of time the reverse John Brunner suffered in the 1886 general election gradually lost its sting. Looking back upon it, he reflected that had he known then as much about the arts of electioneering as he subsequently learned, he might easily have turned a narrow defeat into a modest victory.[1] In any case, he spared no time for recrimination or despondency. Quick to master the lessons of the occasion, he set to work to repair the political machinery that thereafter stood him in good stead. He began by initiating a thorough inquiry into the causes of his defeat and by strengthening the Liberal association in the division. Tom Ellis described to a friend preparations for a Liberal demonstration at Winnington Park on October 2: 'Brunner will be presented with an address—lunch—speechifying, etc.'[2] And on the 13th, in a gala afternoon of entertainments and eulogies of the Grand Old Man, Brunner presided at the opening of the Gladstone Liberal Club in Witton Street, Northwich, where it continues to stand as a monument to its age and to the Brunnerian ascendancy.

These tasks accomplished, he could afford to absent himself from the constituency, secure in the knowledge that the party would be ready to confront the electorate whenever the time came. And he could depend upon Ellis, who doubled as his private secretary and member for Merionethshire, to tend his affairs while he was gone. Without parliamentary duties and, for that matter, with few business obligations to occupy his attention, he revived plans that he had made in the spring of 1885, before his first adoption as a candidate. 'Mr Brunner will very likely take a trip to India before the year is out,' Ellis reported in early autumn, 'so that my hands will be comparatively free.'[3]

Travel held great fascination for Brunner, who had already

---

[1] Brunner to W. Blagg, May 11, 1899 (Letterbook).
[2] Ellis to Daniel, October 1, 1886, Daniel Papers. [3] *Ibid.*

made two visits to the United States, and who soon acquired a habit of biannual holidays on the Continent that was broken only by the first world war. This was the obvious moment for him to indulge his passion on a grand scale. Accompanied by his wife and son, Sidney, he departed on November 4 for Paris, the first stop on an eight-month odyssey that took him through the Mediterranean to Egypt, India, Ceylon, China, Japan, and across North America. He cancelled plans to tour Australia and New Zealand in order to arrive in New York, after an extended stay in the Orient, in time to keep a business appointment. For the edification of those at home, he described in vivid detail the bazaar at Alexandria, where he 'tasted Arab coffee for the first time', the grandeur of Mt Everest, the solemn beauties of Japan, and the excitement of San Francisco.[1] Yet all the while it remained obvious that he would gladly have exchanged his steamship bookings for a return ticket to Westminster. '...Home gossip is already inexpressibly interesting,' he wrote from Cairo on November 21 to Ellis, to whom he appealed for 'plentiful details of what goes on in Winnington and in the Division'. He had spent the better part of the voyage exchanging political views with shipboard acquaintances, but they were a disappointing lot and consequently the time 'was not joyful'. His fellow passengers, he told Ellis, included

two wives of Pasha Nubar, the [Egyptian] Foreign Minister, and Tyrane, a relative of his—an Egyptian Jew...worth half a million, who sent his wife second-class because 'she ate nothing'—a (very) Scotch...medical missionary stationed at Agra, with wife and sister-in-law, a bumptious dogmatical little man full of eastern lore...— [and], besides others,... [a] Judge of the Egyptian International Tribunal, whose great abilities do not procure for him the position they should on account of his great eccentricity and love of bottle...

Like so many Victorian travellers, however dissimilar in outlook or temperament, Brunner carried with him the ideological

---

[1] This paragraph and—except where otherwise indicated—those that follow are based upon Brunner's letter to Ellis, November 21, 1886, and his daughter Grace's various letters to Ellis, January to March 1887, Ellis Papers; also Brunner's reports of his 'Tour Round the World', published in the *Northwich and Winsford Chronicle* on April 2 and 9, and July 2, 1887.

baggage of his age and saw in each society he visited further confirmation of the ideas he held about his own. An inveterate Free Trader, he ascribed the deplorable sanitary conditions among the Egyptian lower classes to a shortage of soap that resulted from that country's import duties. The state of Georgia, he recounted approvingly, had passed legislation regulating the liquor trade which England would be well advised to copy. He was impressed by the beneficence of British rule in India, but chagrined to encounter so 'few Liberals and practically no Home Rulers' among the Anglo-Indian community. But of all the places on his itinerary, he was most enthusiastic about Canada, loyal and progressive, where 'the industry and enterprise of the population constantly tempt the traveller to dream of what the human race at its highest and best is capable'. He called his countrymen's attention to the specific areas in which Canadians had given substance to the lofty slogans of British Liberalism. Perhaps more intent upon proving a point than investigating the situation at hand, he praised Canadians for subordinating their sectarian disputes to a system of free and national education:

The school belongs to all and is free to all. How I long for the day when we shall see fit to adopt in dear old England the system of free schools common to all. It is no doubt absurd to say or to think or even to hope that such schools would abolish and destroy all our differences, but this much is certain, that they make the children more friendly, and that whilst the men and women remain Catholic and Protestant, Episcopalian and Congregationalist, all become less bitter and more Christian.

And, to his mind, the Canadian experience had convincingly demonstrated the practicability of Liberal schemes for Ireland. Given self-respect and a decent livelihood, Irish emigrants to Canada proved as responsible and law-abiding as their neighbors. Furthermore, what could better attest to the validity of the Home Rule theory, he asked, than the federative system that bound together the Canadian provinces for common advantage and, at the same time, left each of them free 'to legislate and to manage internal affairs'?

Ellis, who envied Brunner his 'magnificent holiday', answered his correspondence, kept touch with Northwich Liberals, and sent him periodic reports of parliamentary affairs. 'Coercion, coercion for ever and ever is the only order of the day,' he wrote on January 28,[1] reviewing 'our dismal, repulsive record' of recent legislation. It was all for the best, Ellis consoled him, that he was not present at Westminster to see at close range Chamberlain betray the ideals for which they had once fought side by side:

> I was reading again this morning your former letters, and regretted to find how your hopes of Chamberlain—like those of many of us—have been completely shattered by his conduct during the last few months. He is now given to slandering Gladstone and his followers, and asserts that as a party they are played out. He and Randolph Churchill are bosom friends, and are busily forming a 'National' Party with a programme of unity of the Empire, general land law reform, local self-government, concern for endowments of the poor—but not a word of Disestablishment, Local Option, or House of Lords!

Yet despite what he heard from Ellis and read in the newspapers that were regularly forwarded to him, Brunner maintained—at least in public—a conciliatory attitude toward his former hero. So far as he could tell, he declared, Chamberlain might well have accomplished everything he had 'recently been doing' from a seat on the Liberal front bench 'if he had but had patience...Let us hope that he will again, and that soon, be acting cordially with us. I was loyal to my leader, and...I believe to my constituents. Perhaps some day', he concluded wistfully, 'Mr Chamberlain may be glad of my loyalty to himself as leader.'

'...Overwhelmed with work', particularly Welsh matters, Ellis advised Brunner that he spent nearly as much time at Northwich as in his own constituency. He found the local clubs that Brunner had set up 'working admirably', but it remained 'almost impossible to say whether opinion politically has changed much. The whole country is calm, almost apathetic on Home Rule just now, but I believe that the seeds sown are now dying in order to come up a great and mighty crop. It is the same in our Division.' In Parliament, too, he detected signs that winter of an incipient Liberal revival:

> Yesterday the Tories looked very rickety indeed—Goschen defeated, Iddesleigh dead, Randolph resigned, W. H. Smith weak and nervous, and

---

[1] BP.

Gladstone in fine fighting form. As yet Randolph has no fellow-rebels and the Tories feel safe. But there is an uneasy impression among their own ranks that they are weak in policy and in tactics and they fear the speedy coming of the end...Chamberlain is still wormwood.

By early spring, however, he had lost a measure of his optimism. In terms of both personalities and legislation, the recent parliamentary session had been an unqualified disappointment. '... What was most interesting in the memorable Home Rule Parliament of 1886 is utterly absent from this,' he wrote to Brunner on April 6;[1] 'your stay in Parliament was coincident with the most brilliant and exciting oratorical struggle of the century. We have had nothing but closure and coercion.' The Round Table negotiations between Gladstonian and renegade Liberals had dragged on through the early months of the year, and though Trevelyan was eventually won back, Chamberlain continued to stand apart. Finally, by endorsing Lord Salisbury's repressive policies, Chamberlain effectively put an end to formal attempts at Liberal reunification. According to Ellis, 'Chamberlain's support of coercion is deepening the popular bitterness felt at his conduct in supporting the Tory Government and still attacking Gladstone.' Time, which had failed to heal the party's wounds, was obviously no ally of the Liberals. '...Gladstone's two speeches [against coercion] were very fine,' Ellis reported, 'but the old hero has aged very much. When you return, you will be grieved to notice the change.'

All the while, Ellis was vigilant in his employer's interests. He forwarded regards from Schnadhorst and a number of Liberals in the House, and informed him that 'Irish members are especially warm in their expressions about you'. Liberal newspapermen at Northwich, with whom he conferred, agreed to publicize the fact that Verdin had cast repeated votes for coercion despite frequent campaign pledges to oppose such measures. True, Verdin had enhanced his local popularity by presenting to the community public baths and a pleasure ground which, Ellis feared, might 'more readily appeal to grosser minds than a valuable or even priceless library'. But Ellis was confident that Brunner's return

[1] BP.

93

would go far to remedy the situation, and he offered assurances that 'much solid work has been done in the Division this winter by meetings, lectures, Clubs, and literature, and the soil has been well prepared for your return, when your reception will kindle the enthusiasm of Liberals to the point reached Dec. 1, 1885 '.

With the assistance of Brunner's eldest son, John, who spent his university vacations with him in London, Ellis pored over the past session's division lists and tabulated Verdin's voting record. The member for Northwich, it appeared, had been present for only thirty-five of eighty-two divisions, and many of his votes had been cast in support of one coercion scheme or another. With Ellis's connivance, this information was prominently featured on April 9 in the *Northwich and Winsford Chronicle* alongside an engaging account by Brunner of his world travels. The effect was exactly as the authors had intended. A leader in the *Chronicle* enumerated Verdin's broken promises and concluded:

We frankly ask Mr Verdin to explain the grounds on which he has so grossly deceived this constituency. He pledged himself over and over again to treat the Irish as brothers, to give them equal laws, and to vote for no measure which deprived the Irish of the privileges we enjoy. We say without hesitation that Mr. Verdin's conduct is not the conduct of an honourable and upright representative, and that he is unworthy of the confidence of the electorate of a large and influential constituency like this.

Brunner's letters from abroad—the second of which was published in juxtaposition to 'The Verdinian Record'—were warm, effusive documents that successfully projected an image of continued devotion and concern. They were distinguished by a thoughtful humility and a complete absence of petulance or hard feelings. 'My neighbours...sent me packing, and set me free to see the world,' he began his first dispatch, which appeared on April 2. 'I hope and expect to come back a better and a more useful man, to work for my neighbours and some day again for my country.' He concluded the third and final account of his journey—written at Ottawa on June 8 and published in the *Chronicle* on July 2 to coincide with his homecoming—with the happy observation that he had 'seen a good deal of Her Majesty's dominions in this Her Jubilee Year'. This was no idle boast, but rather a pointed reminder that, like Dilke and other Victorian politicians whose route he had followed, he had acquired new and important credentials for a seat in the Imperial Parliament.

In excitement and opulence, the festivities that greeted Brunner rivalled the local Jubilee celebrations in which he had been unable to participate. The Gladstone Club of Northwich, determined to honor its founder and first president, provided him with a 'jubilee . . . all to himself'. The streets of the town were gaily decorated and hung with banners, brass bands were on hand, and lavish refreshments were served at Winnington Park. To add to the occasion, the events of the day were bathed in sunshine. The train carrying Brunner, his wife, brothers, and five of his children, pulled into Northwich Station at 3.34, and was rushed by a throng of party and company officials who vied for the honor of being the first to extend a hand in welcome. 'Vigorous hand-shaking and cheering was the order of the day for some time,' the *Chronicle* reported. Eventually, the group left the station platform and crowded into ten carriages, Brunner's being the fourth, which formed a slow procession to Winnington Park. 'The population of Northwich turned out in a body, and the cheering all along the road was very loud and quite continuous. At the end of Solvay-road, the cheering was renewed most heartily, and at the bottom of the hill the horses were detached from the [fourth] carriage, the vehicle being drawn at a rapid pace towards the hall by a band of sturdy men.' There, in the shadow of the Brunner, Mond works, some 3000 Northwich residents had gathered, joined by a contingent of 800 from Winsford who had come down the Weaver, equipped with a brass band, in two chartered steamers. Entertainments and speeches lasted well into the evening.

A visitor to Northwich on July 2 would probably have found it difficult to believe that the object of this rousing reception had a year earlier been rejected in his bid for re-election to Parliament. How can this apparent change of heart be explained? To some extent, the welcome accorded Brunner reflected the affectionate regard in which he was held by his neighbors, many of whom would nonetheless decline to vote for him. ' . . . Of course the demonstration was primarily political,' the *Chronicle* conceded;

'but as the welcome...in the town...[showed], all parties joined in doing honour to a family which is universally popular.' Yet, at the same time, the fervor with which Brunner was greeted reflected a widespread disenchantment with the sitting member who, in personal and party terms, had failed to live up to expectations. Here was demonstrable proof that substantial numbers of local Liberals who had adopted a wait-and-see attitude at the last election, or had been seduced by the rhetoric of Liberal Unionism, were now returning to the fold.

The political significance of the hearty welcome he received was not lost upon the man of the hour, who rose to the occasion with a vigorous affirmation of Gladstonian principles and a hard-hitting attack upon 'Coercion Liberals'. There can be no doubt that he intended his address as the first in a campaign that would last as long as the present Parliament. In the general election before last, he recalled, Lady Brooke—the wife of one of the leading landowners in the vicinity—had derided his victory with the comment that the constituency would be a national 'laughing stock' for having chosen a 'German' as its representative. With this incident in mind, he declared his immense satisfaction 'to come back' after a journey around the world 'to the land where I first saw light', and in particular to Cheshire, the scene of his varied successes. '...I have done more for Cheshire', he reminded his audience, many of whom knew the fact firsthand, 'than all the Brookes and all the Mainwarings. My friend Dr Mond and I have filled more hungry stomachs, and founded more happy homes...I do not say this in a spirit of boasting, but in a spirit of thankfulness that it has been put into my power to do it.' But it was the future upon which he wished to fasten his listeners' attention. His travels, he told them, had provided him with new guidance and inspiration, and time and again had made clear to him the validity of Gladstone's Home Rule proposals: '...If you will only follow in the steps of our great leader—our dear and venerated old leader, Mr Gladstone—you will bring about in Ireland that same absence of bitterness between the various religions of Christendom that I have seen amongst the free people of the State of New York.' With respect to his own ambitions, he looked forward to the restoration not only of his former seat, but also of Gladstone to the leadership of Parliament and the nation.[1]

From every indication in both the constituency and the country at large, Brunner would not be disappointed on either score. Liberal Unionism, which a year earlier had seemed the wave of the future, had since revealed itself to be a political backwater. Unable to stand on their own or, for that matter, to deliver to their Conservative allies all they had promised, the Liberal Unionists gradually lost their identity, their scruples, and very often their seats. It was admittedly no easy task to perpetuate an alliance, however tenuous, among politicians as disparate and mutually suspicious as Salisbury, Chamberlain, and Hartington; it was hard enough to maintain a reasonable solidarity between Chamberlain, whose Unionism was idiosyncratic, and Hartington, whose Liberalism was increasingly suspect. Until the close of 1891, when he succeeded his father as Duke of Devonshire, Hartington nominally led the Liberal Unionists in the Commons, and Chamberlain's position was an anomalous one. The Conservatives, for their part, were equally afflicted with a paucity of ideas and a divided leadership. Not for five years—until the general election of 1892—did the British electorate at last have an opportunity to pronounce judgment upon the politics of coercion and to return Gladstone to office for a fourth and final time. But the voters of the Northwich division did not have to wait nearly so long to declare their preference.

Within three weeks of Brunner's homecoming, Robert Verdin was dead of a heart attack and the seat for which they had fought the previous year stood vacant. According to *The Times*, Verdin's fatal condition was known, but Brunner in his speeches and correspondence strenuously denied that he had anticipated the situation that broke upon him. 'He had looked to meeting Mr Verdin in perfect health, and not before the end of this Parliament', he maintained, 'to shake hands with him both before and after an honest political fight.'[2] All of this had changed. 'No

---

[1] *Northwich and Winsford Chronicle*, July 9, 1887.
[2] *Ibid.* August 6, 1887.

steps will be taken in reference to the vacancy till after the funeral,'
The Times announced on the 26th, 'but it is understood that
Mr Brunner will again be the Gladstonian candidate.' The
Manchester Guardian shared that understanding: its London
correspondent reported the same morning the virtual certainty
that Brunner would stand and the fact that 'Liberal members, of
whom a host are ready to travel northwards to his aid, are confident that he will reverse the verdict of last year'.

But if Brunner's candidacy was assumed, it remained an open
question what, let alone whom, he would stand against. Would
the Conservatives oppose him directly, as in 1885, or in league
with the Liberal Unionists, as last time? The *Manchester Guardian*
described the difficulty of finding a suitable Unionist candidate
and the improbability that there would be one: 'Next to the return of a Liberal the Tories dislike the idea of contributing to
strengthening Lord Hartington's little party.' On the 27th the
Guardian predicted that regardless of Brunner's opponent there
would be 'an interesting contest' for the constituency, 'Liberal
in general tendency', which would provide a crucial index to
Liberal fortunes in the country. That day *The Times* reported
rumors that Lord Henry Grosvenor, the third son of the Duke of
Westminster, would stand for Northwich as a Unionist; it confirmed them as fact on August 1. A three-way race, which had
been mooted in some quarters, was presently ruled out by a
decision on the part of the local Conservatives who, 'failing to
secure their own nominee, [threw] in their lot with the Liberal
Unionists and are effectively seconding them in every possible
way'.[1] There followed what was undoubtedly the most dramatic
campaign of Brunner's career, and one regarded by contemporaries as among the most significant confrontations in the annals
of late-Victorian Liberalism.

The strategic importance of the Northwich by-election emerges
most clearly against the background of the other contests that
punctuated the spring and summer months of 1887. Burnley, like
Northwich, replaced a Liberal Unionist with a Gladstonian;
Spalding and Coventry turned from Toryism to Liberalism;

[1] *The Times*, August 5, 1887.

Ilkeston and Bridgeton were held by Liberals with increased majorities, the latter by Sir George Trevelyan, who defended the old cause to which he had returned against a Liberal Unionist; and the Conservative majorities at Paddington, Brixton, Basingstoke, and North Hants were sharply reduced. All of these results demonstrated to one degree or another a growing Gladstonian sentiment; but the poll at Northwich was by far the least equivocal and its effects the most far-reaching.

As a rule, the party in power stands at a marked disadvantage in these isolated contests and takes for granted that it will lose ground. From the election of the 1886 Parliament until its dissolution in 1892, the Gladstonian opposition captured twenty-two seats and forfeited only one. But the spate of by-elections that summer, and particularly the one at Northwich, exceeded the most dismal Tory expectations. They were not simply an embarrassment to the Government, for that much could easily be tolerated, so much as repeated proof that Liberal Unionism was a lost cause and an impediment to effective Conservative action. The Unionists failed, on the one hand, to render material assistance to Conservative candidates and, on the other, to hold their own with Conservative backing. The writing had been on the wall as early as January, when G. J. Goschen had somewhat surprisingly failed to wrest a likely Liverpool seat from Gladstonian hands. Speculation revived as the year progressed that Chamberlain and his fellow 'Radical Unionists' would gravitate back to the Gladstonian camp, while Hartington and the 'Whig Unionists' would convert to outright Toryism. On the eve of the balloting at Northwich, Chamberlain acknowledged the disquieting fact that 'many of the rank and file among the Unionists were uneasy and anxious to know what were really the points of difference' between themselves and Liberals of the other persuasion.[1] Still more, they had profound difficulty justifying to voters and often to themselves their assent to coercion. The outcome at Northwich did nothing to allay their anxieties.

Under the circumstances, Brunner was entitled to be reasonably

[1] Chamberlain to W. H. Smith, August 12, 1887, cited in Hurst, *Joseph Chamberlain and Liberal Reunion*, p. 49; see also pp. 345 ff.

4-2

confident of his chances. He had been defeated last time primarily by widespread abstentions on the part of Liberals who had not been made to see the merits of Home Rule. As the *Manchester Guardian* pointed out on July 27, 'the recent by-elections show nothing if not that the waverers are becoming Home Rulers', and it fully expected Northwich 'to declare, as Spalding declared the other day, against the Tory–Dissentient coalition'. Yet this time Brunner refused to slacken his efforts until victory was in hand. Above all, he sought to correct misapprehensions about Home Rule and to clarify his stand on that issue. In his address to members of the local Liberal association, accepting their invitation to stand, he declared himself 'strongly opposed to the exclusion of the representatives of Ireland from the Imperial Parliament', a provision in the original Home Rule Bill of which Unionists had been especially critical, and he 'cordially welcomed Mr Gladstone's declaration on this point, as also his assurance that any future measure for the purchase of Irish land for the benefit of the tenants shall involve no risk of charge upon the British taxpayer'.[1] Both statements were obviously calculated to answer specific charges levelled by his opponents.

With exactly a fortnight between the date of his official adoption as Liberal candidate and polling on August 13, Brunner had little time to remind the electorate of his qualifications or to convince them of the righteousness of an Irish policy that remained much resented and misunderstood. In large part his campaign was an emotional one that called upon his neighbors to clamber aboard the Gladstonian bandwagon. Three weeks had passed since his return from abroad, he told a meeting at Runcorn on July 30: 'The first thing he [had] heard was the news of the Spalding election. Since that day he had heard more good news of Liberal victories, and he wanted them to add another to those victories to cheer Mr Gladstone's heart.'[2] The walls of the constituency were placarded with broadsides that celebrated recent Liberal successes ('How the Tide is Flowing!!') that presumably 'shew[ed] plainly that the English people are determined on

[1] *The Times*, August 1, 1887.
[2] *Northwich and Winsford Chronicle*, August 6, 1887.

giving Justice to Ireland, and that the Working Men have learnt that the Ballot is Absolutely Secret!!' Brunner's cause received an added fillip on the 6th, a week before polling, with the news from the Bridgeton division of Glasgow that Sir George Trevelyan had easily defeated Evelyn Ashley, a Liberal Unionist. Sir Edward Hamilton, who had been Gladstone's private secretary and who remained a keen observer of the political scene, recorded the Bridgeton return in his diary with appropriate satisfaction, but understood better than most the limitations of its significance:

The Bridgeton Election at Glasgow resulted as was expected in a victory for Trevelyan over Ashley; but his majority was very large and the Govt. are hanging their heads down. The fact is, the 'Liberal Unionist', being neither fish, nor flesh, nor fowl politically, is not understood by the Electors. The turn of the tide, however, such as it is, is probably as much an indication of the unpopularity of a weak and shuffling Govt. as of increased popularity for Mr G.'s proposals.[1]

Lord Henry Grosvenor, Brunner's opponent, had neither the political attainments nor the intellectual gifts of the Unionist who had stood unsuccessfully against Trevelyan. In all fairness to his cause, it must be said that he fell far below the calibre of most Unionist candidates. Only twenty-six years of age, Lord Henry had been chosen in the vain hope that his impressive family connections would compensate for obvious personal deficiencies. There was no love lost between Brunner and the Duke, who had forsaken the Liberal Party and had since added insult to injury by auctioning off the superb Millais portrait of Gladstone that had hung at Eaton Hall. To Brunner, the Duke personified the quintessence of social privilege and narrow class interest, and he did not hesitate to describe him to the electorate in precisely these terms. The Duke, for his part, returned Brunner's enmity, and subsequently refused a neighborly invitation from Gladstone to

[1] Sir Edward Hamilton's Diary, August 6, 1887, Hamilton Papers, Add. MSS. 48646, fol. 120. Ashley, son of the seventh Earl of Shaftesbury, began his public career as private secretary to Lord Palmerston and had since made a name for himself as an author and politician. He attempted five times as a Liberal Unionist to return to the House, where he had sat as a Liberal from 1874 to 1885.

dine at Hawarden to spare himself the unpleasantness of possibly meeting Brunner 'under your roof...'[1]

However much territorial influence it placed at his command, Lord Henry's celebrated paternity was not without its political disadvantages. Coupled with his youth, it laid him open to charges, by no means groundless, that he could not on his own have come nearly so far so quickly. The local Liberal press, quick to visit the sins of the father upon the son, recalled that the Duke 'at the last election...[had] worked harder than perhaps any other man to secure the return of two ultra-Tory candidates for Chester and the Eddisbury division of the county', and it branded Lord Henry 'the crooked son of a politically crooked sire'. On what grounds, it demanded to know, did he purport to be a *Liberal* Unionist? Rather, he appeared in all significant respects 'a good, simple, honest, stupid Tory', who conveniently posed as a Unionist 'to bamboozle the electors of Northwich by egregious nonsense...'[2] Further doubts were cast upon Lord Henry's political allegiance by the revelation that he had served his all too brief apprenticeship as private secretary to W. H. Smith, Conservative leader in the Commons and hardly one to inspire a devotion to Liberal doctrine. It was said on good authority that 'Lord Henry Grosvenor was to have been the selected Conservative candidate for Chester at the next General Election',[3] an altogether more sensible arrangement than for him to stand prematurely at Northwich in the Unionist interest. But regardless of whether he was more a Conservative than a Liberal Unionist, often more a matter of nomenclature than practical politics, Lord Henry had little in his

---

[1] Westminster to Gladstone, August 16 [1887], Gladstone Papers, Add. MSS. 44337, fol. 393. Not that Westminster lacked cause to take offense. At a campaign meeting at Hartford on August 9, Brunner had derided the fact that the Duke, whose annual income exceeded £180,000, 'did not think it beneath him, when Mr Gladstone was Prime Minister, to accept from his hands £2,000 a year for the dignified duty of looking after her Majesty's dogs'. Brunner declared that, 'above all things, he did not want to be a flunkey, to look after either horses or dogs. All the dukes', he was pleased to say, 'had left Mr Gladstone and were supporting the Tory party'. *Northwich and Winsford Chronicle*, August 13, 1887.

[2] *Northwich and Winsford Chronicle*, August 6, 1887.

[3] Letter to Brunner (signature missing), August 11, 1887, BP; the correspondent, probably Philip Salisbury, identified himself as the son of E. R. G. Salisbury, who was returned for Chester in 1857 with the Duke of Westminster, then the Earl Grosvenor.

own right to recommend him. On the day of polling, the *Chronicle* summed up his 'qualifications':

> He is his father's son.
> He is going in his 26.
> He is the son of his father.
> His father's a duke.
> He is a real live dukeling—
> Therefore one of the aristocracy.
> He was born young...

Yet throughout the campaign Lord Henry continued to advertise himself as the representative of 'the true Liberal Party' and Unionism as 'the genuine progressive policy'. Speaking on August 3, he emphatically condemned Home Rule as a scheme 'dictated by Mr Parnell', and he described how 'the real leaders of the Liberal Party, Lord Hartington, Mr John Bright, and Mr Chamberlain, had felt compelled to break away from Mr Gladstone on his Irish proposals...'[1] When confronted with the fact that Unionists had given their approval to illiberal acts of coercion, he argued that Gladstone, in his day, 'had proposed severer measures', a statement that drew a swift and crushing rejoinder from the Grand Old Man, who declared 'that Lord Henry Grosvenor has not the smallest knowledge on the subject on which...he speaks'.[2]

As Lord Henry's platform rhetoric would indicate, the Northwich by-election was dominated by the single issue of Home Rule. For one thing, there was insufficient time to pursue other matters and, for another, neither candidate particularly wished to do so. Each recognized the overriding significance of the Irish problem and counted upon a favorable response from the voters on this score. But the campaign more than made up in intensity what it might have lacked in scope. No other contest since the general election had provided so clear-cut a choice between the policies of coercion and conciliation, and none had taken place

---

[1] *The Times*, August 4, 1887.
[2] Gladstone addressed his remarks to the editor of the *Northwich and Winsford Chronicle* in a letter dated August 8 and published on the 13th. The text was simultaneously released to the national press, which gave it extensive coverage, and appeared in *The Times* on the 12th.

in a constituency more a microcosm of English society. The country looked on intently, convinced that the result at Northwich would determine the future not only of Gladstone's policy, but also of the Liberal Unionist alternative.

Neither side doubted the crucial nature of the Northwich poll: for the Gladstonians, defeat would be intolerable; for the Unionists, a humiliation that would discredit them in Conservative eyes. '...I cannot conceive it possible...that Lord Henry Grosvenor will defeat you...,' one Cheshire Liberal wrote to Brunner, 'taking into consideration how the result will affect the question of Mr Gladstone and of Home Rule...'[1] Even the Liberal campaign song was a reminder of the cardinal issue at stake:

> Men of Northwich, true and brave,
>   'Tis your privilege to say
> Ireland is no more a slave
>   We will break her bonds today.
> All the cruel laws that bind her
>   By your vote may be o'erthrown;
> Tyranny no more shall grind her
>   Once you make her cause your own.

The Unionists called upon the voters to take a stand for law and order and against the dissolution of the Empire. *The Times*, wholeheartedly in the Unionist corner, expected a close race, with those who had held back in 1886 tilting the balance one way or the other: had these former abstainers at last made up their minds on Home Rule, it asked on the 12th, and if so, which way? Most Liberals, too, would have been grateful for a modest victory. At a meeting at Winsford on the 3rd, G. H. Deakin, who presided, called for a Liberal majority of 1500 votes, but Herbert Gladstone, the keynote speaker, admitted he would be satisfied with a majority a third that size.[2]

Politicians followed the Northwich proceedings in the daily press, and many flocked to the constituency in a frantic attempt to influence votes. As *The Times* facetiously observed on the 5th, there was 'no lack of oratory to help the electors in coming to a

1 Philip Salisbury to Brunner [n.d.], BP.
2 *Northwich and Winsford Chronicle*, August 6, 1887.

decision at the polls'. To his delight, Brunner experienced none of his customary difficulty in obtaining distinguished volunteers to speak on his behalf. Herbert Gladstone came twice to extol the virtues of 'my good friend Mr Brunner', and Ellis delivered speech after speech. Henry Broadhurst spent several days in the division, and his open-air meeting at Weston on the 7th was unusually 'well attended and hearty'. That evening there was a 'splendid meeting...at the Runcorn Public Hall', featuring a speech by that redoubtable Radical, S. D. Waddy. 'The effect of Mr Waddy's speech on the whole meeting was marvellous,' James Handley reported to Brunner.

> I have never before seen an audience worked up to such a pitch of enthusiasm. After graphically describing the way in which the poor Irish tenants had had their last shilling wrung out of them to meet the greed of the Landlords...(and he handed to me as chairman actual receipts and promissory notes to prove all he was saying), he compared the Irish to the Children of Israel under Pharoah, when he took away their straw and increased their daily task of brickmaking...

Handley was confident that 'with hearty work up to the last moment it looks like a glorious victory'.[1] Surely he was not in want of assistance. C. E. Schwann, Sir Wilfrid Lawson, and William ('Mabon') Abraham contributed their fiery skills, and Irish members—among them John Dillon, J. J. Clancy, William Summers and John O'Connor—were markedly effective. The Home Rulers did not, of course, have a monopoly upon local platforms, and Lawson noted 'that this county had been invaded by a hostile army—no less than 20 Tory Members of Parliament'.[2] The Unionists announced that Chamberlain would make a last-minute visit to the constituency, and the Liberals threatened to retaliate by bringing in Harcourt or Morley; but Chamberlain instead decided to limit his participation to a written appeal. Gladstone, too, though close by at Hawarden, preferred to 'take another method of communicating his views' and did not appear. Still, there was excitement enough. On the 10th *The Times* counted 'no fewer than 12 meetings' within the preceding twenty-

[1] Handley to Brunner, August 7, 1887, BP.
[2] Speech at Northwich, August 10, 1887, *Northwich and Winsford Chronicle*, August 13, 1887.

four hours, 'and there are nearly a score of members of Parliament on the spot, and fresh relays expected...Both sides profess to be sanguine as to the result, but independent observers believe it will be the closest contest ever fought in Cheshire.'

Polling took place on August 13, a Saturday, affording industrial workers, numerous in the division, greater opportunity to participate. Good weather, 'the heat being moderated by occasional slight showers', also made for a heavy turnout.[1] It was immediately apparent that those who had abstained in 1886 were coming to the polls, but it was not altogether clear on which side. 'The electors were checked off by clerks from the committee rooms of both parties as they entered the polling booths to vote,' *The Times* explained.

The names of those who had polled were then sent to headquarters, where they were again ticked off. The politics of nine out of every ten men polled were known by one or other of the committee men, and thus a tolerably accurate record was kept of how the polling was going. Moreover the local agents..., before the polls closed..., sent round willing scouts to bring up the laggards.

The voting register for the division contained 10,817 names, of which *The Times* estimated that 800 'may be safely taken off to represent deaths, removals or [other] absentees'. Electoral analysts kept a close eye upon traditionally Liberal groups to see how they would respond, and reported that the Irish (some 400 strong) and the lodgers (130 in number and mostly congregated at Northwich) came out early in full force; it did not go unnoticed that the canal boatmen at Middlewich, for some reason steadfast Gladstonians, were absent from their boats at the height of the day.

By and large, balloting 'passed off quietly', despite the constituency's reputation for 'electoral rowdyism'. The walls in every district 'were literally covered with party-coloured bills', and at Runcorn Unionists displayed anti-Home Rule cartoons from *England* and posters that read:

[1] This account is based primarily upon coverage in *The Times*, August 13 and 15, 1887; the *Manchester Guardian*, August 13 and 15, 1887; and the *Northwich and Winsford Chronicle*, August 20, 1887.

only 433 votes fewer than Robert Verdin in 1886, and a few votes more than W. H. Verdin, the Conservative whom Brunner had defeated in 1885. It was clear, however, from the Liberal vote, which had soared, that under the circumstances a Unionist candidate was no stronger and possibly weaker than a Conservative. Tories began to mutter that they would have fared better had they fought on their own account. The *Birmingham Post*, despite its Unionist sympathies, refused to share *The Times*'s delusion that personal and local factors had determined the Northwich result:

Personal regard for Mr Brunner is not enough to account for the change, for at the last election the constituency parted company with him by a decisive majority. The local influence of the candidate again will not account for the transfer of votes, for the influence of the Duke of Westminster, and all that goes with such a connection, must have been very potent on the other side.

Liberals regarded the implicit repudiation of ducal influence as further cause for celebration: 'All the Duke's horses and all the Duke's men have not been able to place Lord Henry Grosvenor at the head of the poll for the Northwich division,' taunted the *Scarborough Evening News* on the 16th; and others jested, with reference to the matter of the Millais portrait, that it was not the Duke who had sold Gladstone, but Gladstone who had sold the Duke.

Gladstone, who during the campaign had for the most part been content to allow others to speak for him, did not hesitate to make political capital of the Northwich victory. As soon as the poll was declared, he communicated to Brunner a warm message of congratulations, adding in a postscript marked 'private': 'I need hardly say you are under no restraint as to your use of this letter.' As he saw it, Northwich had delivered a verdict on behalf of the nation that was 'unequivocal and decisive':

I do not doubt that your personal character and position have much contributed to this result, but your opponent was also very highly favoured in name and associations. And few will seek to disguise the unquestionable addition thus made to the evidence, now somewhat rapidly approaching to a demonstrative character, that the people of England intend to do full justice to the people of Ireland by confiding to them, in a spirit alike generous and wise, the management of their own properly Irish affairs.[1]

Promptly distributed, the text of this letter had appeared by the end of the week in virtually every newspaper, and it was followed in most cases by Brunner's reply of the 17th, worded no less strongly.[2]

Political rhetoric aside, the impact of the Northwich by-election cannot be doubted, though its ramifications may be somewhat discounted. Lord Salisbury was not pressured to resign, nor was the Government reorganized to accommodate new men and new ideas. And the Unionists continued for the time being to stand their diminished ground. Yet the episode did not pass without effects of a more subtle variety. Sir Edward Hamilton, who like nearly everyone else was taken aback by the vote that Brunner amassed ('a far larger majority than even the most sanguine Gladstonian ever anticipated'), concluded with his usual perspicacity:

After every allowance is made for local considerations, the result is most significant. It is clear that Liberal Unionists do not exist among electors, and that Liberal abstentionists of a year ago are resuming their places at the poll ...It is bad tactics on the part of the Govt. to run Liberal Unionist candidates. Such nondescript politicians are not understood. The electors could not understand how Lord H. Grosvenor could professedly pose as a Liberal and yet be acting as Private Secretary to W. H. Smith. There is great consternation in the Unionist camp.[3]

Evidence of this consternation abounded. A cartoon in the August 24 number of *Fun* depicted John Bull, as physician, diagnosing the ailments of Lord Hartington as 'acute Unionitis and inflammation of the Glasgovian and Northwiching membranes. Great loss of power, and general weakness. You must give up business at once.' Others, more sympathetic, thought that the Liberal Unionists might survive the storm provided that they made a rigorous effort to assert a distinct personality and to

[1] Gladstone to Brunner, August 15, 1887 (copy), Gladstone Papers, Add. MSS. 44501, fols. 222–3.
[2] *The Times* published Gladstone's letter on the 18th, and Brunner's the following day.
[3] Sir Edward Hamilton's Diary [August] 17, 1887, Hamilton Papers, Add. MSS. 48646, fols. 125–6.

Though the applause for Brunner at Leinster Hall was long and loud, all eyes were fixed that evening upon William O'Brien, who defiantly scheduled his address for the very hour he had been summoned to appear before petty sessions at Mitchelstown, County Cork, to answer charges that he had delivered 'inflammatory speeches' there a month earlier. O'Brien was found guilty *in absentia* and, under the provisions of the revised Crimes Act, his prosecution was ordered. At four o'clock the next afternoon, a Friday, his colleagues at the Leinster Hall meeting reassembled at Mitchelstown to lead a public demonstration to protest the extra-legal proceedings of which he was the most prominent victim. What followed was a mêlée between the townspeople and the Irish constabulary in which three lives were lost.

Riot, insurrection, or massacre? The authorities, after a perfunctory investigation, returned one verdict; Dillon, Labouchere, and Brunner, recounting their experiences to the House of Commons three days later, another. It is impossible to reconcile the conflicting accounts, each charged with partisan emotion, of what took place at Mitchelstown that afternoon.[1] Action came so fast that so seasoned an observer as the special correspondent for the *Freeman's Journal* was admittedly dazed. 'Never in some considerable experience have I seen police so faced before,' he told his readers, barely able to suppress his intense satisfaction. 'The row began at about half-past-four, and did not last five minutes, but it was made up of a series of Homeric combats, single-handed encounters, which passed as rapidly as a magic lantern.'

Essentially, two versions of the episode emerge with few points of agreement between them. An overflow crowd, variously estimated at between three and eight thousand people, had collected in the town's market place, comparable in size to Trafalgar Square, by the time the speakers (accompanied by 'flags and trumpets')

[1] The present account incorporates material that Dillon, Labouchere, and Brunner presented to the House of Commons on September 12 (*Parliamentary Debates*, 3rd ser., cccxxi, cols. 329–41, 368–85, 410–14) and from Labouchere's analysis of 'The Mitchelstown Murders—the Real Facts' in the September 22 number of his journal, *Truth*. The latter elaborated upon his parliamentary testimony in a letter to Herbert Gladstone on October 13 (Viscount Gladstone Papers, Add. MSS. 46016, fols. 126–7). In addition, *The Times*, *Freeman's Journal* and *Liverpool Courier* have been consulted for the relevant days.

arrived in a party from Dublin. A platform was improvised from wagonettes, assembled along the crest of an adjoining hill to offer an unobstructed view. All the while the police were very much in evidence—their barracks were 250 yards below—but remained at the periphery. Proceedings began peacefully enough. But soon after Dillon opened the program, disturbances broke out. The police, attempting to file through the crowd in order to install an official stenographer upon the platform, encountered violent resistance. Some said they brought this upon themselves by their unreasoned brutality. But, in either case, stones flew, bayonets were unsheathed, and clubbed muskets and blackthorns were wielded. The fighting was fierce, and, once it began, it proved difficult to stop. Members of the crowd, grateful for the opportunity to give the police as good as they had received from them many times in the past, pursued their outnumbered assailants down the hill. One man, implored by a clergyman to desist, replied with Gaelic pugnacity: 'Ah! your reverence; sure you won't stop a poor fellow having another crack at the peelers—only one.' Gunshots rang out from the windows of the barracks, where policemen had taken refuge.

The Times, true to its Tory colors, insisted that the fracas was touched off by mob attacks upon the police that were mischievously instigated by 'English accomplices who have come over [to Ireland] specially to assist them [the Irish] in breaking the law', and who, knowingly or not, 'are to a large extent responsible for the loss of life which has taken place'. This was the theme of Conservative demonstrations all over England, including a massive rally at Trafford Park, Manchester, where a succession of lesser Tory politicians cried shame upon Liberal demagogues who fed upon Irish turbulence, and Lord Carmarthen went so far as to '[wish] to heaven that the bullets' that struck down innocent bystanders at Mitchelstown 'had reached the responsible persons —those on whom, solely and entirely, rested the blame for the occurrence'.

Yet the culprits, if that is indeed what they were, presented an account wholly different in emphasis as well as detail. Home Rulers and bitter opponents of the Crimes Act (Brunner deemed it 'rightly named', for Mitchelstown had shown it 'to be an Act for the legislation of murder'), they sought more profound explanations for the causes of Irish unrest. It was Labouchere's opinion that the local authorities at Mitchelstown, with the Government squarely behind them, had done 'their very best to provoke a collision' so that they might thereupon proceed to deal a final blow to Irish constitutional liberties. Why else had the local constabulary been reinforced that morning with contingents from outlying districts? He conceded that stones were thrown at the police, but only after excessive provocation and defensively, 'with a view to prevent the police from spreading about and continuing their attacks upon the citizens'. Brunner echoed these observations in his address to the House: the assembled residents of Mitchelstown had been 'orderly in the extreme, and as good-humoured as any set of people I ever saw in my life. The meeting was formed, and at the moment that perfect quiet was secured, the police thrust themselves into the midst of the crowd in wedge form.' The police withdrew, regrouped, and charged again. This time, from his vantage point atop a wagonette, he could see 'the police [strike] right and left at the unresisting crowd...It seemed to me an utterly wanton and unprovoked attack on a peaceable and quiet set of people...The people were then fired upon, as I believe, without any orders...' Still more appalling were the bountiful assurances he had received that such incidents were 'a very common occurrence' in Ireland, where power was divorced from responsibility, the agents of the law rarely held accountable for their actions, and the rights of the citizen increasingly ignored.

An official inquiry was conducted in the course of a weekend, and its findings were delivered to Parliament before eyewitnesses had had an opportunity to testify. Understandably, it took little to convince Balfour that the responsibility for the affray rested not with the police, who had done no more than their duty, but with 'those who convened the meeting under circumstances which they knew would lead to excitement and might lead to outrage'.[1]

[1] Speech by Balfour, *Parliamentary Debates*, 3rd ser., cccxxi, col. 327 (September 12, 1887).

Others, who rejected Balfour's principles, emphatically rejected his logic and countered that the inquiry had evaded many more questions than it answered. Had the police fired first or only in retaliation? In either case, by whose authority had they done so, and was the severity of their response justified? Particularly suspicious was the matter of the government stenographer: was it anything more than a deliberate attempt to create havoc? John Morley, when he came to write his *Life of Gladstone* at the close of the century, remained puzzled by the apparent refusal by the police at Mitchelstown to 'choose an easier mode of approach from the rear, or by the side' instead of 'through the densest part of the crowd'; why, he asked, had they 'not got their reporter on to the platform before the business began; and why had they not beforehand asked for accommodation as was the practice'?[1] Fundamental to all of these questions were the sincerity of the Government and the intentions of its policy, both held in profound suspicion.

Even the movements of key participants at Mitchelstown are difficult to ascertain. At what point did they realize what was happening? (Brunner described his bewilderment until someone explained that the police, advancing toward him, accompanied an official reporter.) Had the visitors all along expected the police to force a showdown (as Labouchere later claimed), or were they taken unawares (as Brunner implied)? Did they earnestly seek to restore calm, or actively incite acts of vengeance? Labouchere described Brunner, with Ellis and the Mayor of Cork, 'urging the people to clear the streets for fear of further bloodshed'. But *The Times*, yet to forgive Brunner his presumption in winning Northwich, spoke deprecatingly of him as a cynical adventurer who savored every moment of the crisis he had helped to foment: 'The meeting was broken up, although Mr Brunner, the last recruit of the Separatists, seemed resolved to carry it on, and, affecting an air of cool indifference while the storm raged around, smoked a cigarette with theatric effect on the top of a wagonette

[1] III, 381. 'Half the mischief of *Ireland* all these long years past', Morley reflected still later in a letter to the Earl of Minto, 'had been done by the fuss and bullying of police, etc.' Morley to Minto, March 8, 1906, cited in Koss, *John Morley at the India Office*, p. 98 n.

which served as a platform.' The correspondent for the *Freeman's Journal*, better able to distinguish one bearded Radical from another, identified Labouchere ('the coolest man on the square') as the one with 'a cigarette in his mouth', while 'Mr Brunner was down among the country people trying to find out the extent of their injuries'. According to this report, Ellis, his hand bleeding, had gone off to telegraph the news to London.

The Mitchelstown outrages produced an immediate uproar in British political society and beyond which was sustained by the Government's adamant refusal to conduct a public hearing and by the subsequent quashing of a verdict, delivered by a coroner's jury, that 'wilful murder' had been committed by the police. The parallel with the Peterloo massacre of 1819 was too striking to go unexploited. Morley by no means exaggerated when he declared: 'No other incident of Irish administration stirred deeper feelings of disgust in Ireland, or of misgiving and indignation in England.'[1] This had the immediate effect of solidifying the alliance between Parnellites and Gladstonians, winning for the nationalists 'a much more active sympathy' for their controversial 'Plan of Campaign'.[2]

Simply by his presence at Mitchelstown, Brunner attained new stature among his colleagues and greater notoriety among his critics. Tories had expected no better from Labouchere, whose penchant for rabble-rousing was well known; and Ellis, they reasoned, was both young and a Welshman, susceptible on both counts to Celtic extremism. But Brunner, an Englishman and a businessman of stature, was guilty in Tory eyes of unpardonable behavior. To others, who considered the episode not in relation to personalities, but principles, Mitchelstown appeared all the more ominous. The first significant confrontation that had taken place between the Irish people and the alien authority since the amendment of the Crimes Act, it cast a doubtful light upon the effectiveness of that Act, let alone its justice. The callous manner in which the affair was brushed aside and violent repression

[1] *Life of Gladstone*, III, 383.
[2] F. S. L. Lyons, *John Dillon* (London, 1968), p. 89; Lyons expertly sets the episode within the context of Irish events, pp. 87–90.

condoned was as much an affront to Liberal sensibilities as what had actually occurred. Balfour, so unyielding in public, admitted privately to his uncle, Lord Salisbury, the need to keep tighter rein upon Irish law enforcement officers and revealed steps he had taken to prevent further incidents of this nature.[1] Yet such backstairs maneuvers, however successful they indeed proved, hardly appeased the Home Rulers, who demanded the repudiation of coercive methods. On October 18 Gladstone appealed to the delegates of the National Liberal Federation assembled at Nottingham to 'remember Mitchelstown'. He could rest assured that neither his followers nor their antagonists would soon forget.

'Remember Mitchelstown!' Brunner, for one, did not require prompting from Gladstone or anyone else to take up this new battle cry, which soon resounded from every Liberal platform. With the other parliamentary veterans of Mitchelstown, he spent the remainder of the weekend speaking to various Irish groups. The most important and best attended of his meetings was at Cork on Saturday night under the auspices of the Young Ireland Society, to which he denounced the barbarism of the Irish police and the Government that tolerated, if not perpetuated, such villainies ('a more foul, more base, more despicable Government', Labouchere exclaimed at Cork, 'never cursed a country'). On Sunday he and Labouchere returned to Dublin. They dined early at Dillon's house with William O'Brien, departing in time to board the seven o'clock mail steamer from Kingstown to Holyhead. O'Brien, who came to bid his English companions goodbye, was arrested. 'The whole thing was done very quietly,' according to a report telegraphed to the *Liverpool Courier*, 'and people on the pier were unaware of the import of the conversation.' O'Brien remonstrated that he had had no intention of slipping away, though Labouchere and Brunner had urged him to accompany them to London so that he might defend himself before the House. He spent the night in custody at the Imperial Hotel, and the winter incarcerated in Tullamore jail, where he delighted his friends and infuriated the authorities by preferring

[1] L. P. Curtis, Jr, *Coercion and Conciliation in Ireland, 1880–1892* (Princeton, 1963), pp. 199–200, 435–8.

to sit naked in his cell rather than to suffer the indignity of prison garb.

Brunner and Labouchere, as well as Ellis, who travelled separately by way of Caher, were all present at Westminster the next evening to take part in the previously scheduled debate on governmental interference with public meetings in Ireland. It was a subject on which they had the dubious benefit of their own experience. The parliamentary correspondent for the *Liverpool Courier*, a journal of patently Tory sympathies, watched the Gladstonian benches fill for the occasion. The Grand Old Man, Dr Tanner, and Morley were among the earliest arrivals. 'But before Sir Wm Harcourt rose, Mr Labouchere appeared. So did Mr Brunner, who evidently thinks the eyes of the world are upon him.' Under the circumstances, Brunner's vanity was altogether excusable, for this was hardly the time for reticence or false modesty. When his turn came, he rose to 'give the House the result of my observations, with great respect, and as calmly as possible'. On the whole, his remarks were tempered and not without a certain wry humor.

'When I went to Ireland, and looked around me,' Brunner began his narrative,

it appeared to me as if I were in a country occupied by a foreign enemy. I found a military force in fortified barracks in every petty town...I found houses here and there barricaded; I found the occupying forces regarded with hatred. I found...those who resisted the occupying force [regarded] as patriots.

He had journeyed to Mitchelstown 'in pursuance of what I considered to be a duty', to see for himself the agrarian conditions that O'Brien had decried in his 'inflammatory speeches' a month before. He found, exactly as O'Brien had described, pockets of affluence amid abject poverty, and he cited the case of one proprietor in the district, an infamous exploiter of his tenants, who maintained his exalted station on not less than £20,000 a year ('and as a "chemical Croesus", as *The Times* has the excellent taste to call me, I may, possibly, be allowed to judge upon such matters').

Contrary to Tory allegations, he professed that he made his

visit to allay tensions among the people, whom he, as the new member for Northwich, had wished to assure that relief in the form of a Liberal Government would not be long in coming: 'I wished to tell them that the Party which sits upon the Treasury Bench now was discredited in the eyes of the people of England, and was very certain soon to fall.' But the police had rendered irrelevant his appeal for forbearance. Still, he vowed, he would return to Ireland to continue the mission that had been so brutally interrupted. More than ever he was determined to 'encourage the people of Ireland', despite 'the provocations they have received', to keep faith in their English allies and 'to maintain what I believe, and what they believe, to be their legal rights...'[1]

Four days later, on the 16th, a letter from Brunner was published in the correspondence columns of the *Daily News* that contemplated the grim prospects for Ireland in the winter months that lay ahead. Sir Michael Hicks-Beach, 'who used his great influence in the direction of peace by exerting upon the Irish landlords a "pressure within the law"', had been succeeded at the Irish Office by 'Bloody' Balfour, whose administration pertinaciously defended property rights and showed no mercy for peasant distress. 'The moderating influence of Mr Hicks-Beach [was] absent', Brunner lamented, at the same time that 'prolonged drought' threatened to aggravate agrarian conditions. He therefore invited the readers of the *Daily News* to join him in demonstrating to Irishmen England's abiding concern for their plight. Immediate and ungrudging action was necessary 'to enable the poor and wretched in Ireland to tide [themselves] over the gathering difficulties of their lot..., and to foster the growing love between the two peoples of the two islands, and the nascent hope of better and brighter days to come'. To this end he proposed the establishment of a commission 'of well-known men of the four nations' to collect emergency funds which would be disbursed in Ireland to finance relief projects and to provide legal assistance against eviction. To launch the scheme, he contributed his own check for a thousand pounds.

Brunner's private correspondence with officials at the *Daily*

---

[1] *Parliamentary Debates*, 3rd ser., CCCXXI, cols. 410–14 (September 12, 1887).

News and politicians, Liberals and nationalists, leaves no doubt that his offer was as sincere as the sympathies that had prompted it. The Tory press, as was to be expected, denounced him for this latest act of brazen self-publicity, while the Liberal press, predictably enough, lavished praise upon his 'munificent gift'. A leader in the same day's *Daily News* applauded the 'handsome practical testimony' he had given to his sentiments; while the *Liberal and Radical* initiated a supplementary appeal;[1] and the *Liverpool Mercury* commended the 'sensible conclusions' he had drawn from his unfortunate Irish experiences: 'What has always been wanted...is a closer intercourse between Englishmen and the Irish people,' it asserted on the 17th. 'Such is the work Mr Brunner has striven to do since his recent return to Parliament, and now he proposes to continue it on such a basis as an able man of business would devise.' Curiously enough, it was the Irish who reacted differently from what one might have supposed. Dublin's *Freeman's Journal*, which spoke with pre-eminent authority, was 'profoundly touched' by this generous offer from a man 'who has proved himself a good friend of Ireland'. Furthermore, it welcomed his suggestions ('all excellent') for improving relations between the two peoples. Yet it had grave reservations about encouraging Irishmen to accept material assistance from Englishmen, from whom they asked 'not alms—only justice'.

Brunner's enemies took delight in the *Freeman's* tepid response, which further demonstrated to them the base ingratitude of Irishmen and the futility of conciliatory gestures. They were even more heartened by the publication on the 26th of a second letter from Brunner which acknowledged that 'the response to my appeal...has been practically a negative'. Only three checks were received, all for small amounts, he reported gloomily, and these he returned to their senders with his personal letter of thanks. Noting that the *Freeman's Journal* on the 17th, 'speaking, as it has a right to speak, in the name of Ireland, gave utterance in most dignified tones to an unqualified refusal to accept anything in the shape of alms', he concluded that 'such a reply' had

---

[1] *Liberal and Radical*, September 24, 1887; also G. H. Croxden Powell to Brunner, September 28, 1887, BP.

shown the Irish people 'the more worthy of help, the more deserving of sympathy'. Undaunted, he professed his intention 'to endeavour, through another channel, to perform some of the work sketched out in my former letter'.

There was no shortage of suggestions, not all of them appropriate, as to how Brunner could best apply his thousand pounds. The *St James's Gazette*, which had scorned his original offer as a 'spirited advert', suggested with grim humor on the 28th that he forward his check to the widow of the policeman most recently murdered by Irish patriots. J. J. Clancy, one of the leaders of the 'proclaimed' Irish National League, assured him 'that though the response has not been what you expected, gratitude, deep and undoubted, is felt...in Ireland'. He counselled Brunner, who had solicited his advice, to

send the larger part of the money to John Dillon for the relief of tenants *unjustly* evicted from their homes. I say this, as if you send it to the League it may possibly prejudice you in your constituency. Then I would send some of the money—not a very large share—to the families of the men killed at Mitchelstown. Lastly I would send some to the National Liberal Federation or to the Irish Press Agency or to both for the dissemination of literature on the Irish question in England and Scotland.[1]

Many of the same points had already occurred to Brunner, who raised them in correspondence with Sir Walter Foster, now member for Ilkeston and chairman of the General Committee of the National Liberal Federation. In particular he proposed to Foster that the Federation sponsor a program, which he was prepared to underwrite, to send English working men on fact-finding missions to Ireland. Foster was receptive: 'I should like the Federation to take up some Irish work,' he replied, 'and if my colleagues agree with me, we shall be very glad to accept your generous offer for that purpose.'[2] Although it is not clear what became of this idea, Brunner eventually adopted Clancy's suggestion and presented half the amount to John Dillon. 'Please do not acknowledge the £500 publicly,' he instructed, 'at any rate...until I decide what to do with the balance,' and he inquired as to the

[1] Clancy to Brunner, September 28, 1887, BP.
[2] Foster to Brunner, September 23, 1887, BP.

worthiness of the Irish Protestant Home Rule Association and the National League of Great Britain.[1] Not without considerable risk to his electoral image, he subscribed publicly to the Irish National League: 'You will no doubt understand clearly that I do not mean to imply approval in detail of all the objects of the League,' he told its secretary, Timothy Harrington. 'With its main object, however, the promotion of the happiness, the freedom, and the prosperity of the people of Ireland, I am in heartiest sympathy.'[2]

However rewarding, Brunner's self-assumed role as benefactor of Irish causes was not without its drawbacks. Appeals from the needy, many accompanied by testimonials from parish priests, came in a never-ending stream; and several applicants who were in the vicinity lodged upon his doorstep. Prodded by his wife, he advanced a 'loan' of fifty pounds ('I don't expect to see it back,' he told Dillon) to one Miss Maggie Crotty, who had sent him an especially heart-rending letter. Yet it was obvious that he could not hope to gratify every petitioner. Dillon, who sought to encourage a spirit of greater responsibility among his countrymen, reproved Brunner for his promiscuous alms-giving, which he held to be self-defeating: 'Any one who writes a letter as you did to the papers is sure to be worried by begging letters,' he pointed out. 'Our great object always has been to enable the Irish people to help themselves and to deliver our country from the detestable and humiliating position of constant beggary which it has occupied for so long.' He urged Brunner not to dissipate his funds and to 'consign' the solicitations he received 'to the waste paper basket, and for the future if any Irish man or woman writes you a begging letter remit it instantly to the same place. And if any Irish person should have the indecency to go to your house to beg, get rid of them as soon as possible.' He was 'exceedingly glad' when Brunner decided to dispense his aid through more formal channels and along more constructive lines.[3]

[1] Brunner to Dillon, October 14, 1887 (copy), BP.
[2] This letter appeared, in among other places, the *Liberal and Radical* (September 24, 1887), and the *New York World* (September 17, 1887).
[3] Dillon to Brunner, October 13 and 21, 1887, BP; also Brunner to Dillon, October 14, 1887 (copy), BP.

After acquitting himself in the House, Brunner returned to Ireland to resume his circular tour where he had left off. His speech, essentially the same one he had delivered in Parliament, varied little from place to place; but it grew more compelling with each re-telling. 'He would never rest until the hour of deliverance of the Irish people came,' he vowed on September 18 to a well-disposed audience at Bandon, outside of Cork. In reply to those who asserted that the Irish character was inimical to responsible institutions he defended the Irish as an honest and industrious people: the only thieves who had been present at Mitchelstown, he mischievously protested, were he and Labouchere who had taken home each other's rugs. Besides, a thoroughly responsible administration at Dublin would better cope with any propensity to lawlessness: it would command greater respect from the people, and would more vigorously discipline the Irish constabulary, assigning each man to 'the district where he was born' in order to insure that agents of the law 'would never dare to behave as the police at Mitchelstown did'. Officers who resisted this arrangement, he recommended, should be expatriated to America, where they might give freer rein to their aggressive impulses.[1]

Speaking several times a day, Brunner travelled northward and crossed to England, where he continued his crusade. On the 20th, he addressed a Home Rule demonstration at the New Islington Public Hall, Manchester, with C. P. Scott among those on the platform. By this time he had amplified the account of his Mitchelstown experiences, which was more truculent and markedly less self-effacing. 'Mercy was above the law,' he averred, and he had gone 'to Mitchelstown to stand up for mercy, even if it should be against the law'. He described himself as

[1] *Freeman's Journal*, September 19, 1887; also *Northwich and Winsford Chronicle*, September 24, 1887. Two constabularymen promptly wrote to Brunner, offering to resign if he would assist their passage to America. Michael Davitt, to whom he forwarded the letters, advised him to refuse: 'Mere resignation *now* does not, in my opinion, entitle an R.I.C. man to anything more than a favourable opinion. Before *Mitchelstown*, it did. But, since the murderous action of the Constabulary on that occasion, something else is required besides resignation to entitle him to active sympathy. Men who throw down their arms or batons when called upon to evict wretched tenants or bludgeon people taking part in a meeting give proof of honest indignation, and thereby earn a right to consideration at our hands.' Davitt to Ellis, November 3, 1887, BP.

in your own district to yourself, but in the eyes of the world you are nothing but an ungrateful, blustering, foreign dissenter, whose one hand is against all men, and whose other is deep down in the depths of a well-lined pocket.

Though it was no exaggeration to say that Brunner's pocket was 'well-lined', nothing could have been farther from the truth than the implication that he kept his hand, palm closed, deep within it. It was in fact the extent of his generosity, particularly to causes they found repugnant, that most incited his critics. His offer to endow Irish relief works was a case in point. Throughout the years he identified himself not only as a major contributor to Liberal funds—he was one of the largest single backers of the 1906 election victory—but also as the patron of some of the party's most radical projects.

With the departure of the Whig magnates and the consequent loss of revenues to the party, the Liberals relied increasingly upon men of Brunner's stamp. His assistance came to be taken for granted whether it was a matter of subscribing to National Liberal Club debentures, sponsoring candidates at by-elections, or meeting the payrolls of failing Liberal journals. In 1888 he helped T. P. O'Connor found the *Star*, an outspoken London daily, and two years later he provided the backing to launch the *Speaker* as an antidote to the anti-Gladstonian *Spectator*; these activities will be investigated in the next chapter. The party chiefs turned to him whenever a newspaper, particularly one in the north-west, was on the market; and he helped bring or keep many within the Liberal family. These investments, known to relatively few, were so extensive and diversified that when the *Daily News* changed hands early in the new century, John Edward Taylor, the proprietor of the *Manchester Guardian*, mistakenly presumed that 'our good friend Sir John Brunner is in it'.[1]

Defining Liberalism in its widest possible sense, Brunner gave freely to groups dedicated to goals of social improvement and moral reform, among them various Masonic charities, 'Sunday societies', workmen's clubs, and organizations to assist the homeless, the indigent, and impoverished scholars. His support for higher education was directly inspired by a commitment to a

[1] Taylor to C. P. Scott, January 4, 1901, Scott Papers (copy courtesy of D. G. O. Ayerst).

distinctly Liberal view of society, and his manifold contributions to the party must also be seen in this light. Throughout his career he looked upon parliamentary Liberalism as an agency to propagate specific doctrines, and he asked nothing in return—certainly neither material reward nor personal recognition—so long as the party did not default upon these tasks. When the time came he gladly turned over the *Speaker*, in which he had invested perhaps most heavily, to younger men who stood firm in the faith and who would presumably better realize the journal's potential to accomplish good.

Always high upon Brunner's list of priorities was Irish Home Rule, bound up in his mind with fundamental tenets of social justice and national honor. Though Gladstone's critics on both sides of the House professed to regard Home Rule as a distraction from more pressing domestic problems, Brunner was convinced that an effective Irish settlement would facilitate the solution of those problems either directly or by the precedents it would set. Far from being a vainglorious adherence to abstract principle, Home Rule appeared to him a major step toward re-charting the Liberal Party on a course of more advanced social legislation. For this reason, he often found himself working more closely with Irish nationalists than with his Liberal colleagues, many of whom proved disconcertingly eager to divest themselves of a commitment that had been shown an electoral liability. Because the wealthiest men in Liberal circles tended to be lukewarm Home Rulers, it was increasingly difficult to finance Irish projects. 'We have unlimited energy—the best of men on our side *anxious* to work for us, but we are stymied by want of funds,' E. J. C. Morton, secretary of the Home Rule Union, complained to Brunner. 'I saw the other day...in the papers that the Duke of Westminster had given his *second* subscription of £5000 to the Liberal Unionist Association. Why, we would *contract* to convert all England to Home Rule for £5000.'[1] As in Cheshire politics, Brunner inherited the mantle of men like Westminster who had defected to the enemy. It would be impossible to ascertain the amount of capital he transfused into the Irish freedom movement,

1 Morton to Brunner, August 4, 1888, BP.

ing by Gladstone's guarded silence and by pledges of continued support for Parnell telegraphed from Dublin and America. Ellis received profuse accounts of the Sheffield proceedings from his friends, including A. H. D. Acland, who wrote:

... The cloud of the Parnell business hangs over us (aggravated sadly by the hasty action and stupid words of John Redmond and others who positively leap into Parnell's arms and almost imply that they love him more than ever since the divorce case went against him). Yet the general tone of English Liberalism is splendid and I think this is the best Federation meeting I have seen.[1]

If nothing else, the Federation managed to impress upon Liberal front benchers who were present an aversion to further dealings with Parnell. Morley and Harcourt conveyed this sentiment to Gladstone, who deputized the former to seek out Parnell and to request him to step down for the sake of the cause. Although Parnell, newly re-elected chairman of the Irish parliamentary party, spurned this advice, his political future remained in doubt. Ellis Jones-Griffith, who substituted for Ellis as Brunner's secretary, described continued 'suspense' two days later: 'Mr B[runner] says it is 2 to 1 *on* Parnell retiring.'[2] On the 29th, Parnell issued his manifesto to the Irish people, affirming his intention to remain at the helm. But his effectiveness had been impaired, and he was soon challenged not only by the English parties, but, after an explosive meeting on December 6 in Committee Room 15 of the House of Commons, by a majority of Irish members, who chose Justin McCarthy their leader. Dillon, O'Brien, Davitt, and O'Connor—Brunner's closest contacts among the Irish nationalists—sided with McCarthy.

At this point the fund that Brunner had endowed in October acquired a new purpose, that of strengthening the McCarthy faction of the Irish parliamentary party against the Parnellite rump. 'For the present' the project was 'paralysed', Byles advised him on December 14;

[1] Acland to Ellis, November 21, 1890, Ellis Papers.
[2] Jones-Griffith to Ellis, November 27, 1890, Ellis Papers. Like Ellis, Jones-Griffith was educated at University College, Aberystwyth; he sat in Parliament from 1895 to 1918, and again in 1923–4.

but I feel sure a time must soon come when the expression of substantial sympathy from England will be of infinite value. It will become clear that the present division of Irish opinion is a division of those who trust English Liberalism from those who don't, or who at any rate dare not burn any of their boats to prove their trust. *Then* will come our time. Very likely then we may get some front-bench men with us—perhaps even the G.O.M., and if so, we shall boom. If England then shows that it owns to responsibility for the feeding of the evicted tenants, it will do more than anything else could to wean Irish opinion from Parnell's party to McCarthy's. I hope for your sake this will be so.

I won't write about the terrible time we are going thro'. I know what you are feeling, because I am feeling it all myself so bitterly.[1]

Brunner was dismayed by Parnell's refusal to step aside, by his flagrant misrepresentation of Gladstonian policy, and not least of all by his cruel charges that Gladstone had seized the divorce issue as a fortuitous pretext to disown Home Rule. On February 12, 1891, he dined with Herbert Gladstone, who assured him that Parnell's version of promises Gladstone had made to him fourteen months earlier was completely unfounded:

He told me [Brunner wrote to Ellis] that he read the famous Memorandum which the G.O.M. had before him at Hawarden when Parnell was there—a few hours after the latter left, and had re-read it a week or two ago. Herbert describes Parnell's lying on the subject as stupendous.

There is no *proposal* in it from beginning to end, but only suggestions which came from various quarters.

On the question of Ireland's representation at Westminster under a scheme of Home Rule, for instance, there were five suggestions, all marked with a query (?) to none of which did the G.O.M. pin his faith. This, of course, is confidential.

Brunner bore out *The Times*'s observation on February 6 that 'amongst the Gladstonian rank and file there is a growing feeling of weariness and disgust at the prolongation of the Irish negotiations'. Why, he wondered uneasily, did Parnell's former lieutenants travel to France to seek a rapprochement with him; and why should Liberals compromise their principles to restore an embarrassing alliance? Thomas Sexton, a senior Irish politician, told Brunner that Dillon, passing through London on the 12th on

---

[1] Byles to Brunner, December 14, 1890, BP.

his way to Galway jail, 'had declared to him [Sexton] most solemnly that under no circumstances would he recognise Parnell's leadership', to which Brunner indignantly retorted: 'Why does he [Dillon] not make the statement in his published letter?' The letter to which Brunner referred was part of an open exchange among Irish leaders that had appeared in the press that morning, giving *The Times* cause to celebrate as 'complete and irretrievable' the 'collapse of the Boulogne negotiations' between O'Brien and Parnell. The next day, in a by-election to which *The Times* paid scant attention, the electors of Northampton returned the Liberal candidate with a 'poll 866 more than the highest Liberal vote ever recorded' in the constituency. This 'splendid' result, coming as it did 'the day after the announcement of the final break-up of the Boulogne negotiations', delighted Brunner and demonstrated to him 'the truth of what I have so often asserted...that there is far more funk in the House of Commons than in the country'.[1]

For his own part, Brunner nursed mixed feelings about Parnell. He was too embroiled in the struggle to profess, like Asquith, that had he been born an Irishman 'he would have been with John Redmond in supporting Parnell, and not with Justin McCarthy in opposing him'.[2] Yet like Asquith he recognized Parnell's genius and acknowledged how much the Irish nationalist movement owed him. He continued to prize a superb portrait of Parnell (no Duke of Westminster he), which he presented in 1898 to the National Gallery of Ireland. 'Mr Parnell's past services to Ireland had been so great', he admitted, that he could find 'no word of blame for the generous hearted men who in Committee-room No. 15 had stood up for him so stoutly.'[3] Still, he thought them sadly mistaken in their strategy, and time and again he said so. Ellis, who knew best of all the soul-searching to which Brunner subjected himself, 'often thought' during his voyage 'how sick you must be of all this personal, wrangling aspect of the Irish question when the real Irish question is how to better the poor's

---

[1] Brunner to Ellis, February 13, 1891, Ellis Papers.
[2] Roy Jenkins, *Asquith* (London, 1965), pp. 51–2 n.
[3] Brunner to T. Delaney (of the T. P. O'Connor branch, Widnes, the Irish National League), July 10, 1891. *Widnes Weekly News*, July 18, 1891.

lot and right a nation's wrong'.[1] Brunner never forgot the Irish masses whose suffering gave Irish politics its substance and urgency. Dillon told him of one Irish landlord—'a very hard man' —who had refused any concessions to his tenants and who might be induced to sell his estate: 'If it should appear to me that you can do anything to help the poor people, I shall write to you again.'[2] So long as a comprehensive political settlement of Ireland's affairs remained unlikely, Brunner was prepared to do all he could to alleviate individual cases of distress.

Parnell, refusing to the end to bow to Gladstonian pressures, was presently relieved of his command by a higher authority. But his sudden death in October 1891—'an uncovenanted mercy for his opponents', Dillon's biographer has called it[3]—had an effect more apparent than real. Ireland's uncrowned king left a legacy of bitter recrimination among his former courtiers and one of abiding cynicism among his erstwhile English allies. With a conspicuous lack of enthusiasm, the parties prepared for the general election that came the following July. No one was confident of a meaningful victory, and no one achieved one. The Conservatives, as expected, sustained heavy losses; the Liberal Unionists, heavier ones. The Gladstonians, however, were forced to depend for their majority in the new House upon the votes of savagely divided Irishmen. The situation, though not forlorn, was nowhere as promising as it had been five summers earlier, when Brunner had last been returned for Northwich. He successfully defended his seat in 1892, evoking plaintive memories of his Mitchelstown experience and calling upon his constituents to renew their trust in Gladstone's Irish policy. Confident that the time had come to commemorate Mitchelstown in deeds as well as words, he failed to perceive that others had imbibed antithetical lessons from the same events.

[1] Ellis to Brunner, February 24, 1891, BP.
[2] Dillon to Brunner, September 2, 1891, BP.
[3] Lyons, *John Dillon*, p. 144.

CHAPTER 7

THE SOCIALIST CHALLENGE

Though it was not the least unusual for Victorian politicians, particularly Radicals, to be consumed with a singleminded devotion to one cause or another—employers' liability, disestablishment, the extension of small holdings, or local option on the closing of public houses, to name a few—Brunner successfully resisted the temptation to allow Irish Home Rule, always his governing concern, to become an obsession. During his many years in the House and long after his retirement, his interests, if not always his responses, kept pace with the times and reflected the workings of Liberalism on various levels. And it is in these diverse realms that one may best see how his background and experience influenced his public attitudes and activities.

To whatever extent Brunner's Liberalism was the outgrowth of personal factors, it was never dictated by material considerations, conscious or otherwise. Moral and religious imperatives were at least as important in determining his political response, and often induced him to sacrifice commercial gain or class interest. Such behavior was not uncommon in Victorian society, which cannot be understood without taking into consideration men of Brunner's character and outlook. Yet, much like Gladstone to whose age he belonged, his motives became incomprehensible, even suspect, to a younger generation in revolt against their elders and increasingly susceptible to the suppositions if not the formal doctrines of economic determinism. The passing decades, bringing war and disillusionment, cast into disrepute Victorian theories of progress and left a distrust of ideologies, particularly those with a religious content. As a result, it has become easier to scorn than to appreciate the values of a society distant from our own in every respect save time.[1]

[1] Gertrude Himmelfarb has illuminatingly diagnosed the problem: 'To assign so much importance to ideas, and especially to religious ideas, seems naive to a generation brought up on Marx, Freud, and Sartre. And to find virtue in ideas and religions that

Among the last of the classic Radicals—he died before a new order had truly emerged—Brunner outlived his tradition and the religious fervor that had sustained it through the nineteenth century. He could see in his own children the weakening of non-conformist ties through intermarriage, attendance at the public schools and universities, and worldly success. From the time that he first arrived at Westminster, Radicalism was also challenged by the incipient forces of socialism, an alternative ethic and enthusiasm, that were eventually to dislodge Radicalism from its accustomed place at the left of the parliamentary spectrum. Though Sir William Harcourt might complacently boast in 1889 —significantly the year of the London dockers' strike—that 'we are all socialists now', the spokesmen for the 'New Unionism' took little comfort in the vague collectivism of the Liberal front bench to which the Radicals who continued to dominate the Trades Union Congress appeared unduly deferential. To the few socialists within the House and the greater number outside, Radicalism seemed too anxious to conciliate the enemy and too 'bourgeois' in tactics and temperament. And, to be sure, socialists were often opposed in principle to realizing their goals through the Lib-Lab alliance that their Radical chiefs had painstakingly forged. 'The Radicals are doing our work,' John Burns, at this juncture a self-proclaimed revolutionary, wrote sniffily in his diary; 'it is time we pushed further ahead.'[1] The working-class leaders whom Brunner counted among his friends had to defend their waning authority against attacks from men like Burns, to whom they seemed insufficiently militant. Henry Broadhurst, who occupied the pivotal secretaryship of the parliamentary committee, was in fact denounced by Keir Hardie at the 1887 Trades Union Congress for the assistance he had given Brunner at the Northwich by-election weeks earlier. The fact that Brunner was a large-scale employer of labor, let alone his intimacy with mem-

encourage gradualism, stability, and social cohesion is doubly galling to those who have a quite different order of virtues and values.' 'The Victorian Ethos: Before and After Victoria', in *Victorian Minds* (New York, 1969), p. 299.

[1] John Burns's diary, September 18, 1888, Burns Papers, British Museum Add. MSS. 46310; for socialist resentment of the existing trade union leadership, see Henry Pelling, *A History of British Trade Unionism* (London, 1963), pp. 93–5.

bers of the T.U.C. old guard, made him the immediate target of socialist critics who thought his position in society incompatible with the ideals he professed.

Such imputations pained Brunner, who took pride in the fact that his interests and friendships transcended class lines. His closest political associates tended to be men of humble origin, including Broadhurst, Joseph Arch, Thomas Burt, Michael Davitt, and T. P. O'Connor, any of whom might be considered an unlikely companion for a captain of industry. In particular his collaboration with O'Connor on the *Star*, the organ of advanced Radicalism, strengthened his belief that socialism and Radicalism shared a common destiny. In time he came to enjoy cordial relations even with John Burns, who had retired his red flag and equally offensive straw hat, and to whose 'wages fund' he periodically contributed. Like many others, he later regretted that Burns, whom he had commended as 'the embodiment of the social conscience of the community',[1] proved so fainthearted a reformer. To the extent that Brunner in his later parliamentary years was attached to any one political leader, he was known as a Lloyd George man. But Lloyd George, like Chamberlain before him, forfeited Brunner's allegiance by his flirtations with the Tory enemy. It was in fact Lloyd George's failure to build a progressive alliance that signalled Brunner's decision to support the Labour Party in the closing months of his life.

As soon as his second return to Parliament accorded him sufficient prominence, Brunner found himself the object of incessant attacks in the socialist press. Ironically his assailants chose to ignore his opposition to Irish coercion, at which they too professed great indignation.[2] Among the most vociferous was H. H. Champion, editor of the *Labour Elector*, who was determined to discredit middle-class Radicalism as an agency for reform as well as to remove lingering suspicions of his latent Toryism. By the autumn of 1887 he had grown tired of waiting for Liberal headquarters to take adequate notice of working-class candidates and

---

[1] William Kent, *John Burns* (London, 1950), p. 359.
[2] A Trafalgar Square rally on November 13, 1887, at which John Burns and R. B. Cunninghame Graham, M.P. were arrested, had been called ostensibly to protest the imprisonment of William O'Brien. See Curtis, *Coercion and Conciliation*, p. 201.

ambitions,[1] and he cited Brunner, the Liberal of the hour, as proof of the party's hypocrisy toward the working man.

Champion's allegations, which appeared initially in the pages of the *Labour Elector*, were promptly seized by Tory editors who were pleased to report what one 'thorough-going Radical' thought of another. It amused Brunner that the same Tory journals that now denounced him 'with so much gusto' as a shameless exploiter of labor had, weeks earlier, ascribed his by-election victory to his high standing among his men. Less amusing was a shower of letters, 'many...simply abusive', which 'for the most part...remain[ed] unanswered'. To one, written in a friendly vein, he offered an open reply:

...It is untrue that I have made enormous wealth by 'grinding the faces of the poor,' but through my partner's exceptional ability, and my own exceptional industry...Only a small proportion of our men work in shifts, and amongst those the smallest wage is 24s per week. All steady men in our employ get a week's holiday every year and a week's pay with it. It is absolutely false that on any occasion I ever said one word to discourage the formation of a trades union, either among our men or any others. Lastly it is not true that our business is an unhealthy one. Most of the men who joined us in 1873 are with us still, and I will back them for muscle and sinew against a similar number of Mr Champion's followers any day.[2]

Not easily deterred, Champion kept up his attacks throughout the winter months and dispatched Tom Mann to gather evidence on the spot. Mann took temporary employment at the Winnington works, and decried conditions there in a series of articles that appeared in the *Labour Elector* between November 1888 and the following March. In the spring, Champion urged Henry Broadhurst, whom he addressed 'as the most prominent working class member in the House of Commons', to move a question about a man at the Sandbach works who was fatally injured while 'performing his seventeenth hour of consecutive work'.[3] Though Broadhurst declined to take up the cry, Brunner was moved to

[1] See Champion's correspondence with Arnold Morley, chief Liberal whip, cited in Henry Pelling, *The Origins of the Labour Party* (Oxford, 1965), p. 59.
[2] Brunner to 'a gentleman at Pendleton', October 24, 1887, *Liverpool Daily Post and Mercury*, November 1, 1887.
[3] Champion to Broadhurst, June 20, 1888, Broadhurst Papers (British Library of Economics and Political Science).

the Socialists', and he confessed that before a recent union meeting at Winsford, 'Messrs Champion, Tom Mann and Keir Hardie had talked him over at a Northwich publichouse'.[1]

For the time being, Brunner was reluctant to oblige his friends, including Mond, by replying in kind to his socialist assailants. 'The public', he consoled himself, 'is very quick to see the motive of such attacks, and is rarely influenced by them.' He recalled how 'persistently and maliciously' Joseph Chamberlain had been hounded 'by the Tory party and its tools' in years gone by, and how Chamberlain had won wide sympathy by maintaining his dignity. '...A public man', he reasoned, 'ought not to appear to act too defensively, and 'must not hastily come to the conclusion that attacks upon his private character are a serious danger either to his Party or to the cause he represents.' Yet to his distress, socialist agitators began to encroach upon the local trades union that he paternalistically regarded as 'the direct outcome of [his] public advocacy'. Here was a confrontation between the forces of the old unionism, élitist and conciliatory, and those of the new unionism, different in spirit, tactics, and self-consciousness. Loath to see the movement fall into the hands of irreconcilables, Brunner was relieved when the officers of the Northwich society invited him to take the chair at a general meeting. 'This will show you better than anything I could say', he told a friend, 'the estimation in which I am held by the working men of this neighbourhood.'[2]

Brunner's attitude toward trade unionism might strike the modern student as curious: often ambivalent, it was never

[1] Brunner to William J. Emmott Toze, December 22, 1888 (Letterbook); also Brunner to Broadhurst, December 23, 1888 (Letterbook).

[2] Brunner to Toze, December 22, 1888 (Letterbook). There is every reason to credit Brunner's claim that he encouraged his employees to unionize. 'Last September', he recounted in a speech at the Winnington works on September 21, 1889, 'I had to go to Winsford to address a number of men upon a subject entirely apart from Trades Unions or politics, and I urged them to do their best to form as strong a Trades Union as they could, and why?...I told them that when the Salt Union was formed there would be practically only two large employers of labour in the neighbourhood;...that if any single man in the neighbourhood had a quarrel with any one foreman, all the foremen might join together and refuse to employ that man. I urged these men to band themselves together for their own protection, and I am happy to say that they have taken my advice.' *Northwich Guardian*, September 25, 1889.

unenlightened. At a time when most of his fellow entrepreneurs quivered at the prospect of combination among their men (the very word raised the spectre of jacobinism), he told his employees that 'nothing would please me. . .better than that you should band together for your common good'. This was neither madness nor an idle invitation, but rather the conscious implementation of a distinctly Radical view of what he called industrial politics. He was justly convinced that 'straightforward, honest combination' was more to be welcomed than feared, that it would accredit a responsible working-class leadership with which management could negotiate binding agreements, and that it would lay down guidelines for the settlement of disputes without recourse to strikes and unofficial work stoppages. He was confident that his own position would be strengthened by bringing into existence a countervailing power to which his men could delegate authority and through which he in turn could hold them to a bargain. Eager to redress legitimate grievances, he was glad to open channel of communication. Proud of his record, he knew that if his men compared their conditions with those elsewhere in the chemical industry they would see how little they had to complain about. And, above all, discerning no fundamental conflict of interest between labor and capital, he took for granted that his men were as much aware as he of the inter-dependence of their relationship. 'I am perfectly satisfied', he therefore declared to his assembled employees,

that if you all enter a Trades Union and have regular rules for your guidance, you will never come to me or to my colleagues with any unfair or unreasonable proposals, and I can promise you this, that whenever your Committee comes to us. . .[it] will be met in the frankest and fairest manner possible.[1]

His qualms were few and incidental. He preferred to see his workers affiliate 'with other men in this *locality*' rather than 'with other men in *our trade*', explaining to Mond his reluctance 'to run the risk of being asked for what other alkali manufacturers are not asked for', and confiding his fear that 'too close [an] intercourse between our men and men working in the Leblanc trade. . .might

[1] Speech at Winnington, September 21, 1889, *Northwich Guardian*, September 25, 1889.

so easily be made the means of communicating information to our competitors'. Nor did he discount the fact that he might exert 'far greater influence' upon a local union than upon 'an alkali trade union' that drew its membership from distant works.[1] He was not disappointed by the ultimate arrangement though, so far as he could tell, fewer of his men joined than he would have liked. Still, he held hard and fast to the rule that the company 'would never on any condition whatever' make union membership 'a condition of employment'.[2] For unionism to do its best work, freedom of contract and the rights of the individual would have to be respected by all parties concerned. The subsequent pattern of industrial relations at Brunner, Mond and Company—and to some extent at ICI later on—was a tribute to his vision.

Early in 1889, Brunner was perturbed by reports that a Tory member of the County Council was circulating Champion's calumnies in specially prepared pamphlets. His nerves frayed, he broke his vow of silence to administer a rebuke to the suspected culprit. Even more impetuously and with little more effect, he replied publicly in a polite but barbed letter when R. B. Cunninghame Graham, a socialist M.P., attacked him in the House.[3] Francis Schnadhorst, to whom he sent an advance copy, wisely counseled him not to give Graham the satisfaction of a formal reply: '. . . Whatever he says is always accepted with reserve and incredulity. I hope you won't attach too much importance to it. No one else will.'[4] But Brunner, soon to repent his tactical error, gave vent to his emotions. He had suffered too long and, he believed, too grievously to remain silent.

Graham, who based his speech upon reports in the 'public prints', reiterated familiar charges that Brunner's private practices belied his public sentiments and that the men at Brunner, Mond and Company were underpaid, overworked, and subjected to 'shocking sanitary conditions'. He professed his willingness to

[1] Brunner to Mond, September 22, 1889 (copy), BP.
[2] Brunner to Mond, February 6, 1896 (Letterbook).
[3] Graham had formerly asserted his socialism by laying himself open to arrest with John Burns at a Trafalgar Square rally. Like Burns, he was eventually an admirer of Brunner. The son of a laird and a fervent Scottish nationalist, he ended his career an author of travel stories.
[4] Schnadhorst to Brunner, March 10, 1889, BP.

—with whom he elaborated a strategy that he explained to Mond after the storm had passed. Excepting a handful of workers, 'selected by Jarmay's orders, all the men on the works assembled' at 12.45 on Saturday afternoon, the 21st, to hear an address from their employer, who 'advis[ed] them to become Unionists, and to settle all differences between us and them by open negotiation'. Though he mentioned 'that Champion was coming', he thought it best to say 'nothing of Burns or Tillett'. The response could not have been more gratifying: 'When I spoke of the comparison between our works and other alkali works', he told Mond, 'there were distinct signs of assent from the men and the show of hands according to all who watched was both prompt and unanimous.' To his solicitor, he related that the meeting had closed 'with an *absolutely* unanimous show of hands in favour of "combination, association, and fair-play". After this, I may quote one of my auditors and say " Champion be———".'[1] These extensive preparations were happily in vain, for the week passed without incident. Asquith, who had defended Burns in the criminal courts, assured Brunner from London that his former client, 'who is a sensible man, is too busy with real grievances here to go wool-gathering in your part of the world'.[2] But the dangers had been great, and Brunner had no wish to witness along the banks of the Weaver a repetition of the previous month's events along the Thames.

As previously mentioned, freedom of contract was one of Brunner's cardinal tenets. He no more wished to deprive his men of this God-given right than to allow them to force his hand. Even with regard to welfare benefits, he scrupulously avoided the suggestion of compulsion. 'I cannot yet overcome my repugnance', he wrote to one of his directors, 'to the adoption of any scheme that would require employees to contribute from their earnings to a company-managed pension fund.'[3] Other firms had introduced such schemes for ulterior motives, maintaining discipline by more or less holding hostage the amounts deducted from each man's salary: fines were levied upon pension savings for

[1] Brunner to Mond, September 22, 1889 (copy), BP; also Brunner to Lewis, September 23, 1889 (Letterbrook).
[2] Asquith to Brunner, September 25, 1889, BP.
[3] Brunner to Milner, November 15, 1888, ICI Records.

misconduct, damage to plant, and often as a penalty for premature retirement. This Brunner regarded as a 'despotism, however paternal': 'Not even a conviction of murder would justify such a deprivation.' He proposed more equitable means for the company to fulfill its obligations: perhaps a campaign among the men 'to induce them to save voluntarily through Building Societies, [or] by way of Life Insurance or Friendly Societies', or else the company might 'bargain with an Insurance Company or Friendly Society to receive from us annually and to hold for the benefit of each individual a certain proportion of each man's annual benefits, as long as the man remained in our service'. There was no question but that an employee would receive the full benefits to which he was entitled whenever or under whatever circumstances he left. And it was clearly understood that a pension fund was not a device to bribe, let alone coerce, workers into line.

While the merits of various pension schemes were being weighed, sick benefits were paid according to the same basic principles. A workers' sick club was founded in the early days of the Winnington works, and Brunner took immeasurable pride in its operation.[1] He served by invitation as its president, but his duties were 'confined to taking the chair at the annual meetings'. Policy-making decisions and financial control rested in the hands of a committee, elected by the members who paid dues of four pence a week from their wages. In time of need members received free medical attention and supplies, and weekly sick pay of eight shillings. Boys in the company's employ paid half dues and received proportionate benefits. In 1897 the sick pay was raised to ten shillings for men and five for boys. 'The Company pays the Doctor for attendance and medicine,' Brunner recounted, 'keeps the accounts free of cost to the Club, and pays interest on the daily balance in hand.' It was his view that 'no possible organisation could obtain' for the men 'better value for their money'. The men appeared to agree, and it was Parliament's decision— the Shops' Clubs Act of 1902—and not their own that brought

[1] Brunner to D. W. Hewitt, November 26, 1898 (Letterbook) in which he proposes 'to tender evidence to the Home Secretary's Departmental Committee on Compulsory Shop Clubs'; also John I. Watts, *The First Fifty Years of Brunner, Mond & Co.*, p. 81.

the arrangement to an end. At this point the company assumed complete responsibility for the club, maintaining benefits without deducting contributions. National Insurance, legislated in 1911, expropriated the majority of the club's functions; but the Company continued to provide benefits to those workers not covered by the Act and to supplement the benefits of those who were.

Brunner took the view, with which Mond concurred, 'that we don't do enough for our men'.[1] The remedies he proposed—pensions and sick pay, housing and recreational facilities, free baths and paid holidays—were the product of his social conscience and not, as it may sometimes appear, a capitulation to pressures from below or above. Standing far in advance of the norm, he had little to fear as an employer from state intervention. Yet he was opposed on philosophic grounds to legislation that would 'brutalize' the consciences of the rich by shifting moral burdens to the state. His argument, reminiscent of those heard many times in the century, was that legislative interference tended to drive a wedge between masters and men, robbing the former of their sense of responsibility and the latter of their self-respect. Rather than increase the number of factory inspectors, he would inflict more severe penalties upon 'manufacturers and owners of workshops' who neglected to 'keep their establishments in good order'.[2] The effect, he trusted, would be the same, but the emphasis decidedly different. From his perspective, governmental regulation appeared more an impediment than an inducement to progressive change; it would impose a standard of mediocrity, inhibiting those like himself who wished to proceed beyond. And, by its very nature, legislation could not take adequate account of the infinite variety of industrial experiences and relationships.

Yet, unlike the orthodox Gladstonians in his party, Brunner was not unilaterally opposed to state intervention in industry, merely to what seemed to him an indiscriminate use of it. He conceded wide realms in which parliamentary action would be useful, even necessary, and he long and ardently advocated a measure for

---

[1] Brunner to Milner, November 15, 1888, ICI Records.
[2] *Parliamentary Debates*, 4th ser., xcv, cols. 673 ff. (June 17, 1901); also cviii, col. 1039 (May 30, 1902).

compulsory arbitration, 'convinced that it would have a whole-some effect' upon employers less tolerant and percipient than he of working-class aspirations. 'There were districts in the country', he noted with surprise,

where the feeling between the two classes was still of the old-fashioned variety,... [where] employers still refused to meet the representatives of the workmen, with the result that the employers had a somewhat uneasy conscience, and the employed and their representatives a feeling of irritation...[1]

One way or another, the balance would have to be redressed and a working relationship restored. To the same end, and citing his own experience, he supported legislation in 1897 to compensate injured workmen. His company, he boasted to the House, had anticipated such a measure by sixteen years, and had in that time 'paid compensation in every case of injury without asking who was at fault'. The good will had been incalculable and the accident rate had been halved. Compensation was paid directly from company funds, avoiding insurance companies who were known to 'pay as little as possible, and fight every case when there was a chance of defeating the workman'. Admittedly, this was potentially a more costly arrangement, but the directors were determined that 'no such intermediary should come between them and their employees, on the ground that good relationship between them was extremely valuable and should be maintained'.[2]

Early in 1895 Brunner, Mond and Company instituted the eight-hour day, once the cry of Championite disruption. As one trade union pointed out, the company did not concede 'the 48 hours week pure and simple...to all their employees unconditionally': only artisans worked a weekly total of 48 hours (from 7.45 to noon and 1.00 to 5.30 five days a week, and from 7.45 to noon on Saturdays), while semi-skilled laborers worked $49\frac{1}{2}$ hours, and unskilled men 50 hours. Several unions, jealous of their status, balked at the arrangement, but Gustave Jarmay, the director in charge, explained that a chemical works could not operate on the same basis as 'an ordinary Engineering shop', and

[1] *Parliamentary Debates*, 4th ser., XLII, cols. 436 ff. (June 30, 1896).
[2] *Ibid.* 4th ser., XLIX, cols. 763 ff. (May 18, 1897).

that for the time being the experiment was the best that could be tried. Jarmay took pains to bring

before everybody's notice, that the proposed step is not taken with a view of raising wages, but the shortening of the hours is simply being adopted as a means of improving the quality of work done during the same period, and that we expect every man to turn out as much and better work than he is now doing per week.[1]

Five years of intensive study had given every reason to believe that a reduction in hours would be accompanied by improved efficiency, and that the company might expect more willing, regular, and (Brunner would add) sober service from its men. Humanitarian considerations were important, and need not be labored, but the decision to adopt an eight-hour day was essentially a practical one. Of course Brunner was convinced, and rightly in his own case, that the cause of humanity could best be served by the pursuance of enlightened self-interest.

The Brunner–Mond achievement was all the more notable in a trade where management proved infamously recalcitrant. To the best of the Home Secretary's knowledge, there were '1569... cases in which men employed in chemical industries worked for an average of 12 hours a day 7 days a week. This was the industry with the most such *reported* offences.'[2] The number of actual cases was assumed to be far greater. Brunner regretfully concluded that 'as long as our competitors go on with twelve-hour shifts and other abominations' he could not afford to act as generously as he would have liked.[3] Hoping to induce them to follow his example, he contributed a lengthy letter on the subject of work hours to *The Times* on February 7 and later circulated his observations in a privately printed pamphlet. In those 'industries in which workpeople are necessarily employed seven days a week', he saw 'a strong case...for legislative control'. But he thought it best to limit, at least for the present time, intervention to the specific areas 'in which it is obviously and for many reasons most needed'. For this reason he declined to vote for bills to ex-

[1] Jarmay to Mond, January 24, 1895 (copy), BP; also Jarmay to Brunner, February 7, 1895, BP; also Jarmay to Brunner, February 8, 1895, BP.
[2] Speech by Asquith, March 14, 1895, *Parliamentary Debates*, 4th ser., XXXI, col. 1049.
[3] Brunner to Mond, February 6, 1896 (Letterbook).

tend the forty-eight hour week to miners, who worked on the average fewer than six days a week, and to bakers, who he insisted would 'defeat their object' by asking too much.[1] He feared, as did many respected trade unionists, that the unilateral adoption of an eight-hour day would reduce productivity and depress wages, and he therefore urged his parliamentary colleagues to proceed sympathetically, but cautiously, judging each case upon its merits.

In Parliament as in industry, Brunner hoped to draw the teeth of socialist critics by anticipating the more reasonable of their demands and by showing a readiness to negotiate upon the others. In essence, this was the policy of the *Star*, a Radical daily founded in 1888 with the ambition of ending 'the stupid ostracism of socialists' and, at the same time, getting them to 'abandon... much of the wild talk, the "viewy" aims, the impracticable methods which they had inherited from German sources'.[2] Brunner's connection with the *Star*, by all accounts a close one, eludes precise definition. He was among several wealthy Radicals whom Labouchere persuaded that an evening paper was urgently needed to propagate their views in the metropolis. T. P. O'Connor, the editor to whom the *Star* owed its phenomenal success, recalled that two of the richest members of the Liberal Party were brought together by him—they seemed to him to look like 'two goats preparing for a fight'—and agreed between them to provide half the £40,000 to float the venture; but 'one of them entirely changed his mind', and 'the other, after long negotiation', came through with only half the promised amount.[3] Though Brunner's financial status and bearded countenance might lend themselves to such a description, his records show that he gave generously to the *Star* and, on numerous occasions, privately to its editor. It was in fact Brunner who, on behalf of his fellow directors, conveyed the terms of O'Connor's appointment to him.

[1] J. L. Hammond to Thomas Ashton, January 21, 1899 (Letterbook); Brunner to George Scales, March 12, 1900 (Letterbook); Brunner to W. Carr, April 24, 1900 (Letterbook).
[2] *The Star*, January 17, 1889.
[3] O'Connor, *Memoirs of an Old Parliamentarian* (2 vols. London, 1929), I, 254. John Barry identified one of the two would-be benefactors to T. M. Healy as James Williamson, the future Lord Ashton, who insisted that the directors have full power to dismiss O'Connor, who would resign from other commitments. Healy to his brother, August 27, 1887, in Healy, *Letters and Leaders of My Day* (2 vols. New York, 1929), I, 276.

The first issue of the *Star* appeared on January 17 and achieved a record circulation of 140,000 copies, which virtually doubled within two years. O'Connor, who continued to sit for his Liverpool constituency, assembled a staff that boasted such names as H. W. Massingham and Robert Donald. Bernard Shaw, another brilliant recruit, was an embarrassment as often as an asset. The correspondence columns provided a forum for Fabians, Championites, and even Friedrich Engels, all of whose activities were duly reported. Designed to bring together the divergent forces of socialism and Radicalism, the *Star* rode two tigers (one considerably tamer) and as a result neither very comfortably. This inner tension revealed itself in conflicts within the editorial staff, within the directorate, and, most acutely, between the two; evident from the start, it was aggravated by the wave of industrial unrest at the close of the decade, when O'Connor was suspected of showing too much sympathy for striking unions and of giving wholesale support to Labour candidates for the London County Council. He faced continual opposition from his directors, who sought to pressure him into resigning (they could not dismiss him outright), and who in 1891 succeeded in buying him out.

Where did Brunner stand on this matter? His appointment diaries for 1889 and 1890 reveal frequent meetings with O'Connor at the *Star* offices and at the House; and there are ample references in his correspondence, all laudatory, to articles O'Connor had written. Certainly the attempt to stimulate a more progressive Liberalism by waging a 'war on all privilege' was one he would naturally approve. Though he wrote perhaps brusquely to O'Connor that he 'had not time or energy to spare for all this worry', it is not true, as O'Connor's biographer has inferred, that Brunner 'gave him no help' in his struggle.[1] Brunner's support was financial, administered in a series of £500 advances which O'Connor used to increase his shares and thereby to fortify his position.[2] There is no indication that he continued his affiliation with the *Star* after O'Connor's departure.

There is still better evidence of Brunner's sympathies. The

---

[1] Hamilton Fyfe, *T. P. O'Connor* (London, 1934), p. 154.
[2] O'Connor to Brunner, February 6, 1889, August 7 and October [23], 1890, BP.

Speaker, of which he was the sole and acknowledged backer, pursued the same line as the *Star* toward the ideas and aspirations of organized labor:

We must assimilate Socialism: if 'Liberal' is not to become a mere shibboleth, a term as meaningless as 'Democrat' or 'Republican' in American party politics, we must take from Socialism what is good and reject what is bad or doubtful.

Unfortunate in this time of transition is the plight of many Liberals obliged to adapt themselves to new practices, while retaining, at all events nominally, old principles.

The Liberal of forty years ago knew the exact functions of the State. He could define them. The Liberal of today cannot. The former could tell the limits of law; we, to our misfortune, cannot. Political economy then spoke decisively about the duty of *laissez-faire*; now its voice is silent or ambiguous.[1]

O'Connor, who recognized this affinity, commended the *Speaker* as the best of the weeklies.[2]

In the summer of 1889 Brunner was approached by the veteran Liberal journalist Wemyss Reid, with whom he presently entered into 'a financial partnership'.[3] The *Speaker*, a weekly journal of party opinion edited by Reid, was born the following January, barely in time to send greetings to Gladstone on the occasion of his eightieth birthday. Higher in tone than the *Star*, it was aimed at a more exclusive readership which, it was hoped, might be diverted from the anti-Home Rule *Spectator*. But despite the quality of its features and the renown of its contributors, it never matched its rival in influence or circulation: sales reached a modest 4000 at the end of the first year and crept up falteringly thereafter. Unlike the *Star*, it never cleared a profit, and Reid was forced to appeal to his partner at regular intervals for supplementary amounts as high as £1000 to meet payroll and printing expenses. Resigned to a financial loss, Brunner was disappointed only by the *Speaker*'s failure to carry greater weight. At the century's end he was glad to hand over its modest resources to a group of

---

[1] This plea 'to effect the assimilation of Socialism and Liberalism' (unsigned) appeared on May 10, 1890. It was a far cry from its categoric pronouncement five years later that Labour ought to be 'fought instead of courted'. July 20, 1895.

[2] The *Sun*, December 13, 1891.

[3] Brunner to F. G. Hawkins, his solicitor, September 23, 1889; and Brunner to the manager, City Bank, London, October 17, 1889 (Letterbook).

younger Liberals, among whom was J. L. Hammond, his private secretary, who succeeded to the editorship.[1] Financial troubles continued to plague the publication, which in 1907 was rechristened the *Nation*—Massingham, who began on the *Star*, became editor—and eventually incorporated with the *New Statesman*.

Under its original management—from January 4, 1890 to October 7, 1899—the *Speaker* was the organ of what may best be described as unconventional Gladstonianism. It never wavered in its loyalty to Home Rule, making references and drawing analogies to Mitchelstown at every turn; at the same time, it was equally dedicated to the Newcastle Programme of more advanced social legislation to which Gladstone had given grudging assent. Brunner, who was kept abreast of all editorial decisions, entirely approved. 'I was very glad of our talk the other night,' Reid wrote to him on March 10, 1891. 'You will see from the first leader next Saturday that I am pushing our programme forward. I am sure that one is needed by the party.'[2] Early issues reflected this policy of Gladstonianism with a difference: in addition to articles by Dilke, Bryce, Dillon, O'Brien, Bradlaugh, and Haldane, there was a series of articles on London government by Sidney Webb. Others who frequently contributed were Frederic Harrison, J. M. Barrie, and Oscar Wilde. Gladstone, given a standing invitation to 'write on any literary or social subject which interests him',[3] provided a long and abstruse obituary of a German theologian for the third number. The *Speaker* had few kind words to spare for the Liberal Unionists and caused 'a sensation' (to the delight of its editor) with the revelation that Hartington, by this time Duke of Devonshire, had with seeming disloyalty tried and failed to form a ministry in 1880 before Gladstone emerged from retirement.[4] It was sympathetic to trade

[1] F. W. Hirst, *In the Golden Days* (London, 1947), pp. 202–3.
[2] Reid to Brunner, March 10, 1891, BP.
[3] Reid to Herbert Gladstone, November 18, 1889, Viscount Gladstone Papers, British Museum Add. MSS. 46041, fols. 113–14.
[4] 'The *Speaker* has, at one bound, taken its place in the front rank of journalism,' Reid boasted to his partner, informing him that 'I made my statement at the request of Mr Gladstone.' Reid to Brunner, February 26, 1892, BP. See also *The Times*'s leader, February 25, 1892.

unionism and, at least until the disastrous general election of 1895, to labor as an independent political force.

Brunner's newspaper proprietorships, a diversion and not a vocation, complemented his work as an industrialist and parliamentarian. He undertook these obligations strictly as a service and, as such, they were intended to influence opinion within the party no less than in the country at large. The last decade of the nineteenth century was one of dislocation and agonizing reappraisal for Liberals, Brunner included, who suffered the humiliation of prolonged opposition and the ignominy of internal strife. The renaissance that lay ahead was not anticipated by the most sanguine of them, and meanwhile there were frequent changes of leadership and challenges to time-worn doctrine. But these were also the years in which the groundwork, organizational and ideological, was being laid for eventual recovery; and it is in these spheres that his activities can be studied with greatest profit.

CHAPTER 8

FROM GLADSTONE TO
CAMPBELL-BANNERMAN

As an employer of labor, Brunner was continually vexed by the
activities of socialists who permeated the trades union movement, eschewed traditional bargaining methods, and threatened to
disrupt the tacit Lib-Lab alliance. As a politician, he was no less
concerned with unionists of the other variety. He discerned an
essential conservatism in the English working classes which, he
rightly feared, posed a far more dangerous threat to progressive
Liberalism than the catchwords of revolutionary socialism. It
was to this conservative strain in popular opinion that he ascribed
the defeat of Liberal proposals for Home Rule and, later, the jingo
fervor that inflicted irreparable damage upon Liberal unity and
national honor.

As member for the Northwich division, Brunner worked
strenuously in Parliament and out to commit his working-class
constituents to the Liberal cause. He was prepared to risk the disapprobation of some of the nonconformist elders by sanctioning
the installation of a billiard table in the Winsford Liberal club as
a means to compete with the attractions of the Primrose League.
At the same time he remained keenly aware of the need for more
serious and far-reaching efforts to win the confidence and support
of a younger, less deferential generation. To this end he campaigned for parliamentary legislation that can best be understood
with reference to local situations.

With the establishment of a flourishing chemical trade along
the Weaver and the founding in 1888 of the Salt Union, an
amalgam of salt producers on a joint-stock basis, the problem of
land subsidence reached acute proportions. Essentially a Cheshire
problem, subsidence occurred in salt-producing areas as far
afield as Worcestershire and Lincolnshire. Erosion, caused by the
unrestricted pumping of brine, brought the collapse of extended

surfaces, many in densely populated areas. 'In Northwich alone' an authority on the subject has written of this period,

nearly 400 houses and other structures of the value of over £100,000 were more or less seriously injured by this subsiding of the ground, while in the surrounding district, acre after acre of land had sunk and become covered with water, forming huge lakes of the extent and depth sufficient to float the largest vessel in the British navy.[1]

The wreckage at Northwich included the first Brunner public library, which began to sink and crumble soon after its opening in 1885. Without governmental regulation, pumping continued unchecked and its victims were rarely if ever adequately indemnified.

From his earliest days in Cheshire, Brunner was convinced that those who profited from the salt trade should be prepared to assume obligations to the community in terms of self-restraint and compensation. Fully aware of the cost to his own company, which pumped brine in connection with the Solvay process, he urged the levying of 'a tax upon the salt made, or the brine raised, in the district to pay for, or to be applied towards paying for the damage done by the pumping of brine'.[2] Among those he held chiefly responsible were the officials of the Weaver Navigational Trust, who administered tolls and traffic on the river. Dating from the reign of George I, the Trust was a 'secret' and self-perpetuating body of approximately one hundred 'peers, clergymen and country gentlemen' whom Brunner identified without too much exaggeration as 'the owners of Cheshire'. In the summer of 1888 Brunner failed in his bid to enter this charmed circle: nominated by a small band of reforming trustees, he obtained only five votes to finish last in a field of seven candidates. Largely indifferent to claims for compensation, the trustees instead applied surplus revenues to the relief of county rates (and thereby to the 'relief of the rates on their own property') and to the endowment of three churches. In 1893–4 Brunner took an active hand in promoting legislation to reconstitute the Trust.[3]

---

[1] Albert F. Calvert, *Salt in Cheshire* (London, 1915), p. 325. Photographs of the effects of subsidence at Northwich appear on pp. 1159–1200.

[2] Brunner to (?), November 9, 1878 (Letterbook).

[3] Brunner to T. Ward, August 7, 1886 (copy), BP; also the *Northwich and Winsford Chronicle*, August 13, 1887; also Algernon Fletcher to Brunner, August 7, 1888, BP; also Brunner's circular letter to members of Parliament, June 1, 1893 (printed), BP.

As soon as he was returned to Parliament a second time, Brunner began to canvass support for a Royal Commission on the subsidence problem. He laid his case before C. T. Ritchie, president of the Local Government Board, whom he further attempted to pressure with periodic letters to *The Times*.[1] The greater number of his constituents, including several prominent within the Salt Union, shared his view that only a full-scale public inquiry would achieve a satisfactory settlement. At a meeting on February 14, 1889, the Winsford local board ('representing the largest salt manufacturing district in the world') passed a resolution calling upon him to secure 'just and reasonable...compensation...in respect of damage occasioned by...brine pumping'. The Northwich local board expressed itself in identical terms.

As the clerk of the Winsford local board observed, Brunner's petitioners addressed him 'in the first instance as the member for this Division, but there will be very considerable difficulty in separating you...from the firm of Messrs Brunner, Mond & Co'.[2] To a lesser extent Brunner experienced comparable difficulty. He and Mond agreed 'that legislation is necessary', but neither wished to be held responsible for the neglect of others, let alone for the effects of earlier pumping. Brunner urged 'an annual charge per ton' upon brine pumped in the district, with revenues to be deposited in a special compensation fund. To this amount he proposed to add the profits of the Weaver Trust. Others had suggested that this surplus be applied to a reduction in tolls, but Brunner, though he stood to gain from cheaper shipping on the Weaver, gave priority to the redress of legitimate grievances.[3]

Here was one crusade against privilege in which Brunner had the approval and assistance of many of Cheshire's landed magnates. His petition for a Royal Commission, dated July 15, 1889, was signed by the Duke of Westminster, Lord Egerton of Tatton, Lord de Tabley, all but two of the county's members of Parliament, and by twenty-eight other members—among them Herbert Gladstone and John Bright—who took special interest in

[1] *The Times*, October 4, 1888 and February 9, 1889.
[2] J. H. Cooke to Brunner, March 13 and 19, 1889, BP.
[3] Brunner to Mond, March 17, 1889 (copy by J. F. L. Brunner), BP.

the matter. In an address to the Local Government Board that accompanied the petition, Brunner recalled an abortive attempt eight years earlier to obtain remedial legislation. Its opponents had mounted a costly campaign ('I am credibly informed [they] spent over £5000') and the bill 'went no further than the Commons'. It had then been alleged that the salt trade, suffering a depression, could not afford the burdens of compensation: that, Brunner professed, 'is notoriously no longer the case'. It was also argued in 1881 that the use of underground water could not be restricted: 'It is an abuse of terms', Brunner replied, 'to describe brine as water...' And finally, critics of the earlier measure had insisted that 'through the operation of a geological law' subsidence would continue even if pumping ceased: 'In all history and literature', Brunner declared, he had heard nothing so silly, except perhaps the story of a party of American tourists in the Alps who, told by their guide 'that a glacier began to descend the mountain from the time of its formation', decided 'that as they were not in a hurry, they should go home to New York by glacier'.[1] The urgency of the situation was best illustrated by the news telegraphed to him at Westminster on July 18: 'Serious subsidence Leftwich road last night. Timber decking only support of road and this may go any minute.'

The *Manchester Guardian*, bringing to bear its immense influence, stressed the need to distinguish, as local officials had never done, 'between those who directly suffer and those who directly benefit from the industry'. Its leader on August 3 noted approvingly that spokesmen for the salt trade had taken an important step in conceding a link between brine-pumping and the subsidence problem. Yet the *Guardian* doubted whether the issue was one that warranted the attention and expense of a Royal Commission. The Government, taking the same view, appointed a Select Committee that heard evidence through March and April 1891.[2] Its product, the Brine Pumping (Compensation for

[1] Petition of July 15, 1889 (printed), BP; also draft copy of address, August 1, 1889, BP.
[2] Report on the Select Committee the Brine Pumping (Compensation for Subsidence) Bill; with the proceedings and evidence; 1890–91 (206), XI. 219. *Parliamentary Papers*.

Subsidence) Act of that year, met most of Brunner's expectations. He assured the chairman and members of the Northwich local board who voted him a resolution of thanks that his work had been 'a labour of love', and enjoined them to implement the new legislation 'fairly and honestly' in order to reduce friction and tensions.[1] J. H. Cooke, writing to him on behalf of the Winsford local board, thought it

all the more creditable to you, and therefore all the more deserving of our thanks, that you have introduced and supported this measure, although it has been one which will cost the Co. which bears your name a very considerable sum of money each year.[2]

It was a source of pride as well as amusement to Brunner that his achievement as a parliamentarian imposed financial penalties upon him as an industrialist:

I can honestly claim to have done more for my constituents than any [other] Member of Parliament living or dead, for I have worked hard to obtain from Parliament an Act which involves me in a liability to pay from £800 to...£1000 every year, and attaches that liability to my property for ever.

Every penny of this money will go to my constituents, and my contribution in money to the cost of the passing of the Act, not to speak of the time and the thought I have had to bestow upon it, has been far and away the largest individual contribution.[3]

Not that he regarded the levy upon his firm as 'either an unfair burden or a very serious one'. His only reservation about the Act was its failure to appropriate the toll revenues of the Weaver Trust for compensation, a defect he ascribed to the self-interested opposition of the salt trade.[4]

In each of the parliamentary battles he waged, Brunner demonstrated the same contempt for those who enjoyed privilege without commensurate responsibility. Hoping to see local institutions more representative and receptive to social needs, he gave unstinting support to Ritchie's Local Government Bill of 1888, which he anticipated would effectively dislodge the landowners

[1] Brunner to Winsford local board, August 15, 1891 (copy), BP.
[2] Cooke to Brunner, July 29, 1891, BP.
[3] Brunner to S. W. Cross, March 21, 1892 (copy), BP.
[4] Brunner to James Cowley ('not for publication'), August 15, 1891 (copy), BP.

who had hitherto dominated Cheshire politics.[1] He sent Ritchie detailed suggestions and encouraged him to persevere with a comprehensive measure: 'I don't think you fully realise the strength of your position today, and I want to assure you that the Government can do just as it pleases in this matter.'[2] Always willing to achieve his ends in concert with politicians of other parties, Brunner was annoyed by certain Liberals, 'sadly lacking in patriotism and loyalty to principle', who indulged in 'factious opposition' to so worthwhile a measure.[3]

It was with particular regard to education that Brunner sought to reform local government. There could be no significant advance in this crucial sphere until school boards, subject to elected county authorities, were created and assigned responsibility for matters now in the hands of competing denominational agencies. He did not overlook the fact that his company 'would have to bear a very considerable proportion of the rate' for a school board in its neighbourhood, but he did 'not grudge the outlay'.[4] With Ellis's assistance, he compiled and published a study of education in Cheshire in which he urged the newly created county council to pay greater attention to technical and commercial instruction, to encourage children to remain in school past the age of fourteen, and to better 'superintend the general working of institutions receiving or requiring county aid'.[5] With J. L. Hammond, who succeeded Ellis as his private secretary, he published a revised edition in 1896, appraising the achievements of the previous six years and calling for increased appropriations for educational projects. He defended the school board system to critics who alleged that it failed to provide for the spiritual welfare of its charges, citing statistics which made 'abundantly clear that religious teaching, other than instruction in distinctive doctrines, is

---

[1] For the effects of the Act upon Cheshire society and administration, see Lee, *Social Leaders*, pp. 55 ff.   [2] Brunner to Ritchie, April 21, 1888 (draft copy), BP.
[3] Brunner to Thomas Forgan, May 16, 1888, ICI Archives. On the same day, Brunner wrote to Edward Milner: 'I certainly am ready to "pass the Bill", but unluckily there are not enough Members of my way of thinking.' ICI Archives. Brunner struck the second phrase about 'factious opposition' from the letter he wrote to Ritchie on April 21, 1888 (draft copy), BP.
[4] Brunner to the Rev. M. P. Vaughan, April 7, 1890 (Letterbook).
[5] *Public Education in Cheshire* (Manchester, 1890), *passim*.

carefully provided for in board schools'.[1] His object was to obtain universal and compulsory education, Christian in its morality, but unsectarian in its dogma.

Brunner's attempts to relieve the Church of its 'effective control' over education in the county embroiled him in successive controversies with Anglican clergymen, of whom the most prominent was Francis John Jayne, Bishop of Chester.[2] In the autumn of 1896 he engaged the Bishop in a heated correspondence, later made public, regarding his proposal to endow a school at Barnton where many of his employees lived and where there existed only a Church-run National School. Nonconformists, he declared, 'should have the right to a religious education for their children in consonance with their religious opinions'. The Bishop, citing the cost that would devolve upon local ratepayers, instead applied to the Education Department for funds to enlarge the existing facilities. Brunner asked him to withdraw the request, and offered to provide the sum of £800 'in perpetuity' to indemnify 'the Church people of Barnton' who might be 'compelled to pay a School Board rate...in addition to... the maintenance of their own school buildings'. Moreover, he advised the Bishop, he 'cheerfully undertook' the responsibility to maintain the proposed voluntary school if allocations from rates proved insufficient. His offer was, however, politely rejected, and each party proceeded to accuse the other of seeking 'to introduce religious animosities into Barnton'.

'I have never in my life acknowledged that a Bishop as Bishop had any greater right in such a case than anyone else,' Brunner bluntly informed his antagonist. 'At the same time I regard my right to take an interest in the education of the children of Barnton as absolute, and by no means limited by any distinction as to employment or religious creed.' He pointed proudly to the fact that nonconformists at Barnton had often sent their children to his school at Winnington rather than enroll them where the Church provided religious instruction and appointed teachers:

[1] *Public Education in Cheshire* (Manchester, 1896), pp. 31–3.
[2] The following account, except where otherwise noted, is based upon Brunner's letters to the Bishop, October 1 and 14, November 7, and December 4, 1896 (Letterbook).

Sir John Brunner and Dr Ludwig Mond: Silver Anniversary portrait

Winnington Hall in the 1860s: a school for ladies. The stucco façade was later removed and the Tudor framing restored

Winnington Hall in the twentieth century surrounded by the Brunner–Mond works

Cartoon of Brunner in 1909
drawn by Arthur Hacker, R.A.

'Who shall be teacher is more important to the people of Barnton than who shall be Prime Minister.' Though his campaign to obtain scriptural education on an unsectarian basis was typically (though not uniquely) Unitarian, Brunner denied that it was his intention to build 'a "frankly denominational" Unitarian school'; there would be room for children of any faith, though he assured the Bishop of his willingness 'to limit my building so as to leave with you all the children whose parents prefer a Church of England training'.

The passing months brought mutual recrimination, but no compromise. '...I have very little confidence in the Bishop's straightforwardness,' Brunner confided to a friend, 'and he evidently trusts me as little as I trust him.'[1] Finally, on December 4, Brunner broke off negotiations by announcing plans to persevere with the construction of a voluntary school at Barnton. The copy conveyance he presented to the managers of the new school when it was opened early in 1898 testified to the earnestness with which he had waged his struggle:

...The Committee shall not either directly or indirectly make or institute any inquiry into or pay any regard to the sectarian and theological opinions or views of any...teacher either before or after his or her appointment, and ...no religious test of any kind shall be imposed upon any teacher...The education to be given...shall be of the kind usual in a public elementary school...[It] may include a reading and explanation of the Bible, but be in all respects absolutely unsectarian.[2]

The enrollment at the Barnton school, which the Bishop of Chester had sought to limit to 150, exceeded twice that number by the close of the century. By that time Brunner looked with amusement upon his 'tussle' with Bishop Jayne, a worthy adversary, with whom he had since cooperated on several occasions 'for good-fellowship and the advancement of his neighbours'.[3]

In addition to the elementary schools he built and helped to maintain, Brunner gave generously to University College, Liverpool, which later became the University of Liverpool and he, for

[1] Brunner to Algernon Fletcher, October 22, 1896 (Letterbook).
[2] Copy Conveyance, January 8, 1898, BP.
[3] Speech by Brunner at Winsford, November 3, 1899, in J. H. Cooke, *The Diamond Jubilee in Cheshire* (Warrington, 1899), p. 184 E.

a time, its pro-chancellor. In memory of his father, a longtime resident of greater Liverpool, and his son Sidney, a student there at the time of his death, he endowed a chair in economic science in 1891. Later he endowed chairs in subjects as diverse as physical chemistry and Egyptology. His close relationship with this institution, initiated by his son's death in 1890, was furthered by his purchase of Druid's Cross at Wavertree, a Liverpool suburb, the following year. He moved his family from Winnington Hall, to which he returned only as a visitor, and henceforth divided his time between Wavertree and a house he leased in Ennismore Gardens, South Kensington.

Sidney Brunner, his father's second son, had been a sickly youth and of the three boys had remained closest to Brunner's side. Tuberculosis developed and, for three days early in 1890, his family had waited anxiously at his bedside. He made a remarkable recovery and by March was strong enough to journey to the Continent to be 'out of England's east winds for a time'. He remained abroad, principally in Switzerland, through the summer months and, 'feeling and looking very well and happy', joined his father and older brother on September 6 for a holiday with the Monds at Bellagio in northern Italy. Two days later a boating party ended in tragedy. Sidney, robbed of breath by his long illness, drowned in an attempt to rescue his brother, who had grown tired and called for help. Brunner looked on helplessly from another boat, kept at a distance by high winds. His oldest son, who safely reached shore, 'blamed himself bitterly', though Brunner knew 'he would have done as his brother did, if it had been the other way'. The body was recovered two days later and buried at Bellagio, to which Brunner could never bring himself to return. 'I try to think of his beautiful bright happiness as he joined me,' he wrote to Ellis three years later, 'and to be humbly thankful that one was saved.'[1]

Parliamentary duties were a welcome intrusion upon Brunner's grief. He threw himself into the task of drafting his Compensation

[1] Grace Brunner to Ellis, January 22, 1890, Hilda Brunner to Ellis, January 29, 1890, Brunner to Ellis, September 9, 1890 and October 29, 1894, Ellis Papers; also Brunner to ?, March 7, 1890 (Letterbook); also appointment diary, 1890, BP.

for Subsidence Bill, and into the renewed battles for a tithes bill and Irish Home Rule. By the following February politics had re-captured something of its flavor, and his spirits lifted. There were flattering rumors, which later proved unfounded, that the Tories had decided not to oppose him at the next general election. 'I must study Welsh to speak for you in Merionethshire,' he boasted to Ellis, 'as I shall have nothing to do.' But the best medicine was the bracing air at Westminster and the company of those whom he found there. 'On my way to town I was reading the "Welsh Notes" in the *Manchester Guardian*,' he recounted to Ellis,

and I noted that Lloyd George is considered a comparative failure in the House, and completely eclipsed by Sam Evans. When I reached the House very late, lo and behold, there was Lloyd George doing his level best to give the lie to the *Guardian*, by fervency of tone and vigour of gesticulation. I was greatly amused.[1]

The next general election was a prospect that Brunner had con-templated with satisfaction as early as 1889, when he made a modest wager of ten shillings with another backbencher 'that [the] Home Rulers [will] have a majority in the next Parliament'.[2] As the life of the 1886 Parliament ebbed, he assumed an increas-ingly active part in the financial affairs of his party. On a visit to Oxford in April 1891 he heard that the local Liberal association lacked the funds to contest an imminent by-election. Brunner defrayed expenses, and the Liberal candidate, though unsuccess-ful, became well enough known to capture the seat in the follow-ing year's general election.[3] Arnold Morley, chief Liberal whip and 'trustee of Party funds', appealed to Brunner, one 'of the more wealthy members of the Party', to do all he could 'to make Mr Gladstone's final effort as complete a success as his devotion to the cause of Ireland and the Liberal Party deserve'. Brunner responded generously, taking special interest in the contests in the north-west.[4]

---

[1] Brunner to Ellis, February 13, 1891, Ellis Papers.
[2] Undated entry, appointment diary, 1890, BP.
[3] Autobiographical notebook (1909), BP.
[4] Arnold Morley wrote to Brunner on December 30, 1891, that Francis Schnadhorst 'thinks that £300 ought easily to be subscribed' by Liberals in the Knutsford division of Cheshire; to this sum he was prepared to add the same amount from party coffers, leaving Brunner responsible for the £500 balance. BP.

In the months ahead Brunner worked to solidify the alliance of Radical groups upon whose support he depended. On October 24, 1891, he presided at a national meeting of temperance reformers at the Town Hall, Crewe; and on November 7, in a public letter to 'every licensed person in Cheshire', he attacked the tied-house system by which the publican was obliged to sell whatever quality drink the brewer delivered, and declared his determination to secure compensation for the employees and tenants of public houses whose licences were not renewed. To the non-conformists and trade unionists he made equally vigorous appeals. And he had his usual brush with the establishment, this time in the person of the Reverend F. W. France-Hayhurst, rector of Davenham, who denied him the facilities of the Davenham National School for a Liberal meeting; such a refusal, Brunner protested, 'makes the use of the title "National Schools" a mockery'.[1]

As in his first parliamentary campaign, Brunner was opposed in 1892 by an outright Conservative rather than a Liberal Unionist. The *Liverpool Courier*, conceding on February 13 the difficulty of removing a man 'ready armed and mounted on the high horse', expected this fact to work against Brunner. His opponent was George Whiteley, a cotton manufacturer from Blackburn, former chairman of the Blackburn Conservative Association, a Churchman who feared that unsectarian education would 'bring up a nation of Atheists', a proclaimed enemy of Home Rule, and a friend of the publicans. The *Warrington Examiner* cynically wished Whiteley well in his 'hopeless task', predicting on the 27th 'that he...will be very much behind at the finish, and out of breath, if not out of money'.

It was not an uneventful so much as a predictable campaign. Brunner, perceiving his opponent's weakness, thought it best to 'leave him alone', and concentrated instead upon answering charges in the Tory press that his company, fearing that the previous autumn's coal strike would drive up prices, had taken the precaution of discharging large numbers of men. To the contrary, he maintained, his company had 'bought and put into

[1] Brunner to France-Hayhurst, January 9, 1892 (copy), BP.

reviewing the honors list, singled out Brunner as 'a man whose name is synonymous in Cheshire with the best and most generous form of public spirit'. The *Westminster Gazette* paid tribute to him as 'a great favourite in the House of Commons'. Wemyss Reid, recently knighted, accompanied his letter of congratulations with a depressing balance sheet for the *Speaker*. The most touching messages came from those who knew him longest. George Brocklehurst recalled their student days at St George's House and wondered, 'What would the old "Dad" say, if he were alive?'[1] Robert Holt, the Liverpool shipper who declined a similar honor for himself, nonetheless 'rejoice[d] much' in Brunner's as a friend and a fellow Unitarian.[2] Also on the list was Henry Irving, the celebrated actor, who received a knighthood and whose granddaughter married Brunner's grandson and the eventual heir to his title.

Weeks after the publication of the honors list, the Liberal Government resigned. Lord Rosebery came away with few happy memories of his brief premiership besides the Derby his horse had won. His Cabinet had been racked from first to last by ideological disputes and personal animosities. Without effective leadership, Liberal politicans confronted the electorate in July 1895 in a hopelessly confused state, 'each with his own cure for the ills of the nation': Home Rule, Welsh disestablishment, workmen's compensation, local veto, House of Lords reform.[3] The party's distress was reflected most acutely in the number of top-ranking members who lost their seats, some never to return to the Commons. The Unionists, with a commanding majority of 152, began a decade of uninterrupted rule.

Brunner's predicament at Northwich, though not nearly so grave as that of most Liberals, was in many ways typical. Early in the year he sensed a loss of support among several groups upon which he had depended for his last majority. A new vicar at Winsford, he informed Ellis, had captured the support of several former Liberals with 'lantern-light entertainments and lectures on

---

[1] Brocklehurst to Brunner, June 18, 1895, BP.
[2] Holt to Brunner, May 26, 1895; also Roscoe Brunner to Brunner, May 27, 1895, BP. It is worth noting that Holt's son accepted a baronetcy in 1935.
[3] Peter Stansky, *Ambitions and Strategies* (Oxford, 1964), p. 176.

behalf of the Church Defence Assoc[iation]'.[1] To counteract this mischief, he arranged a visit on April 4 from Lloyd George, who could be depended upon to outdraw any rival attraction. Local temperance groups were disappointed by his failure to press more ardently for local option, and he was forced to defend himself with a testimonial from Sir Wilfrid Lawson, whose credentials as a temperance reformer were beyond reproach. Fearful of 'over confidence' among the Liberals, he prepared and circulated an election address that embraced every issue of the day and, significantly, paid greater tribute to Gladstone than to the party's present leadership. The first imperative, as he saw it, was 'the abolition of the veto of the House of Lords', a cause he advocated 'not as a Revolutionist but as a consistent Reformer':

Upon this greatly to be desired reform depend all others—Home Rule for all the three Kingdoms and for Wales—Reform of the Land Laws, involving security for the farmer and for every other trading tenant—the Transfer of the Power to Regulate and Control the Traffic in Intoxicating Liquors from the hands of irresponsible magistrates into those of the people themselves—Protection of Life and Health for workpeople—Equality of Voting Power in the Election of National Representatives—Disestablishment of the Welsh Church, and all measures having for their object the improvement of the social condition of the people.[2]

His brother, wishing him luck on the eve of battle, anticipated a hard fight: 'the extent of the constituency is sufficient to make it so'.[3] The late date fixed for polling also threatened to work against him. By the time that the electors of Northwich cast their ballots on the 24th, word had been received of Harcourt's defeat at Derby and Morley's at Newcastle. Like many others, they had fallen victim to 'The Trade' (the organized liquor interests), the militant defenders of Church education, the forces of independent labor, the effects of a trade depression, and, not least of all, to growing imperialist sentiments. Brunner, who faced each of these challenges to one degree or another, fared considerably better, leading his Tory opponent, Thomas Ward, by 1638 votes. 'I put more *personal* effort into the fight than ever before', he sub-

[1] Brunner to Ellis, January 11, 1895, Viscount Gladstone Papers, Add. MSS. 46022, fol. 93. [2] Printed pamphlet, BP.
[3] Henry Brunner to Brunner, July 14, 1895, BP.

178

sequently reflected, 'and I had my reward.'[1] He celebrated his victory with a family holiday on the Continent. But in view of his party's plight, there was little to celebrate.

With a characteristic blend of detachment and disdain, Lord Rosebery watched his party go down to defeat. His leadership, though it survived the debacle, grew increasingly tenuous. Realizing as much, he abruptly dropped the reins a year later. The issue that ostensibly precipitated his withdrawal concerned the massacre of Armenians in the Ottoman Empire. While Rosebery adopted a wait-and-see attitude, content to leave matters in the hands of the Unionist Government, Gladstone broke his silence to demand strong action against the still unspeakable Turk. Rosebery, who did not disguise the relief with which he divested himself of an unwelcome legacy, declared Gladstone's intervention and the conduct of rank-and-file Liberals a betrayal of his leadership.

Like many within the party Brunner had been incensed by Turkish atrocities and dismayed by Rosebery's reluctance to speak out. In the closing days of 1895 he delivered an address at Chester that anticipated many of Gladstone's arguments. Ellis, by this time chief whip, attempted to reconcile him to Rosebery, whom he considered 'quite right' in his refusal to 'advocate definite and irrevocable action without knowing the facts'. Furthermore, Ellis pointed out to Roscoe Brunner, the popular mood militated against a bold policy:

England knows the Armenian horrors and believes them...But bloated armaments and the Peace Society together have made the masses of the people very much alive to the inexpressible horrors of war and inclined them to 'peace at any price' in the bad, callous sense. I think this, for a generous nation, is horrible, but it is true.[2]

Brunner, with an uneasy eye upon events in South Africa and along the Nile, was not convinced of his countrymen's pacific inclinations. Instead of a Kitchener, he longed for a 'Cromwell', who would equate 'National Duty' and moral principle. 'I do not feel bound, as Lord Rosebery does, to keep silence,' he proclaimed to the editor of the *Chester Chronicle*.

[1] Brunner to W. Blagg, May 11, 1899 (Letterbook).
[2] Ellis to Roscoe Brunner, January 1, 1896, Ellis Papers.

The more I think of the subject the more do I feel the shame of our position.

When the German Emperor published an injudicious and offensive telegram we were all ready for war to avenge the insult.

Surely the Sultan has insulted us far more grossly and yet in his case the fear of war is to keep us silent. The German Emperor is not like the Sultan, an enemy of the human race, and...defiance of him has hardly any justification except anger at a piece of impudence, whereas action against the Sultan would be justified before God and Man.[1]

With the passing months he grew more furious in his detestation of the Sultan and more impatient with Rosebery. 'I see you praise Lord Rosebery for his action or non-action with regard to Turkey,' he chided Ellis on October 2, six days before Rosebery unexpectedly announced his retirement. 'My tongue refuses, and I am becoming more and more restive under the unwholesomely secret methods of the Foreign Office.' Reviving Radical arguments of an earlier vintage, he declared that any 'material advantage got by the maintenance of the Turkish Empire is the very wages of sin...' And foreshadowing Radical criticisms of Sir Edward Grey in the next decade, he deprecated 'the "continuity" of our Foreign policy, of which we Liberals have professed to be so proud, [and which] denies all play to our enthusiasm for human liberty...'[2]

Lord Rosebery's resignation from the party leadership, which left Sir William Harcourt more or less in command, created more problems than it solved. The Liberals provided only a fitful and an invariably ineffective opposition, incapable of stemming the jingoist tide that ultimately swept the nation into war in South Africa. Returning from a golfing holiday at Cannes (there had been 'two cloudy days with partial rain, and for the rest of the thirty-two, uninterrupted sunshine'), Brunner reported 'great apprehension...about the Soudan business', and a dissipation of the 'old bitterness against Liberals,...possibly...because we are no longer dangerous'. An education bill promulgated by the Government struck him as 'malicious and ill-intentioned', and the 1896 Budget incurred his wrath by proposing cutbacks in educational appropriations and in the interest paid on Post Office

[1] Brunner to F. Coplestone, January 22, 1896 (Letterbook).
[2] Brunner to Ellis, October 2, 1896, Ellis Papers.

'I have had an awful job,' he wrote to Hammond in the wake of the campaign.

> When I, during the first week, addressed the Liberal organisation, I found that *nearly every* man believed the story that B.M. & Co. would not take on men over 30 years of age.
> My reception by *them* was therefore deadly cold.
> You may imagine how outsiders felt.
> In the end I could not *kill* the lie...
> Luckily for me my opponent was a blunderer of the first order, otherwise I should have been beaten.[1]

As it was, Brunner scraped by with a diminished majority of 699, roughly the same margin by which his son was defeated at Hyde.

Having escaped annihilation, a fate that their enemies had fully intended for them, the Liberals were disappointed by their failure to make the slightest indentation in the Unionist majority. The election returns gave fresh impetus to a movement in the direction of Lord Rosebery who, after exiting in 1896, continued to stand enigmatically in the wings, his every utterance carefully weighed for clues to his political intentions. Brunner, although he took strong exception to the content and tone of Rosebery's recent public statements, sought to minimize differences and thereby avert a formal rupture between the official party leadership and the Liberal Imperialists who clustered around Rosebery. He rebuked H. W. Massingham for an attack in the *Daily News* upon Sir Edward Grey, one of Rosebery's principal lieutenants. At the same time, he deprecated the fact that Lord Rosebery had spoken in terms of two competing 'schools' of Liberalism with regard to the Boer War: 'May we not all of us, Tories and Liberals alike, claim the right to judge for ourselves... whether the war at its beginning was wise or unwise, and this also as regards methods: past methods, present methods and future methods?'[2] If the Liberal Party was to maintain even the vaguest semblance of unity

---

[1] Brunner to Hammond, October 18, 1900, Hammond Papers. Brunner armed himself with a resolution passed unanimously on September 28 by approximately one thousand of his employees, who instructed Alfred Mond 'with full liberty to make what use he may think fit of it' on behalf of his father's partner. *Liverpool Daily Post*, September 27–9, 1900.

[2] Letter to the editor, *Daily News*, July 18, 1900.

in these troubled times, it would be necessary to defer to individual conscience.

Brunner, who fitted comfortably into none of the party's warring factions, stood a reasonable chance of mediating between them. He sided with the Gladstonians on Home Rule, though in most other areas he found them too categoric in their pronouncements. On foreign and imperial questions, he tended to follow Sir Henry Campbell-Bannerman's left-of-center course. And on education matters, so important to him, he recruited his few Liberal allies from among the Roseberyites, lukewarm Home Rulers and supporters of the war. Actively involved with Lord Derby in plans to transform the University College at Liverpool into a full-fledged university, he chaired a meeting on October 25 at which R. B. Haldane joined him to argue the need to keep pace with German advances in technical education. Soon afterward Brunner invited Lord Rosebery, whom he was not alone in regarding as 'the most powerful of living voices', to speak at Liverpool in an attempt to 'overcome the tremendous inertia of the mass of people, and the horror of rates'. The visit, he stressed, would be 'strictly non-political'. Still, certain members of the Liverpool Reform Club doubted the wisdom of trafficking with Rosebery, who had recently spoken at Chesterfield of the need to 'clean the slate' and reformulate Liberal doctrine. Brunner remonstrated that Rosebery had delivered at Chesterfield 'not only an eloquent and a patriotic speech', but 'from beginning to end a Liberal speech', and he asked the membership of the club to extend a cordial welcome to their former leader. Rosebery came to Liverpool for a two-day visit on February 14; he touched only fleetingly upon educational questions and, much to Brunner's embarrassment, called anew for a disavowal of Home Rule and a 'clean slate'.[1]

Brunner's devotion to higher education reflected, at least in part, his conviction that British society was neglecting the resources at hand in favor of dubious ones to which it aspired in

[1] Brunner to Rosebery, November 10, 1901 (Letterbook); Brunner to John Lea, chairman, Liverpool Reform Club, December 19, 1901 (Letterbook); *The Times*, February 15 and 17, 1902.

far-flung continents. The country was consequently losing commercial ground to younger nations with a better sense of priorities. 'Every great business...in Germany or the United States
has at its command the best university-trained men to carry it
on,' he told a large meeting at the Liverpool University Club.
English firms, however, were sadly deficient in 'men of trained
intellect', and the prosperity of the entire Empire was bound to
suffer for it. As a remedy he proposed the establishment and
endowment of new universities 'at the national cost':

> In other ways we are spending money like water, and we are imposing the
> repayment of it upon posterity. I doubt whether posterity will get much
> advantage from the expenditure, but I pass that by; but in this direction, if
> we spend money, we may do so with an extremely clear conscience. We may
> borrow the money and ask posterity to pay because posterity will gain the
> advantage.[1]

He carried his campaign to the floor of the Commons, interrupt-
ing debate on trade with Persia to express 'regret that the public
mind is so much occupied in the consideration of affairs which are
of so small importance in comparison with the enormous extent
and value of our trade at home'. Before the Speaker could suppress his outburst, Brunner was able to chastise his colleagues for
going 'absolutely crazy on these matters' and to remind them
that they could better promote trade by constructing 'a free
canal from the Mersey to the Humber' than untold railways in
Persia and Uganda.[2]

In July 1902 the aged Lord Salisbury resigned the premiership
and retired to Hatfield for his remaining months. He bequeathed
to A. J. Balfour, his nephew and successor, a legacy that included
a pacified South Africa, a new monarch on the throne, and a
strong mandate recently renewed at the polls. Yet he also left the
seeds of problems that were to vex Balfour's ministry throughout
its stormy life and discredit it in the general election three years

[1] *Liverpool Courier*, May 31, 1901. 'I have often said that every penny I have has come
from the application of science to industry,' Brunner told the Commons on October 7,
1909, urging the Government to follow the German example of subsidizing scientific
inquiry. 'I ask if we do not follow, how are we to compete?' *Parliamentary Debates*
(Commons), 5th ser., XI, cols. 2250–2.
[2] *Parliamentary Debates*, 4th ser., CI, cols. 627–8 (January 22, 1902.)

later. When Balfour assumed office he found several important measures—including an education bill—already in the mill. Not that he merely executed his uncle's policies; but his qualified successes, much like his outright failures, were to a large extent dictated by the nature of the Unionist alliance Lord Salisbury had forged.

The education bill that Balfour inherited as a piece of unfinished business was proved in time a sensible measure that brought greater efficiency and standardization. Nonetheless it drew the fire of nonconformists by extending the Church's virtual monopoly upon education in rural 'single school' areas, and by contributing out of rates to the maintenance of Church schools. The Liberal front bench, in a rare display of unity, opposed it; and even Chamberlain, within the Government, was known to nurse misgivings. Like many, Brunner feared that the bill would provide the means to propagate Anglicanism at the expense of the nonconformist ratepayer. He urged greater parental control over a child's education and greater popular control over local education authorities. Confronted with the imminent abolition of school boards, which he had long regarded as a means to escape Church dominance, he thought he might 'dodge this abominable act' by buying the village school from the board he had helped to found at Moulton and converting it into a voluntary school. But that of course was no answer to the larger evils implicit in the bill. He appealed to the Government for compromise, adding that he could think of no occasion in his long parliamentary career 'in which there was such a strong wish on both sides to make peace'. When this strategy failed, he accurately prophesied that the Unionists would pay for the proposed legislation in nonconformist votes.[1]

The issue of imperial preference also antedated Lord Salisbury's departure from Downing Street, though it came to the fore during Balfour's tenure with the resignation of Joseph Chamberlain, a convert to Tariff Reform, from the Cabinet on September 9,

[1] Letter to the editor, *The Times*, July 19, 1902; also *Parliamentary Debates*, 4th ser., cxiv, cols. 204–5 (November 5, 1902); Brunner to Algernon Fletcher, May 1, 1902 (Letterbook); *Parliamentary Debates*, 4th ser., cx, col. 399 (June 30, 1902); cxi, col. 1398 (July 28, 1902).

1903. Brunner, who took an amused view of the Government's distress, doubted the necessity 'to offer any monetary advantage to the Colonies, and...did not believe that the love of the Colonies for the Mother Country was simply "cupboard love"'.[1] There were, in his opinion, moral as well as material benefits to be derived from a continued adherence to Free Trade, which had served Britain so splendidly in so many ways. For one thing, protective duties would require the administration of a large and meddlesome bureaucracy. For another, the introduction of tariffs would subject legislators and civil servants to 'an irresistible temptation'. Here is an argument, quintessentially Victorian and classically Liberal, worth examining.

Replying in 1896 to protectionist arguments that had been raised in Parliament and the press by Sir Howard Vincent, an official of the United Empire Trade League, Brunner cited the ease with which he and other 'wealthy business men' in the House might propose 'import duty after import duty' to augment their private fortunes 'at the cost of their fellow countrymen'. He recalled a case he had mentioned in debate a decade earlier of a certain 'import duty which would, if imposed, have restored a lost mining industry in Ireland and, at the same time, increased the profits of my firm by half a million a year'. He remained content to forgo such opportunities in order to preserve 'purity in politics' and disinterested service among politicians. 'Human nature being what it is,' he explained on a subsequent occasion, 'I firmly believe that to "the wielders of the powers of jobbery and corruption" the temptation is irresistible.'[2] A bleak but not unreasonable view in an age when the governments of protectionist countries—France and the United States in particular—were regularly rocked by scandal, it was one he shared with countless

---

[1] *Parliamentary Debates*, 4th ser., CIX, col. 200 (June 9, 1902).

[2] Letter to the editor, *The Times*, October 27, 1896; letter to the editor, the *Westminster Gazette*, August 20, 1903. Brunner followed the same procedure in his business, where he instituted a 'system of bookkeeping...as close and as accurate as it could possibly be made...to prevent all imposition, all fraud, on the part of everybody in the service of the Company...I have always interpreted the Lord's Prayer', he professed, 'not only as a petition that I myself might be freed from temptation, but as a command not to put temptation into the way of others.' Typescript of undelivered inaugural address, Liverpool University, BP.

Free Traders of both parties, including George Cadbury, who acknowledged that 'Protection appeals to every selfish interest, especially among the wealthy manufacturers' like himself.[1] Brunner was likewise convinced that tariffs would imperil foreign relationships and domestic prosperity, and from his knowledge of alkali industries on the Continent, he tellingly disputed Chamberlain's bald assertion that Tariff Reform would bring higher wages to the working man.

Brunner was not one to deny that the Free Trade system had served him well, but he insisted that all it had taken was initiative and a receptivity to new ideas. Critics never ceased to remind him that his firm benefited enormously from a private protective arrangement with Solvay and Company, beneath whose preferential wing it had been sheltered since birth. Needless to say, he did not see the situation in quite this light, and argued that, in any case, there existed a world of difference between an entrepreneurial monopoly that evolved as a response to market conditions and one maintained artificially by governmental controls. In an industry subject to particularly heavy German and American competition, Brunner, Mond and Company managed not only to hold its own but also to expand its markets. Brunner's was largely responsible for the fact that in 1904, after Great Britain had been eclipsed as a manufacturer of chemicals, she continued to produce fifty per cent of the world supply of soda ash.[2] And Brunner's had attained its phenomenal success—its output rising from 800 tons in 1874 to 77,500 tons in 1885 to 240,000 tons in 1903—in a period widely regarded as one of general economic decline.

But he did not allow his personal security to blind him to the situation of which Tariff Reform, as Chamberlain preached it, was as much a symptom as a proposed cure. Contemporaries, counting the monopolies that Britain had lost to fast-developing rivals, were convinced of a trade depression about which scholars have since debated without end. Concern was doubtless genuine,

---

[1] A. G. Gardiner, *Life of George Cadbury* (London, 1923), p. 80.

[2] H. W. Richardson, 'Chemicals', in Derek H. Aldcroft, ed., *The Development of British Industry and Foreign Competition, 1875–1914* (London, 1968), p. 278. Richardson (pp. 302–3) confirms Brunner's view that a failure to promote advanced research contributed significantly to the relative decline of British industry in these years.

but was it—all things considered—justified? Export industries, though their growth rates had slowed, were not declining. Commerce, though not realizing its potential, was hardly languishing. Brunner, though he dismissed the crisis in national confidence as 'a political bogey conjured up to frighten us into an act of folly', recognized the need to allay popular anxieties with something more than 'a simple negative to the specious proposals of the Protectionists'. To his 'infinite regret' Free Traders in both parties were strangely reluctant to 'come forward with any alternative' to Tariff Reform, leaving the protectionists a clear field. A Free Trader, Brunner was no orthodox Cobdenite. He urged his allies to reply not defensively with the 'worn-out shibboleths' of the 1840s, but aggressively with a bold program that applied past principles to present problems. He proposed active Government assistance for 'our industrial population': improved and less expensive transport, a vast expansion of public works, the encouragement of technical training and scientific research. 'All these things', he told Sir Alfred Jones, president of the Liverpool Chamber of Commerce, 'we leave to private enterprise', in whose path 'we put all sorts of obstacles' including unfair rate assessments, disproportionate tax burdens, and antiquated property laws. He took special interest, as did many chemical manufacturers faced with mounting railway costs, in the repair and further development of inland waterways; as early as 1893 he had investigated the terms by which New York State acquired the Erie Canal, and in 1913, old and infirm, he crossed the Atlantic to inspect construction at Panama. 'Remember,' he instructed the readers of the *Westminster Gazette*, 'that whilst our internal trade has multiplied a hundred fold, we have not made a new road for seventy years, and have suffered our canals to dwindle, and sometimes actually to disappear.' All of these projects would require large capital outlays—'borrowing for investment—a sound business transaction'; but Brunner professed that he, 'for one, should be heartily glad thus to dilute our National Debt, which, so far, represents warlike expenditure alone.'[1]

[1] Letter to the editor, *The Times*, July 14, 1903; Letter to the editor, the *Westminster Gazette*, August 20, 1903; Brunner to Jones, February 6, 1904 (Letterbook); Richardson, pp. 300–1.

SIR JOHN BRUNNER

Brunner assumed it as his task to galvanize Sir Henry Campbell-Bannerman. Here was a golden opportunity to unite Liberals of all denominations and, at the same time, to drive further the wedge between protectionists and Free Traders in the Unionist camp. 'My dear Leader,' he began his plea to Campbell-Bannerman on November 15, 1903:

I need not tell you that, however unreasonable it may be, there is a great deal of discontent among the business people of the United Kingdom, and that it all helps Joe [Chamberlain].

What I want to impress upon you is that unless our Party offers something to these people, that discontent will before long prove our ruin as a Party and disaster to the country...

My deep conviction is that we have ridden the policy of 'laisser-faire' to death, and that the time has come for you to announce its abandonment on our behalf—as a 'worn-out shibboleth' if you like. The result of our holding to it so long is that we are behind hand in all sorts of ways.

Haldane has been preaching sound doctrine on our lack of scientific teaching and of course...I am heartily in sympathy with him, but his remedy will begin to act a generation hence, and the rule-of-thumb manufacturers, typical of our countrymen, want something immediate.

Now I propose, to begin with, but only to begin with, that we shall follow France and nationalise our inland water-ways and maintain them toll-free...I have written a letter to the 'Times' about the matter which I hope will appear tomorrow.

Until you have had time to post yourself up in the subject all I ask is that *you will make a thoroughly bold* (I will accept a cautious announcement as a beginning, with gratitude) announcement on the policy of 'laisser-faire', but I implore you to do that much at the earliest opportunity. *It is the only thing that can rescue us from the terrible dangers of Protection.*[1]

His letter to *The Times*, which appeared the next day, developed the same general themes. It expressed confidence that the electorate would reject Tariff Reform, which was no solution to the nation's difficulties. Nor, for that matter, was the old notion of *laissez-faire*, 'the product of the disgust with Government meddling so loudly voiced by the free traders in the "forties"'. Brunner called for nothing less than an extensive program of 'active Government aid to trade', beginning—but only beginning—with the overhaul of the nation's decayed canal network.

[1] Brunner to Campbell-Bannerman, November 15, 1903, Campbell-Bannerman Papers, Add. MSS. 41237, fols. 203–4.

Though others defended Free Trade far more eloquently and with infinitely wider effect, Brunner's words carried weight, coming as they did from a successful man of business. Unremitting in his efforts, he addressed himself not to tradition, for which in itself he cared little, but rather to practicalities of which he commanded a firm grasp. He made it a point not to raise imperial issues, for these he considered a distraction from the situation at hand. Though he 'threw back in the teeth of any man the imputation that he was a Little Englander', Brunner was nonetheless insistent that 'there were better ways of spending public money than scattering it in all parts of the world except at home...'

On February 11, 1904, in a speech to the Commons that won plaudits from the *Manchester Guardian*, Brunner seconded John Morley's Free Trade amendment to the royal address and diagnosed the ills of British industry. His observations attest to his perception about problems endemic in the British industrial order and destined to grow more acute with the passing decades. Certain trades were suffering not for want of protective tariffs, and certainly not for want of colonial markets, but for reasons wholly unrelated. These were in most cases trades dating from mid-century or earlier that relied upon plant and methods equally outmoded. Their owners, dependent upon 'rule-of-thumb' and suspicious of expertise, had failed to make adequate renovations to their works, to install new machinery, and to adopt the latest marketing techniques. But all the blame did not rest with management. Production was adversely affected—and 'he had no hesitation in saying [this] in the presence of friends...who represented organised labour'—by the parochial concerns and 'old-fashioned ways of some of the trades unions'. Cautious by nature and defensive by instinct, unions too often 'drove hard bargains' that had the effect of holding back 'output', limiting 'unduly...the number of apprentices', discouraging 'new designs' and the introduction of labor-saving 'mechanical appliances'. Far too many workdays and export contracts had been lost as a result of industrial unrest for which he held responsible the intransigence and narrow self-interest of both sides. He implored Parliament, before it went so far as to encircle the Empire with a tariff wall, 'at least [to] let the employers and employed meet together in a friendly fashion and set their house in order'.[1]

Campbell-Bannerman, who had all he could do to quell mutinies among his troops, was neither equipped nor disposed to meet the challenge as vigorously as Brunner wished. Along with seven other backbenchers, all active in industry and commerce, Brunner soon called upon his leader to repudiate formally Lord Percy's recent statement to the House 'that a Free-trade Government could do nothing for trade'. If allowed to persist, such a feeling might easily cost the Liberals the next general election. In content and tone, the petition was unmistakably Brunner's work. It reviewed the wide realms in which foreign governments had 'done great things to help internal and external trade', and it professed hope that the Liberal Party—its arrival in office only a matter of time—would pledge its efforts and sufficient 'national funds' to the same policies,

to the improvement of scientific education on the one hand, and on the other hand to the improvement of our roads, of our canals, and of our harbours, and the adaptation of our rivers for internal navigation, which will, by cheapening the cost of the transit of goods, greatly assist both home and foreign trade.[2]

Not until the following November did Campbell-Bannerman oblige his petitioners, and then only to a limited extent. He closed a key speech at Edinburgh on the 5th with an anticipation of the time when 'we shall be able to point. . . to the resources of our country more fully developed'. Brunner, notwithstanding his disappointment that specific mention was not made of canals and roads, wrote gratefully that the peroration had 'warmed my heart'. *The Times*, he observed, had entirely missed the point of the speech, and 'hit out wildly' with the argument that the English people would have to choose between 'governmental encouragement. . .of industry' and do-nothing Liberalism.[3] Campbell-

[1] *Parliamentary Debates*, 4th ser., cxxix, cols. 1113 ff. (February 11, 1904); also cxxxiii col. 1525 (April 28, 1904).
[2] Petition dated House of Commons, May 6, 1904, Campbell-Bannerman Papers, Add. MSS. 41242, fols. 1–7. The other signatories were Sir Francis Evans, Sir W. H. Holland, D. A. Thomas, Sir Charles Maclaren, Sir James Kitson, Sir Michael Foster, and Sir Christopher Furness.
[3] Brunner to Campbell-Bannerman, November 8, 1904 (Letterbook).

Bannerman did not reply to Brunner's letter until he had had the opportunity 'to gather the views of one or two others', who agreed with him that it was best for Liberals to maintain a guarded silence while Unionists continued to discredit themselves. An astute tactician—as Liberal leader he had had to contend with some of the most skilful intriguers in the business—he did not think the time had come to tip his hand. Besides, he was enjoying too much the spectacle of Unionist disruption to divert attention to his own party, its vital energies sapped by more than a decade of internecine strife. 'What you quote of the taunts of *The Times*, repeated by others, to the effect that we have no alternative to Chamberlain, rather should persuade us the other way, should it not?' he asked rhetorically.

They wish to tempt us into putting forward some scheme, in rivalry with his. I would argue against his scheme on its own demerits: but at the same time recite many reforms connected with land tenure, education, transit, etc., which would be beneficial, and indeed are urgently necessary. This is not quite the same thing as setting up an image to be worshipped in competition with his. It may not satisfy your ardent Chambers of Commerce, but I think in the circumstances it is the wiser course to take.[1]

Optimistic, but not unaware of the hurdles that lay ahead, Liberals prepared for their emergence from a decade in the political wilderness. Some of the old-timers had passed from the scene; others had removed themselves, to one extent or another, from it. Would it be possible for Campbell-Bannerman to form a cohesive ministry from the disparate talents at his disposal? Balfour, hoping against hope that delay might exacerbate differences among his opponents, held precariously to power until the next-to-the-last moment. All the while Liberals, coming perilously close to fulfilling his cynical expectations, engaged in furious debate about the composition of the next Government and the causes it would embrace. Brunner's attitude toward his party's improved prospects was in many ways typical.

Nearly two years before the parties were pitted in electoral combat, Brunner quietly set to work to fortify Liberal organization in the north-west and to line up qualified candidates. 'It is my

[1] Campbell-Bannerman to Brunner, November 23, 1904, BP.

intention', he revealed, 'to help in the payment of election expenses where necessary.' Though it is agreed that he was one of the principal financiers—according to some the principal one—of the 1906 Liberal victory, he operated unobtrusively through varied and often indirect channels; this was, he recognized, 'a matter...which will have to be handled very delicately'.[1] He advised Herbert Gladstone late in 1905 that he had recently sent 'a good deal of money' to the Free Trade Union, adding: 'I will send you a cheque for £5000 at the New Year, and if later on you tell me that you are in dire straits, I will with pleasure go further.'[2] As usual his total contribution is impossible to calculate, but he left no doubt with what inestimable pleasure he rejected a Tory offer to let him stand unopposed if he withheld his support from other Liberals.[3]

Brunner contributed considerably more to the struggle than money, though his own seat was secure. For a man of immense wealth, he waged a campaign that was manifestly anti-capitalistic; but, then, the chemical Croesus was never a conventional capitalist. He decried Chamberlain's proposed 'food taxes' as a burden upon the poor, and he cited recent events as proof that the Boer War had been 'fomented and urged on by a body of capitalists of various nations resident in Johannesburg'. It is worth mentioning that his criticisms were free of the anti-semitism that was so often insinuated into rhetoric of this nature. It had been a war not for principle, but for plunder, and the beneficiaries of the nation's 'enormous sacrifice of blood and treasure' were the gold magnates—the 'Randlords', he called them—whose privileges had been secured and on whose behalf Chinese coolies were now being imported 'to work in a condition of slavery' at wages under two shillings a day. Whether the system of Chinese indentured labor, sanctioned by the Balfour Government, was one of 'slavery' as Lloyd George and others declared in the House of Commons, or 'semi-slavery' as Lord Ripon averred more cautiously in the Lords, remains an academic question. An insult and

[1] Brunner to W. Handley, February 4, 1904 (Letterbook).
[2] Brunner to Gladstone, December 19, 1905, Viscount Gladstone Papers, Add. MSS. 46063, fols. 222–3.
[3] The *Manchester Guardian* reported this offer on January 13, 1906.

a shock to the British worker, it provided the Liberal Party with a tremendously effective cry, which Brunner and others raised as a means to resurrect the alliance between Radicals and trade unionists.[1]

The popular outcry, the stinging by-election defeats, and the disputes among his followers failed to dislodge Balfour from office. A vote against the Government on July 20, 1905, passed without his resignation, for which Brunner waited in vain. Trying to read the Prime Minister's inscrutable mind, the Opposition press came slowly to the conclusion that he would resign at a particularly inopportune moment, presenting Campbell-Bannerman with the unenviable assignment of forming a ministry before confronting the voters. Brunner, who kept in close touch with his chief, volunteered his services in the probable event of 'a purely "Dissolution Government"' that would 'hold office until after the General Election *and no longer*...I could not afford to remain in the Government, but I am quite willing to give up my holiday to serve you.'[2] His presence in a 'caretaker' administration would have been a distinct asset: he commanded the loyalty of an important segment of back-bench opinion and the affection of virtually all Liberals. Balfour, however, did not choose to act until early the following December, when it looked very much as if an accommodation between Campbell-Bannerman and the Liberal Imperialists—Asquith, Grey, and Haldane—was out of the question. To his disappointment and Campbell-Bannerman's relief, the wayward Rosebery failed to emerge from the shadows, while the other Liberal Imperialists were one by one persuaded to contribute their prestige and talents to the new Government.

There is little need to recount the familiar details of the Liberal Party's spectacular victory at the polls in January 1906, an episode only slightly less remarkable than the party's steady deterioration in the decade that followed. Elated by the Liberals' return to office, Brunner campaigned throughout Lancashire and Cheshire

---

[1] Brunner's letter to the Electors of the Northwich Division of Cheshire, April, 1904 (printed), BP.

[2] Brunner to Campbell-Bannerman, July 22, 1905, Campbell-Bannerman Papers, Add. MSS. 41238, fols. 51–2. Brunner was impelled to write by a piece H. W. Massingham had written in that morning's *Daily News*.

to obtain a majority sufficiently large to realize long deferred party goals. Addressing a group of businessmen in the Abercromby division of Liverpool, he professed that he and Lever, who was standing as a Liberal in the Wirral division of Cheshire, supported Free Trade not because it profited them, but because they wished to save themselves the 'filthy temptation' that tariffs would introduce. 'Rich as he was,' he told an audience at Chester the following week, 'he would become infinitely richer by a Protective system, but the poor would become poorer.' And at Warrington, 'in the capacity of a capitalist', he urged the return 'of a brother capitalist, Mr Arthur Crosfield, and...advise[d] the democrats...[that] when they got a capitalist tamed to be sure to keep him'.[1]

Brunner's opponent at Northwich in this, his final contest, was Colonel B. N. North, one of six brothers who had fought in South Africa, a defender of the 1902 Education Act and the Chinese Labour Ordinance, and a vigorous champion of Tariff Reform, which he welcomed as a means to 'bring the foreigners to their senses'. North received strong support from the local 'Church party', which, the press reported, was 'straining every nerve for the Conservatives'.[2] But he was no match for Brunner, who rode the crest of a national wave to amass a majority of 1792 votes. Polling day on the 23rd did not, however, pass without mishap. Brunner fell and badly injured his right knee, forcing him to remain bedridden at Winnington Old Hall for several weeks and to miss the opening of the new Parliament. By February 12 he was able to walk 'a few steps between two doctors', though he suffered a 'slight attack of pleurisy'. On March 8 he travelled 'up to town' for the first time, and four days later he belatedly 'took the oath, just after A. J. Balfour', who had lost his Manchester seat in the general election and was returned for the City of London at a by-election in the meantime.

Brunner's appointment diary for the succeeding months provides less a record of his political engagements than an index to his physical debility: '12 May. Walked down stairs (halfway)

---

[1] *Liverpool Courier*, January 5, 1906; *Manchester Guardian*, January 12, 1906; *Liverpool Daily Post*, January 15, 1906.
[2] *Manchester Courier*, January 23, 1906.

each foot alternately, without sticks for the first time in 15 weeks, 3 days.' Though he was not particularly old in years, he was afflicted with ailments that curtailed his activity and necessitated periods of enforced leisure. From the early years of the century, his golfing holidays on the Continent or at Bournemouth, prescribed by his physician, grew more extended. Often he would conscript a son-in-law to share his game, at which his persistence failed to bring distinction. It was his practice at whatever hotel he stayed to book an entire floor so that his children and grandchildren might arrive in constant procession. Although it was not the least unusual for him to interrupt his holiday to return to London for a meeting or a vote, one may safely say that his days of regular back-bench attendance were over.

It was widely expected that he would lighten his burdens by taking a peerage, which was proffered to him on more than one occasion. The Conservative *Liverpool Courier* reported approvingly on December 7 that this would be 'one of the early acts' of Campbell-Bannerman's premiership: 'Bluff, breezy, and almost boisterous at times, Sir John engages the sympathies even of his strongest opponents by his English honesty and downright pugnacious determination...We lament his politics, but we appreciate his qualities...' But Brunner could not deny himself the pleasure of sitting, however erratically, in the Liberal-dominated chamber from which he anticipated so much. He was encouraged not only by the size of the Liberal majority, which exceeded his most sanguine expectations, but also by the arrival at Westminster of a phalanx of Labour members, to whom he, like his son, looked to give 'impetus to labour legislation...The House of Commons is better for their presence.'[1]

Though he refused a seat in the Lords, he gratefully accepted a privy councillorship conferred upon him in June. His recent injury made it 'absolutely necessary that I should humbly appeal for his Majesty's gracious permission that I should be excused from kneeling' during the ceremony at Buckingham Palace on the 30th.[2] Herbert Gladstone, now Home Secretary, 'particularly

---

[1] J. F. L. Brunner, 'Industrial Politics', in *The Policy of Social Reform in England*, p. 69.
[2] Brunner to Sir Almeric Fitzroy, June 28, 1906 (copy), BP.

delight[ed] in seeing this great honour [conferred] upon one who all through somewhat troublous and depressing times contrived to keep up the flag firmly and evenly'.[1] Walter Runciman, launching his ministerial career as parliamentary secretary to the Local Government Board, celebrated the fact that this 'best of all honours...leaves you still in the House of Commons—whence even the youngest of us would miss you sadly'.[2] And Sir Robert Hudson, secretary of the National Liberal Federation and a longtime friend, wrote puckishly: 'You always were right honourable, but I rejoice that I may now describe you as such each time I write you a letter.'[3] C. P. Scott, editor of the *Manchester Guardian*, sent private congratulations and published a leader that applauded Brunner's appointment to the Privy Council as 'a recognition not only of his staunch Liberalism and his great public service, but of his high position as one of our few great intellectual businessmen —a type that is unhappily too rare in this country'. Brunner, though he enjoyed such adulation, was too much a Radical and a man of practicalities to exaggerate the importance of the honor he had received. At a dinner given for him at the Liverpool Reform Club the following autumn, he recounted how he was sworn as a privy councillor 'not to reveal any of his Majesty's secrets'. He had kept his oath, he was proud to say, 'because his Majesty had been advised by his constitutional adviser not to tell him any'.[4]

Did Brunner regret his decision to remain a commoner and a member of the lower house? A year later he sportively 'consoled myself for not having a Peerage by shortening my signature', and henceforth no longer used his middle initial.[5] It is more than doubtful that he would have been comfortable in 'another place', the graveyard for so many Liberal measures in these years; but continued service in the Commons was not without its hardships and frustrations. The expected benefits of the 1906 election victory were often elusive, and meanwhile there were persistent

---

[1] Gladstone to Brunner, July 1, 1906, BP.
[2] Runciman to Brunner, June 29, 1906, BP.
[3] Hudson to Brunner, June 29, 1906, BP.
[4] *Liverpool Daily Post*, October 19, 1906.
[5] Brunner to Hammond, September 16, 1907, Hammond Papers.

reminders of Liberal incapacity. 'This Parliament must be a refreshing contrast to the last—but aren't you beginning rather to hate the name of Education?' Scott asked him early in the first summer of Liberal rule.[1] Brunner vowed 'to bring strong pressure to bear against the policy of thinking the attainment of knowledge the only thing that was not worth finding money for'.[2] Yet Liberalism proved sadly deficient in schemes for higher education, and his personal contributions to Liverpool University, the National Physical Laboratory, and other institutions were no substitute for active governmental support. The 1906 education bill was almost as keen a disappointment to him as its destruction by the House of Lords, and the Government's failure to introduce an immediate Home Rule measure was beyond his comprehension. There were, of course, redeeming features to the 1906 Parliament, among them an amendment to extend employers' liability. But from an early date he had the uneasy impression that the Government was too often led by the least Liberal of its members in directions contrary to the Liberal tradition.

Unlike many who felt this way, Brunner was no doctrinaire Gladstonian but the advocate of a progressive Liberalism, sensitive to the welfare and aspirations of labor. 'He was not a Socialist, but he claimed to be as sincere as any Socialist in his desire to benefit the great mass of their fellow-countrymen.' He doubted, not the morality of socialism, but its practicability: so far as he could tell, socialism was 'impossible of attainment by the hands of men; it required angels...He had sat opposite a few gentlemen in the House of Commons who called themselves Socialists, and he had not seen any wings sprouting yet.' There were good grounds, he admitted, 'for socialising the national defence, the Post Office, roads, lighting, and even railways, but a Socialist state, to be managed by officials, meant the negation, denial, and abolition of freedom'. Brunner's remedy was 'True Liberalism', which would encourage enterprise at the same time that it dedicated itself to 'the salvation of the helpless and suffering'.[3]

[1] Scott to Brunner, June 30, 1906, BP.
[2] George B. Bidder, Marine Biological Association, to Brunner, November 13, 1906, BP.
[3] Speech at Liverpool Reform Club, October 17, 1906, *Liverpool Daily News*, October 19, 1906; speech at Middlewich, February 13, 1908, *Manchester Dispatch*, February 14, 1908.

Brunner gave warm endorsement to the social reforms that were executed in the prewar years by Liberal Governments under Campbell-Bannerman and Asquith: non-contributory old-age pensions, an eight-hour day in the mines (a measure introduced by his son, newly elected member for the Leigh division of Lancashire), labor exchanges, and national insurance. These, he reasoned, were compatible with Radical—if not necessarily classical Liberal—tenets in that they promoted the economic freedom of the wage-earner. He continued his campaign for state assistance to trade, speaking on the subject whenever the occasion presented itself. 'If he could gain adherents... in the fight upon which he had entered in old age,' he told an enthusiastic audience at Hanley, 'then he would have done an extremely good work.'[1] His chief ally within the Cabinet was Lloyd George, whom Asquith promoted in 1908 from the Board of Trade to the Exchequer, and with whom he shared a nonconformist heritage, a disdain for inherited privilege, an avid interest in the problem of rates, and an aversion to jingoism and armament spending. Justly impressed by Lloyd George's 'imagination, sympathy, and courage' at the Board of Trade,[2] he remained through the early wartime years a self-professed 'Lloyd George man', who looked to the fiery Welshman to impart energy and Radical morality to their Liberal colleagues. Lloyd George in turn recognized Brunner's high standing within both party circles and the business community, and welcomed his support in the struggle for the People's Budget. 'Tomorrow and Tuesday the debate will range over the whole Budget,' he advised Brunner on May 2, 1909.

A word on development would be most welcome of all as it is my pet child. I wish the party would back me up in putting surpluses into a reserve for development for canals, light railways, etc. It is so much better and more businesslike to pay out of such a reserve than always to be 'on the borrow' whenever we have a small job on hand.

You might say a word also about the general fairness of sparing the poor by putting the burden on the shoulders that can afford to bear it.

Many thanks for your readiness to assist. I felt sure you would help.[3]

---

[1] Brunner, *The State and Trade* (Chester, 1908), pp. 15–16.
[2] *Parliamentary Debates*, 4th ser., CLXXVII, col. 150 (June 27, 1907).
[3] BP.

Brunner obligingly provided a spirited defense of Lloyd George's proposals coupled with a scathing attack on Tariff Reform, which many members across the House thought a better solution to national problems. He returned to the fray the following November, when the Budget had its third reading. He likened the Budget to a 'Development Bill' that would 'broaden and expand' trade with the revenues it collected from its levy upon unearned increment; and, especially by 'benefiting the poor', he anticipated that it would 'increase the demand for goods and increase trade and employment', thereby accomplishing more than any protectionist scheme, the dubious benefits of which would accrue to certain groups and classes.[1] This proved most fittingly Sir John's last speech to the Commons. The peroration of his parliamentary career, it conveyed better than any previous address his warm affection for the House, his sense of moral justice, and his abiding concern for humanity. 'This heavily-bearded veteran of politics and industry', the *Daily News* wrote the next morning, 'scored the success which always attends sincerity.'

The rejection of the 1909 Budget by the House of Lords came as a surprise to few, a relief to many, and a welcome event to some. It plunged the nation into a constitutional crisis that occasioned a general election early in 1910, the first of two that year. For the first time in a quarter century, since the creation of a seat at Northwich, Brunner did not stand in the Liberal interest. Weeks before his final appearance in the House, he informed his constituents of his intention to retire when the present Parliament was dissolved. He had reached his decision, he revealed, more than a year earlier on the advice of his wife's physician and his

[1] *Parliamentary Debates* (Commons), 5th ser., IV, col. 985 (May 4, 1909); XII, cols. 1710 ff. (November 2, 1909). Brunner reminded one correspondent, who reproved him for his support of Lloyd George, that he had 'expressed himself pretty forcibly' in the past 'on the unfair exemption of large country houses' (Brunner to 'Mr Hughes', January 21, 1910 [copy], BP). From his travels in 1888 he wrote to Edward Milner: 'Monmouthshire, by the way, which I understand belongs almost entirely to the Duke of Beaufort, looks very poverty-stricken. Ruined cottages abound, new buildings nowhere to be seen, roofs and gates out of repair, and the most wretched houses I ever saw in England. A marked change as soon as you enter Herefordshire.' Brunner to Milner, May 26, 1888, ICI Archives.

own.[1] Notwithstanding his intense disagreement with Liberal leaders over armaments and foreign policy—matters which we shall examine presently—he disclaimed any ideological motive and identified himself as a 'faithful supporter' of the Government.

His health did not permit him to campaign as widely or vigorously as in the past, but he circulated a series of open letters on behalf of Liberal candidates and the principles at stake. The crucial issue, as he saw it, was the dispute with the House of Lords, long an object of his indignation. 'The man who votes for the Lords and against the Commons..., no matter what his position in life, will be denying his own manhood,' he declared to the members of the newly reformed Liberal association at Wigan whom he urged to cooperate with Labour to realize a common goal.[2] To the electors at Northwich, of whom he 'took formal leave' on October 9, he professed that it had been his rule in politics as in industry to accord 'even handed justice to all men alike'. He urged them to follow his example and to assume the responsibilities of democracy:

Did they intend that they would govern through their elected representatives in the House of Commons—or did they intend that the men gathered together in that ridiculous institution at the other end of the lobby should govern? He said seriously, bound to every syllable, the House of Lords as at present constituted was not only the most ridiculous but was the meanest and most mischievous institution in all the country.[3]

Reluctant to leave his flock unshepherded at so critical a juncture, he took consolation in the fact that his older son transferred his services from Leigh to Northwich. J. F. L. Brunner kept the seat in the family until 1918, when it fell to a 'couponed' Unionist; his son, Sir Felix Brunner, contested it as a Liberal in the general election of 1945.

Again there was talk of a peerage. At the conclusion of an informal luncheon at the House, Thomas Cochrane, a Tory

[1] Lady Brunner, for whose health her husband had recently bought Silverlands in Surrey, died on April 4, 1910. Brunner wrote to his son at the time of his retirement that her 'end is not far off, and she now longs for it'. Brunner to Roscoe Brunner, December 29, 1909, BP.
[2] *Liverpool Courier*, December 23, 1909.
[3] *Manchester Guardian*, October 11, 1909.

member, expressed 'sorrow' at Brunner's impending retirement and deduced 'that the translation of Sir John Brunner might be to a not very distant spot, and if he survived the fate of that doomed institution they might have fleeting glimpses of him walking across the lobby'.[1] Brunner's was the first of 249 names on a list that Asquith drew up in the summer of 1911 to submit to the King in the event that it proved necessary to pack the House of Lords.[2] But aside from a wish to take part in the destruction of aristocratic power, Brunner was reluctant to go to the Lords and hoped he could 'escape being "elevated"'. He told his younger son:

I saw Alec. Murray [the Master of Elibank and chief whip] last Thursday and told him frankly and plainly that I wanted no reward for what I had done, that if he wanted men to carry the [Parliament] Bill in the Lords I would go there with joy, but that if it were to be merely the granting of honours I should prefer to be left out...

If the passage of the Bill were absolutely assured, they would present to the King a short-list of highly distinguished men with myself at the head...

My main reason for hanging back is the fear that my grandsons should grow up to be snobs.

A few days later he sent word that he had 'definitely declined to be one of the small group of "distinguished men"'. The more he had thought about taking a title—at one point he had considered 'Lord Everton'—the less attractive it became. 'Verily the House of Lords is a snobbish institution,' he exclaimed, outwardly relieved to sound more like his old self. 'Possibly if hereafter they are *all elected*, its tone may mend.'[3] Murray, who refused to accept Brunner's decision as final, informed him that 'the Prime Minister will invite you to join the Upper House on the first occasion that he submits a list to the King'.[4] J. F. L. Brunner urged his father to reconsider on the grounds 'that in the House of Lords you will make for yourself opportunities of doing good work and you will enjoy being once more in the middle of things political'.[5] Unable to make up his mind, Brunner called upon

[1] *The Times*, November 5, 1909.
[2] Jenkins, *Asquith* (appendix A).
[3] Brunner to Roscoe Brunner, July 31 and August 2, 1911, BP.
[4] Murray to Brunner, August 8, 1911, BP.
[5] J. F. L. Brunner to Brunner, December 9, 1911, BP. Brunner noted on this letter: 'On receipt of this, I wrote to Lucy [his daughter-in-law] saying that I would accept.'

John (now Viscount) Morley 'to ask him if I could do any good work in the Lords'. Morley, who never ceased to regret his removal in 1908 to 'another place', cautioned his old friend not to commit the same mistake. His advice was heeded. A week later Brunner 'saw [the] Chief Whip and told him I did not wish to be in [the] list of new peers New Years Day'.[1]

Out of office, Sir John Brunner (as he remained) was far from being out of politics. In February 1910 he sought and obtained election from the Chertsey division to the Surrey County Council. Not too proud to end his public career at a level where most politicians began theirs, he campaigned earnestly if not arduously for the honor to serve his neighbors, solemnly reciting his qualifications which far exceeded the demands of the office. But more important as an indication of the veneration he received was his election in November 1911 to the presidency of the National Liberal Federation. Bringing to this office a vigor that belied his years, he made it a powerful instrument in the forlorn campaign to arrest the drift to war. This, the last and most urgent of his crusades, is the one that best reveals the components of his Liberalism. At the same time, it illuminates the forces to which the Liberal order fell victim in August 1914.

[1] Appointment diary, December 7 and 14, 1911, BP.

CHAPTER 10

PEACE, RETRENCHMENT AND REFORM

In all the years of disillusionment and defeat Sir John Brunner never doubted either the moral righteousness or the political practicability of his cause. Liberalism, he was convinced, fostered a spirit of individual enterprise that built character at the same time that it stimulated the greatest material prosperity. It inculcated a respect for institutions while it labored to achieve equality before the law. It championed the rights of oppressed peoples, defended principles of civil and religious liberty, and lifted burdens from the poor. And it was pledged to the removal of restraints and restrictions between classes as well as nations. In the first decade of the twentieth century the opportunity seemed at hand to translate lofty principle into fact. 'The Liberal Party had triumphed with a vengeance,' one historian has recently written of the 1906 general election. 'The promised land had finally been reached and the fruits of victory were at last within their grasp. It all seemed too good to be true...'[1] Indeed it was. As Brunner came gloomily to learn, Liberalism in office was not necessarily Liberalism in practice.

His extra-parliamentary activities continued in the prewar decade to be multifarious and exacting: he contributed his waning energies to the agitation for an equalization of rates to include undeveloped or vacant property, to the campaign for canals and other public works, and not least of all to various committees for housing and land reform. Various tenants' associations benefited from his generosity; the Hampstead Garden Suburb was among his favorite projects; and the Co-Partnership Housing Council, of which he briefly served as president, named its Bloomsbury headquarters 'Brunner House'.

Increasingly, Brunner's attention was drawn to the international arena. Crucial to Liberalism's success, indeed to its very

[1] Peter Rowland, *The Last Liberal Governments* (New York, 1969), p. 30.

survival, was the maintenance of European peace and a spirit of internationalism that had lately showed signs of evaporating. It was surely not accidental that Free Trade doctrines were challenged at the same time that pressures mounted from abroad. The country's continued prosperity and security—to the Liberal mind the two were inseparable—required nothing less than the full exertion of her moral influence in diplomatic councils. Alliances were to be avoided, but opportunities for intercourse were to be welcomed. Brunner was a longtime benefactor of the Inter-Parliamentary Union, whose sessions he regularly attended and which he valued as an agency to promote understanding and forbearance. Before the negotiation of the 1904 entente, he was invariably a guest and often a host at dinners on behalf of Anglo-French rapprochement; for the next decade he worked indefatigably, but with less gratifying results, on behalf of Anglo-German friendship.

The Ministry of All Talents that Campbell-Bannerman proudly assembled in the final weeks of 1905 revealed itself time and again as an unwieldy coalition of diverse and competing factions; this proved even more the case after April 1908, when the ailing Prime Minister was succeeded by H. H. Asquith, whose casual leadership too often invited dissension. From their earliest days in office, the Liberals were divided by a wide range of issues, but by none so much as matters of foreign policy and defense. The issue of naval construction, particularly, turned Cabinet members against one another and the rank and file. An important segment of party opinion, perhaps insufficiently represented within the Government, sought to halt spiralling estimates and thereby lessen tensions with Germany. Among these individuals Brunner attained special prominence, first as an elder statesman of the back benches and after 1911 as president of the National Liberal Federation. Like many, he never forgot that Gladstone had ended his long career in a bitter struggle to resist naval increases 'that will be taken as plunging England into a whirlpool of militarism'.

Usually identified as Liberal Economists, those within the party who took a stand against military and naval appropriations were not so much practitioners of 'penny-in-the-slot politics' as the conscious defenders of a moral tradition. Brunner, for example, went on record that 'his object was not to reduce his taxes, but to have the money raised by taxation better spent'.[1] Though their patriotism was impugned, these men were convinced, and not unjustly, that they served the higher interests of the nation. They were a heterogeneous group, often bitterly opposed to one another on other matters; that, in large part, accounts for their inability to project their views and their ultimate failure to determine policy. Their social and economic backgrounds varied, as did their extra-parliamentary interests. Several were men of formidable intellect, while others betrayed a crude anti-intellectualism. The entire group, however, was infused with a strong nonconformity that was manifest even among those who professed no religious commitment. A great many were ardent temperance reformers, and more than a few were active in the land values campaign. Many were old-timers who had won their spurs in combat with jingoes of an earlier vintage and whose energies were largely spent. A significant number were of foreign extraction and some of them were associated with foreign trade. The vast majority were stronger in their allegiance to Campbell-Bannerman, whom they mourned as 'dear old C. B.', than to Asquith, whose Liberal Imperialism they found hard to forgive and who moved in a society foreign to most of them. 'Campbell-Bannerman,' Beatrice Webb had observed with her usual blend of bigotry and acumen, 'nominally a "sane" Imperialist, is at heart a "Peace man", with all the old Liberal principles and prejudices writ large on his mind—retrenchment in public expenditure and no compulsion at home and abroad.'[2] Some remained lifelong Liberals, though not of any one persuasion; most were pushed toward Labour or even Toryism by the war they were powerless to avert.

On December 21, 1905, Campbell-Bannerman began his premiership by addressing a rally at the cavernous Albert Hall. His remarks, many of them inaudible, included the solemn pledge that

[1] *Parliamentary Debates*, 4th ser., CLXX, col. 1050 (March 7, 1907).
[2] Diary for February 20, 1900, cited in Philip Poirier, *The Advent of the British Labour Party* (New York, 1958), p. 166.

Liberal England would take her place 'at the head of a league for peace'. Brunner, for one, could not have been more pleased, and waited anxiously for the Government to carry out the mandate it received at the polls the following month. Unfortunately the terms of that mandate were confusing: the same electors who had voted for peace, retrenchment, and reform were soon clamoring for dreadnoughts. As John Morley, who shared Brunner's despondency over the naval race, candidly admitted, 'The Liberal victory...was, to the best of my belief, mainly due, in the huge extent of it to furious detestation of Balfour and his tactics. No great issue was really settled.'[1]

Although he recognized the authority that Sir Edward Grey's imposing presence at the Foreign Office conferred upon the new Government, Brunner nursed profound misgivings about Grey's notion of a 'continuous' diplomacy that would follow guidelines established by the previous ministry. In Gladstone's day disputes over foreign policy had been the stuff of party politics, an opportunity for Liberals to assert their identity. As one who drew inspiration from the Midlothian campaigns, Brunner wondered why twentieth-century Liberals should deprive themselves of a free hand by accepting wholesale the presumptions, mistaken and often pernicious, of their Unionist predecessors. Without taking the slightest exception to the formal provisions of the 1904 entente with France, he suspected that Grey attached a military significance to the agreement that even its author, Lord Lansdowne, had not intended. A disciple of Lord Rosebery (though he was immune from his mentor's francophobia), Grey aroused fears that, like Rosebery in Gladstone's later Governments, he would operate as a free agent at variance with Liberal principles.

Unlike most Radical critics of Grey's diplomacy, Brunner did not level comparable attacks against R. B. Haldane, another member of the Liberal Imperialist triumvirate, whose War Office policies he generally admired. He had come to know Haldane through their ventures on behalf of technical education and to appreciate his efforts to allay Anglo-German tensions. Haldane's cutbacks

[1] Morley to Lord Minto, January 24, 1908, cited in Koss, *John Morley at the India Office*, p. 69.

in military outlays, modest by any standard, were sufficient to appease Brunner, who recognized the difficulties under which the War Secretary labored and who was impressed by the way he defied vested interests in his drive for efficiency. Brunner instead concentrated his fire upon the Admiralty, where the two-power standard remained gospel and where successive Liberal first lords —Lord Tweedmouth, Reginald McKenna, and Winston Churchill—were overwhelmed by the arguments of their sea lords and seemingly inebriated by their first official scent of salt air.

In March 1907 the House of Commons considered for the first time naval estimates submitted by the Liberal Government. Spokesmen for the Opposition attacked them for whittling down the ambitious program set down in the Cawdor Memorandum of December 4, 1905; indignant Radicals, on the other hand, doubted whether the Government had gone nearly far enough. The *Manchester Guardian*, giving solemn voice to Radical concern, urged a policy consistent with the aim of the second conference on disarmament at the Hague, where representatives of forty-six nations were scheduled to convene in June 'the first meeting of the Parliament of Humanity'. J. A. Murray Macdonald, a dour Scotsman who sat for the Falkirk Burghs, promptly moved to reduce naval manpower by 8000. His motion was seconded by Brunner, who reminded Campbell-Bannerman of the pledge he had made at the Albert Hall on the eve of electoral battle: the present estimates, he declared, 'were not in consonance' with that 'never-to-be-forgotten speech'.

The Little Navyites, as their critics derisively dubbed them and as they came in time to identify themselves with pride, were as various in their strategies as in their motivations. Some placed emphasis upon a balanced budget; others sought to lavish upon social reforms the money wasted upon 'bloated armaments'. Inside Parliament and out, Brunner was among the most authoritative of them. More pragmatic and politically experienced, he made his point no less sharply for the subtle irony in which it was usually sheathed. Neither a pacifist nor a unilateralist, he sought a navy that did not exceed the nation's defense needs to the extent that it posed a threat, real or imagined, to any foreign power. While others denounced the two-power standard as a national conceit, Brunner urged only its adaptation to changes that had occurred in the diplomatic situation since it was devised in 1895. Japan, as a result of a 1902 agreement, was now an ally; France, as the result of the 1904 entente, was no longer a potential enemy but 'our friend'; and British relations with Russia 'were better than they used to be' and steadily improving. He therefore found the navy 'infinitely larger than was necessary for a two-Power standard', and he professed that 'his dearest wish was to go back to that standard' from which over-anxious Tories had deviated. He implored the Government to demonstrate its good faith and to set a good example to other nations by narrowing the margin by which the British fleet maintained its historic paramountcy.[1]

There were good grounds, military as well as ideological, for the argument that Brunner advanced. Sir John Fisher, first sea lord and father of the Dreadnought policy, confided to Lord Tweedmouth that the country's 'present margin over Germany (*our only possible foe for years*) is so great as to render it absurd to talk of anything endangering our naval supremacy, *even if we stopped all shipbuilding altogether!!!*' And Asquith, whose membership in the 'big navy' wing of the party is beyond question, informed the Prime Minister that he was 'much disquieted' by the announcement of naval 'construction far beyond any real necessity'.[2] Brunner shared these misgivings, and furthermore believed that by overreacting to a remote German challenge, Great Britain was in fact helping to create the situation she most dreaded. As a man of business, he saw nothing dangerous in a trade rivalry which, in his opinion, added to the desirability of Germany as a partner and a friend. Like Norman Angell, whose *Great Illusion* appeared in 1910, he saw war as an economic absurdity and capitalism a force for peace. Nor did he see any reason to deny

---

[1] *Parliamentary Debates*, 4th ser., CLXX, cols. 1050–2 (March 7, 1907); for the reception of the 1907–8 estimates, see A. J. Marder, *From the Dreadnought to Scapa Flow*, I (London, 1961), 125 ff.

[2] Fisher to Tweedmouth, September 26, 1906, Marder, ed., *Fear God and Dread Nought* (London, 1956), II, 91; Asquith to Campbell-Bannerman, December 30, 1906, cited in Jenkins, *Asquith*, p. 168.

Germany the self-indulgence of a high seas fleet that would, if anything, appease her ego at the expense of her economic growth. Britain had more to learn than to fear from Germany: as the Prussian experiment had shown, a society could advance most quickly toward power and prosperity by marshalling its full resources, physical and intellectual, behind a 'national policy' of public works and social reform.[1] There was no reason, however, to emulate Prussian militarism, which he trusted was on the wane, and he strongly opposed proposals that military training should be a part of the curriculum at Liverpool University.

Brunner spent the Easter recess at Cannes, from which he had abruptly returned for the debate on the 1907–8 estimates. Before his departure he renewed contact with Campbell-Bannerman, whom he saw frequently after he returned in mid-April. He dined at Downing Street on the 27th and returned the Prime Minister's hospitality that summer. In between he kept a string of appointments with ministers, journalists, and like-minded backbenchers among whom he hoped to advance the cause of disarmament. One of his closest associates was Murray Macdonald, who came to Silverlands in the early autumn to draft 'a respectful but earnest appeal' to the Prime Minister; within a few days they had collected 136 signatures, a number that they were convinced 'could have been considerably increased' had there been the time and opportunity 'to prosecute a personal canvass among all the supporters of the Government...' (see Appendix 1). It was not thought necessary to publish the letter for it to have effect.[2]

The threat of a Radical revolt in which Conservatives might cynically join to bring down the Government caused a panic within the Cabinet, where the estimates were discussed from January 21 to February 12. Tempers ran high and resignations were threatened. In the end a compromise was reached by further

[1] *Parliamentary Debates*, 4th ser., CLXXVII, cols. 150–2 (June 27, 1907).
[2] Murray Macdonald and Brunner to Campbell-Bannerman, November 4, 1907, Campbell-Bannerman Papers, Add. MSS. 41240, fols. 138–9; also Murray Macdonald to Arthur Ponsonby, the Prime Minister's private secretary, November 4, 1907, Campbell-Bannerman Papers, Add. MSS. 41240, fols. 136–7. Sir John Fisher, who saw an advance copy of the letter, praised it to the King as 'one of the best papers I have read...It is quite true.' He ascribed credit for it to Brunner. Fisher to King Edward, October 4, 1907 (apparently misdated), Marder, ed., *Fear God*, II, 141.

paring Haldane's army appropriations and by reductions in the navy estimates too diminutive to affect new construction. Unappeased, the Little Navyites on the back benches decided to persevere with their plan to move an amendment to the Address. On February 7 Lord Northcliffe's *Daily Mail* gleefully contemplated the prospect of no fewer than 130 Radical and Labour members who would follow Murray Macdonald and Brunner ('his principal ally') into the lobby. The Liberal *Daily Chronicle*, which by party standards took a 'big navy' line, appealed the same day for 'a stronger sense of party loyalty' on the part of those who, in their misguided zeal, would destroy the Government to reform it.

Reports of discord within the Cabinet were assiduously carried to Radical critics outside, who accordingly intensified their pressure. With Murray Macdonald, Brunner attended meetings nearly every afternoon in one room or another of the House. The endorsement of the executive committee of the Liberal members of Parliament was obtained for a manifesto calling for a curtailment of expenditure on armaments. After the publication of the navy estimates on February 24, they held a series of interviews with Asquith, who attempted to temper their resistance. But on March 2, as promised, Murray Macdonald moved:

That, in view of the continued friendly relations with foreign Powers announced in the gracious Speech from the Throne, this House trusts that further reductions may be made in expenditure on armaments, and effect be given to the policy of retrenchment and reform to which the Government is pledged.

Brunner hailed the motion as a 'zealous, logical, calm, and temperate statement', which he duly seconded. 'Let us return', he urged his fellow members, 'to the days of manly restraint, reticence, and moderation, and let us abandon bluff,' and he aimed several barbs at journalists who earned their keep by perpetually 'nagging at Germany'. Asquith immediately followed with an expression of 'complete sympathy...with the intention and the motive of my hon. friends', and an amendment that cut the heart out of their motion. Instead of calling for 'further reductions', which seemed too strong an indictment of the Government, the successful amendment called only for 'such economies...as are consistent with the adequate defence of His Majesty's dominions'. The original motion was defeated by a vote of 320 to 73, with members of the Opposition solidly against it.[1]

Neither Brunner nor his friends took lightly their opposition to the Government, an opposition that laid them open to charges of coquetting with the Kaiser and compromising national security. Again and again, he felt obliged to explain that it was 'no pleasure …to act the part of "candid friend"', which he assumed in the best interests of the party and the country.[2] J. E. Ellis, a venerable Liberal of Quaker background, kept a diary for these weeks that provides a record of his activities as well as an index to his moral distress: 'This matter of armaments', he wrote on February 4, was 'much exercising my mind…After thinking it over earnestly', he reached 'the rather painful conclusion [that] it was my duty to vote for the [Murray Macdonald] amendment (want of confidence)'. The next day Ellis was heartened by Campbell-Bannerman's announcement—and Murray Macdonald's acceptance—of an offer to discuss 'substantial reductions' in the forthcoming estimates: 'This makes it incumbent on us to do all we can in the direction of reduction.' On the 6th he went to see Asquith, Lloyd George, and Lewis Harcourt, each of whom he tried to impress with the backbench commitment to peace and economy. The party leaders whom he consulted failed to convince him—did Lloyd George and Harcourt indeed try?—to withdraw his objections, and subsequent developments merely strengthened his resolve to support the dissidents. On March 2, Ellis attended the House to hear

Macdonald's resolution about Armaments reduction. Asquith's amendment thereto. Much mental perturbation among supporters of the Government, myself included. Rather a painful evening. Macdonald's and Brunner's speeches good. Voted with minority of 73 against Government…Well satisfied on the whole that I did so, especially after Balfour's speech [defending the estimates].[3]

[1] *Parliamentary Debates*, 4th ser., CLXXXV, cols. 365 ff. (March 2, 1908). A. M. Gollin helps to explain Brunner's allusions and to identify his targets in *The Observer and J. L. Garvin* (London, 1960), p. 55.
[2] *Chester Chronicle*, January 30, 1909.
[3] A. T. Bassett, *The Life of J. E. Ellis, M.P.* (London, 1914), pp. 240–1.

'On its success in ultimately reducing military and naval expenditure the future of Liberalism will largely depend,' the *Manchester Guardian* presciently observed the next morning in a leader that revealed the ambivalence of its own position. On the one hand, it could not contain its relief that the Government had withstood the assault; but, on the other, it was profoundly disappointed with the final declaration, which said little: 'Well, of course. Nobody wants to leave the country inadequately defended.' The fact could not be ignored that in 1908, 'a year of profound peace', a Liberal Government (no less!) had proposed 'to spend sixty millions, or six millions more than we spent on normal military and naval services in 1901, the worst year of the South African War'. The only consolation was the fact that the amended motion, like the original, stressed 'continued friendly relations with foreign Powers'; this provided an area 'of agreement sufficiently spacious for all genuine Liberals, in and out of Government, to stand on'.

In large part, the *Guardian* hinted broadly, the problem lay in Murray Macdonald's unsympathetic delivery. His matter-of-fact observation that 'the resolution was moved in no spirit of hostility' elicited a blunt rejoinder from Asquith and peals of laughter from the Tory benches, where certain members 'seemed to interpret it as a manifestation of the comic spirit'. Brunner's contribution was decidedly the more impressive: the same 'young lions' who had greeted Murray Macdonald with rude comments found in his remarks

material less for derision than for ironical applause, which swelled into positive acclamation when this candid friend, turning to Ministers, warned them against living in a fool's paradise, and pointed out that if every member who sympathised with the motion were to vote in its favour the Government would certainly be in a minority.

So far as the *Guardian*'s correspondent could judge 'from the demeanour of the Liberals no less than [that] of the Nationalist and Labour members, the boast was no idle threat'.

Asquith's role in these proceedings reflected not only the strategic importance of his place at the Exchequer but also the fact that the Liberal leadership, to which he had long aspired, was expected to fall to him imminently. There had already been symptoms of the illness that would bring Campbell-Bannerman's resignation and death in April. Asquith's advent was accepted as inevitable even by those who had mixed feelings about it. Brunner, however much he admired Asquith's parliamentary gifts, had grave reservations about a Liberal Imperialist at the helm of party and national affairs. And, so far as he was concerned, no one could take the place of Campbell-Bannerman, with whom he had weathered so many storms. Supremely conscious of his position as heir apparent, Asquith tried as best he could to conciliate the various Liberal factions whose allegiance he was due to inherit. *The Times*, unsympathetic to his plight, scolded him for assuming 'the not very enviable part of Mr Facing-both-Ways', defending the two-power standard in practice while regretting it in principle.

On April 22 Brunner was again summoned home from Cannes, where he had gone the day after the Commons vote, by a telegram informing him of Campbell-Bannerman's death. The next day he was back in London and, a week later, in the chair at a meeting at the Reform Club, where he introduced the new Prime Minister to the assembled members of the parliamentary Liberal party. Though his function was largely honorary, his remarks were not the least perfunctory. Many of those present had gathered in the same room nearly a decade earlier to elect Campbell-Bannerman their leader. The distance that the party had since travelled was enormous. On that occasion, Brunner recalled, Sir Wilfrid Lawson ('a genial and a tender man, but a sturdy Radical') sat in the chair, 'and he hoped he might without egotism say...that the presence in that chair [today] of another sturdy Radical meant something at any rate'. After a nostalgic tribute to Campbell-Bannerman, he paid cordial welcome to Asquith, who he trusted 'would prove as admirable a leader of the House of Commons as Sir Henry had proved'; in particular, he hoped that Asquith would be as 'determined' as his predecessor 'to maintain the dignity and the power' of the elected chamber, increasingly challenged by the House of Lords. He took the occasion to urge the new Prime Minister to conduct a foreign policy faithful to the spirit of Campbell-Bannerman's Albert Hall speech ('He did not think he ever read in his life an address which touched the hearts of the best among them as that speech did'); and he renewed his appeal for the party to jettison 'that policy of the Manchester School that was called the *laissez-faire* policy', and to adopt instead 'a liberal trade policy—a sane, a wholesome, and a sound trade policy' that put national resources to creative use.[1]

The Opposition press thought it curious, if not ominous, that the new Liberal commander first addressed his troops at a meeting at which a 'staunch cosmopolite and Little Englander' presided. Those who troubled themselves to investigate Sir John's antecedents took delight in pointing out how little the son of a Swiss could possibly know about matters of naval security. The *Observer*, which should have known better, attacked him on May 3 as a 'naturalized' subject who 'remains in instinct and imagination an alien in spite of himself'. Even more damaging, it inferred that Brunner's speech signalled a retreat from Free Trade:

> This is doubtless a very significant declaration. It admits that even among professed Free Traders our existing Fiscal System no longer rests upon a basis of conviction... Cobdenism, as Sir John Brunner expounds it, is part of the retail trade of domestic politics—liable to be abandoned for a more paying line. From the point of view of tactics Sir John Brunner is undoubtedly right. He represents the practical opinions of which the Chancellor of the Exchequer is the most brilliant and the most incalculable exponent. Mr Lloyd George, like Sir John Brunner, believes in internal reorganisation upon the German model.

The *Spectator*, a leading organ of Free Trade Unionists, denounced Brunner as a traitor to the common cause for his Reform Club remarks. And Lord Lansdowne, who led the Unionist majority in the House of Lords, criticized his suggestions as a half-way house between Free Trade and Tariff Reform. Brunner was more surprised than annoyed by the misunderstandings to which his statements had given rise. By no means did he think them inconsistent either with anything he had previously said or with cardinal Liberal tenets. 'I want a constructive trade policy', he declared in a *Morning Leader* interview, 'as an antidote to the

[1] *The Times*, May 1, 1908.

poison of Tariff Reform.' In a letter that appeared in *The Times* on May 25 he replied publicly to Lord Lansdowne with detailed proposals for 'an active policy' that would indeed fortify the Free Trade system:

Distrust of collective action and complete reliance on the springs of individual enterprise marked the progress of English commerce in the nineteenth century. But I fear that unless we now bestir ourselves to meet new conditions these same characteristics will produce a decline in the twentieth.

Brunner's critics were more astute in their perception of his affinity with David Lloyd George, whom Asquith promoted to the Exchequer in this reconstructed Cabinet. In his diary for the spring and summer months of 1908, Brunner recorded frequent appointments with the new chancellor, who remained a zealot for naval economy, a subject they presumably discussed. At the same time he cooperated with other Liberals within Parliament and out of doors to achieve the same goals. J. Allen Baker, member for East Finsbury and one of several Quaker businessmen prominent in the Anglo-German friendship movement (Joseph Rowntree was another), received financial support for a reception for visiting German churchmen. This project, typical of most of the efforts that were made, was expected by its sponsors to achieve quick and far-reaching results. Useful in a limited sense, it had no diplomatic ramifications, a fact that Baker ascribed to the loss of Campbell-Bannerman.

The German Emperor did nothing to make easier the task of those Englishmen who endeavored to allay suspicions of him. His ill-considered intrusions into British politics—his exchange of letters with the doddering Lord Tweedmouth in February 1908 and his infamous *Daily Telegraph* interview in October— provoked a demand for accelerated Dreadnought construction. The German fleet's first Atlantic maneuvers that summer, followed by a series of unsettling international crises, focused attention upon the fast approaching naval estimates for 1909. Invasion fears, strong throughout this period, reached a new intensity. As the year drew to a close, the Cabinet was savagely divided over laying down four extra ships or six, while an inflamed public opinion responded by chanting 'We want eight and we won't wait.' It was a cry that continued to reverberate through the first half of 1909, applying pressures that nearly brought down the Asquith Government.

Convinced that this agitation was fomented by unscrupulous politicians and journalists, Brunner assumed it his mission to help the Government withstand the clamor by encouraging the expression of countervailing sentiments. He had good reason to believe that top-ranking ministers, despite their public postures, welcomed such assistance. 'As you know,' Asquith had recently reminded Reginald McKenna, who succeeded Tweedmouth at the Admiralty, 'I have for a long time been growingly sceptical (in the matter of shipbuilding) as to the whole "Dreadnought" policy...There is much money in it—and more than money.'[1] Brunner could not have put the matter better and often argued the case with similar logic. At a time of economic depression, an expanded naval program would leave insufficient revenue for the social welfare schemes to which Liberals were committed. This situation could hardly have escaped the attention of Tory politicians, who agitated for higher and higher estimates at the same time that they balked at increased taxation.

Brunner was not at Westminster when Parliament opened on October 12, but at Winnington, where he had gone to consult with his directors about schemes 'to employ more men' at a time of hardship and economic uncertainty.[2] No sooner had the session begun than the Tory press and politicians were calling upon the Prime Minister to define the two-power standard, hitherto left wonderfully vague, in the strongest possible terms. Brunner, who spent his autumn mornings sitting for a portrait by Sir Hubert von Herkomer, spent the greater part of each day consulting with Murray Macdonald, Ellis, Arthur Ponsonby, Sir W. H. Dickinson, and other Radical opponents of naval increases. He suffered a profound disappointment on November 12 when Asquith, prodded by Arthur Lee and other Tory members, agreed to

[1] Asquith to McKenna, July 4, 1908, McKenna Papers (The Library, Churchill College, Cambridge).
[2] Appointment diary, BP. The *Westminster Gazette* reported on November 16 Brunner–Mond's attempt 'to re-employ men formerly in our service', and plans for 'new work ...to create more employment'.

define the two-power standard in terms of two keels to one, as 'a predominance of 10 per cent over the combined strengths, in capital ships, of the two next strongest powers'.[1] Still, the Government—which had yet to reach a decision—refused to reveal its construction plans before the appropriate time in the next session.

On December 2 Brunner and Murray Macdonald had 'an interview with Asquith on the Two-Power Standard question, ... and...informed him of our having been deputed to convey to him profound dissatisfaction with his acceptance of Arthur Lee's definition'.[2] Brunner's pique did not prevent him from attending a dinner in the Prime Minister's honor nine days later at the National Liberal Club; every attempt was to be made to keep the quarrel within the family and to preserve the party as an agency for good. Yet he was quite specific that he intended to apply every available pressure to hold the forthcoming estimates below the figures for 1907–8, and to prevent the Government from leading the party to dissolution and the nation to disaster.

Brunner and his confederates were not without allies within the Cabinet: Lords Morley and Loreburn, Lewis Harcourt, John Burns, and, at least for the time being, David Lloyd George and Winston Churchill. These ministers waged a stiff but uncoordinated campaign against the designs of the new first lord, Reginald McKenna, an apostate from their ranks. McKenna had the support of the Liberal Imperialists who now occupied the three vital departments—the premiership, the War Office, and the Foreign Office—and he expected Asquith to 'instantly resign' in the event that either House failed to support his estimates.[3] Lloyd George, the most dynamic and best placed of McKenna's opponents, meanwhile implored the Prime Minister to 'save us from the prospect of sterile and squalid disruption' over 'the very crude and ill-considered Admiralty demands'. On February 2, in a letter of uncharacteristic length and detail—his crabbed penmanship covered thirteen pages—he argued that:

[1] Marder, *From the Dreadnought to Scapa Flow*, I, 146; it is upon this invaluable source that much of the present account is based.
[2] Brunner to 'Mr Hoyle', December 13, 1908 (copy), BP.
[3] McKenna to Asquith, February 2, 1909, Asquith Papers.

8

KSJ

There are millions of earnest Liberals in the country who are beginning rather to lose confidence in the Government for reasons we are not altogether responsible for. When the £38,000,000 navy estimates are announced, the disaffection of these good Liberals will break into open sedition and the usefulness of this Parliament will be at an end.[1]

Throughout the early weeks of the year there was a pitched battle within the Cabinet that further illustrated the Liberal Party's strange propensity for self-destruction. 'The crisis is still on and getting more serious,' C. F. G. Masterman's wife wrote on February 16. 'Morley has not been "squared", but is still firm... Winston and Ll. G. are fighting for all they are worth, certain that the party is behind them, as the Liberal Press certainly is.'[2] Finally, on February 24, both sides accepted a compromise that provided for the construction of four Dreadnoughts in the coming year and held out the possibility of an additional four should the need present itself. It was a solution, credited to the Prime Minister, that testified to the weakness of the Little Navyite position and perhaps, too, to a failure of both strategy and stamina on the part of those involved.

Disheartened by the collapse of support within the Cabinet, which now stood united, Brunner and his allies nonetheless refused to capitulate. There was no longer any serious chance that they might prevail in a Commons vote. 'Estimates presented upon the authority of a Cabinet', Asquith later wrote,

in which the advocates of peace and economy, and the enemies of militarism, were known to have a predominant voice,... could not, in principle and as a whole, be opposed by the Liberal Party.[3]

Yet, men of principle, they continued to act out of principle. Men of faith, their performance was an act of faith, a vain hope that they might inspire others with their courage. The construction of four Dreadnoughts was a foregone conclusion; but they might well discourage the construction of the supplementary four or, if nothing else, they might inhibit Admiralty plans for subsequent years.

[1] Lloyd George to Asquith, February 2, 1909, Asquith Papers.
[2] Lucy Masterman, *C. F. G. Masterman, A Biography* (London, 1935), p. 124.
[3] Asquith, *The Genesis of the War* (London, 1923), p. 109.

But it would be wrong to dismiss Radical opposition to Mc-Kenna's estimates as a quixotic attempt to tilt at windmills. That it appears in retrospect to have been futile, even injurious, does not detract from the high principle and profound concern that motivated it. Brunner was convinced that Great Britain could better protect herself against Germany by endowing a school of naval architecture and design than by clinging to the 'antiquated formula' of a two-power standard, which was foisted upon the Government by 'the London press and London society'.[1] A letter he addressed to the electors at Northwich received wide coverage in the national press. In terms of wealth, seniority of experience, and electoral strength, he was in a far stronger position than most others to take an uncompromising stand. Lord Weardale wrote on February 3 to applaud his efforts ('Your letter ought to rally the stalwarts') and to take stock of the situation:

It looks as if we are going to have a large increase in the Naval Estimates, and unless pressure is brought to bear on the Government, the 'blue funk' members of the Cabinet will succeed.

Of course the battle will have to be fought in the House of Commons. But unless something can be done to arouse the party in the country, and get an active backing for those Members who will oppose the Estimates, I am afraid the influence of the Whips will be too strong for most of them.

On the grounds that it was 'hopeless to expect official organisations of the party to take such action', Weardale proposed to re-activate the National Reform Union, which 'has always been sound on these points, and being independent, can and will move if we can get financial support for it'. Both he and Sir William Hartley had given £100, and he invited Brunner, as an 'old peace-loving Economist', to do at least the same. He pointed out that men like Murray Macdonald, 'whom we can best rely on in the House', could not afford to contribute: 'So our clientele is necessarily limited.'[2]

Never one to put all his eggs in a single basket, Brunner was also committed to the maintenance of the Lancashire and Cheshire

[1] *Manchester Guardian*, January 11, 1909; *Chester Chronicle*, January 30, 1909.
[2] Weardale to Brunner, February 3, 1909, BP.

Liberal Federation, which he had been instrumental in founding the previous autumn. A year later it merged with the pre-existing North Western Liberal Federation—covering Cumberland and Westmorland—to become the Lancashire, Cheshire and North Western Liberal Federation. It met for the first time in the library of the Liverpool Reform Club on January 27, and one of the first orders of business was Brunner's election as president. A resolution was unanimously passed expressing confidence in the Government, appreciation 'for the far reaching measures of social reform which have already been carried into effect', and a determination to see to a successful conclusion the struggle with the House of Lords. Brunner, who did not as a rule attend meetings, was annually re-elected president in absentia. There were no contributions to the Federation's treasury larger and none except Lever's as large as his. Several of Brunner's allies in the anti-armaments campaign—Lord Weardale among them—took a dim view of this proliferation of regional bodies, which they feared might diffuse party opposition to Cabinet policy. Brunner, however, seeking to tap hidden reserves of Liberal power, contemplated an agitation with the widest conceivable base.

In large measure, Brunner deluded himself in his expectation of grassroots support from the party and a widespread reaction outside. More than he suspected, Liberals were prepared to defer to their official leadership and the country was genuinely alarmed by the vague German threat. Typical of Liberals of an earlier age—for example, those who accompanied Gladstone on what Disraeli called his 'pilgrimage of passion' against the 1876 Bulgarian horrors—he was consumed by a burning sense of self-righteousness that militated against an accurate assessment of political realities and led him to overestimate the strength of his position. This false impression was also fostered by Tory spokesmen, who insidiously exaggerated the influence of the Little Navyites within the Liberal Party in order to tar the party as a whole with the brush of defeatism. Yet such an interpretation accords these individuals a prominence in prewar political society to which they are not altogether entitled. However well intentioned and eloquent, they remained—as we shall see—fitfully led and hopelessly divided. Capable of inflicting considerable embarrassment upon the Government, they could not afford to proceed too far for fear that they might deliver themselves into Tory hands. What, in that event, would become of old-age pensions, Welsh disestablishment, national insurance, Indian reforms, and Home Rule? Like all politicians at one time or another, they were forced to swallow either their pride or their principles to protect a host of secondary objectives. Even had outside forces not overtaken them in August 1914, they were too much the victims of party structure to dictate national policy.

This is not to say that, in the opening weeks of 1909, the Liberal Economists were negligible. By some reports, they numbered as many as 140 and could muster additional support from the Labour and Irish benches. With his Cabinet at sixes and sevens, a spate of by-election defeats, and intensified Tory attacks, Asquith could ill afford to dispense with support from any quarter. Yet he moved cautiously, intending to concede more shadow than substance. Sir John Fisher assured J. L. Garvin of the *Observer* that they had nothing to fear from either the Prime Minister or McKenna, upon whom he relied 'to blind their own extremists'. Asquith's statement that he would attempt to hold naval increases to six million pounds was, according to Fisher, no more than 'an artful dodge to conciliate the Brunner party & let them suppose the Admiralty demands had been reduced'. Though Fisher continued to press for the construction of eight Dreadnoughts, he admitted that he thought six 'sufficient...and if the Germans should have made the progress that is possible but not probable *we shall have the eight!* but don't allude to this as it will utterly humbug Asquith in playing his game with his Brunner party'.[1]

On the 8th, Brunner sent Asquith a letter of 'calculated indiscretions' which the Prime Minister promised 'to bear in mind':

I am quite sure that you are right when you say that now that the Germans find themselves confronted with the actual cost of Naval Expansion and

---

[1] Fisher to Garvin, February 3, February 11, and March 11, 1909, cited in Gollin, *The Observer and J. L. Garvin*, pp. 68–73; the second of these letters suggests that Asquith had conveyed the terms of his compromise formula to Fisher long before he presented it to the Cabinet.

other such luxuries, they are beginning to have serious doubts whether the game is worth a candle, and, still more, as to whence they are to procure the new and necessary tallow.[1]

He was also in touch with Asquith's wife, the irrepressible Margot, who thought he might add to the diversity of her political dinner parties. An invitation to one of Margot's celebrated soirées was, however, small consolation for the disappointment he suffered on March 12 with the publication of the estimates for 1909–10. Unappeased, he joined a band of Radicals—the self-styled Reduction of Armaments Committee—who vowed their determination to divide the House.[2] It was decided by sessional ballot that J. Allen Baker would move an amendment to the estimates when they were presented on the 16th, and Arthur Ponsonby, A. H. Scott, J. F. L. Brunner, and Richard Holt volunteered to rally the dissidents as whips. Baker, who stoutly resisted 'indirect and subterranean efforts to get him to withdraw', was prevented by illness from carrying out his fiat. At the last moment he was replaced by A. G. C. Harvey, a singularly unhappy choice.

In any case, Harvey's task was an unenviable one. Asquith drew the teeth of his Radical adversaries by disclosing to the Commons German plans for an accelerated shipbuilding program. Balfour, the Tory leader, assisted him with exaggerated predictions of German strength that were emphatically denied the next day in a statement by the German admiralty. But the work had been done. The opponents of increased estimates were 'taken aback' and, according to the sympathetic correspondent for the *Manchester Guardian*, they 'appeared confused and their strategy uncoordinated'. Harvey, who came to the conclusion that the Government had adequately proved its case for increases, could not bring himself to move the amendment that stood in his name on the order paper. Fewer than three dozen Radicals, Brunner among them, ultimately joined Labour and Irish members to vote in a minority of eighty-three against the estimates as they stood.

---

[1] Asquith to Brunner, February 10, 1909, BP; Brunner's letter, of which he did not apparently keep a copy, does not survive among the Asquith Papers.
[2] Elizabeth and P. J. Noel Baker, *J. Allen Baker* (London, 1927), pp. 156–60; also the *Manchester Guardian*, March 16, 17, and 18, 1909.

Fisher crowed with exultation: 'We have engineered the great radical majority into an obedient flock—Brunner and Co. are wiped out!'[1]

By the time that Brunner spoke on the 17th, he could no longer have expected to sway votes. But conscience demanded that he point out to his colleagues the folly of their ways:

It is a sight to make the gods weep that two great and reasonable nations should be discussing which can excel the other by a week or two, or a month or two months, in the building of an ironclad... During this year, when there has been an enormous increase in the Army Estimates and the Navy Estimates, we have reduced our grants for Universities. Oh! the shame of it. Oh! the pity of it.[2]

On this modest score, he was successful. F. W. Hirst, one of the four chief propagandists for the cause (the others were Scott of the *Manchester Guardian*, Massingham of the *Nation*, and Gardiner of the *Daily News*), thought that Brunner 'and one or two others [had] carried the evening', and proposed a special '*Economist* supplement treating all the Estimates—Army, Navy and Civil Service—critically and showing waste'.[3] Brunner volunteered to contribute toward expenses. Hoping that it might still be possible to bring Asquith round, he urged the Prime Minister to redeem the situation with a bold stroke:

The situation is critical and requires a big man to deal with it.

That we may find that man in you is my dearest wish. On the one side there is the risk of causing some embarrassment in the German Embassy here and in the German Foreign Office.

On the other is the glorious chance of an instant relief in the international situation and of an ultimate relief from the crushing burden upon two Empires, and lastly a smashing blow to Toryism.

I have pondered over this and am convinced that you will succeed if you will disclose in the House

(1) That you are convinced beyond shadow of doubt that the House is unanimous in desiring that we should live on terms of amity with Germany.

---

[1] Fisher to Garvin, March [19], 1909, cited in Gollin, *The Observer and J. L. Garvin*, p. 75.

[2] *Parliamentary Debates* (Commons), 5th ser., II, cols. 1101–2. The passing of the 1909 estimates, Lord Morley lamented, 'ends an era—the era of Gladstonian retrenchment. The Liberal League has beat us.' Cited in Koss, *John Morley*, p. 71.

[3] Hirst to Brunner, March 17, 18, and 22, 1909, BP.

(2) That the House is by overwhelming majority, irrespective of party, desirous of a mutual limitation of armaments through friendly agreement.

I wish you God Speed.[1]

At month's end, 'with wife, doctor, nurse and maid', he left for Cannes, where he continued his campaign by correspondence.

A letter to the editor of *The Times*—written on April 2 and published three days later—signalled a new tack. In it, he took issue with Grey's pronouncement that the controversy over enemy property at sea was irrelevant to the navy estimates. Condemning the policy of 'legalized piracy' that prevailed among nations at war, Brunner argued that if Britain were 'to enter into a solemn agreement with the maritime nations of the world to abolish' the so-called right of capture, she would be relieved of her obligation to police the seas and could reduce her fleet accordingly. The suggestion had moral as well as financial merit: 'As a commercial man, I declare emphatically that I should infinitely prefer the protection of recognised international law to the protection afforded to us by our Navy.' One strong-willed Radical backbencher had set down a motion on the subject for the 21st, and Brunner begged the Prime Minister to 'allow the House to vote' on it 'free from Government pressure...If not, it will be a great opportunity missed. If you do, you will I think be surprised at the amount of support the motion will have.' He recalled to Asquith the party meeting at the Reform Club a year earlier, and especially his appeal for 'a Liberal *Trade* policy', with which this motion was consistent. 'I do not believe that it is yet too late', he told him once again, 'but I am absolutely convinced that failing the adoption of such a policy we shall be smashed at the next General Election. Worse than that, we shall deserve to be smashed.' He stressed the need for Liberalism to show imagination and initiative at home and abroad, and suggested railway nationalization—not merely amalgamation as the Government had recommended—as a good beginning.[2]

[1] Brunner to Asquith, March 2, 1909 (copy), BP.

[2] Brunner to Asquith, April 6, 1909 (copy), BP. The opponents of naval increases were by no means of one mind on the matter. C. P. Scott complained to L. T. Hobhouse on August 22, 1908, that 'Ll[oyd] G[eorge] is unhappily as much opposed as any of the Jingoes to the abolition of the right of capture of private property at sea—the real key of the situation'. Scott Papers (copy courtesy of D. G. O. Ayerst).

'I am full of high politics here,' Brunner wrote excitedly to Lord Crewe, to whom he furnished a report of his activities:

Firstly I wrote a letter to the 'Times' of the 5th on the question of the capture of private property at sea.

Then Lord Reay [who had been a British delegate to the Hague Conference] called here on Friday last [the 9th]. I was out, but later went to him at the Hotel des Anglais where he told me he was very much pleased with my letter and we had much interesting talk.

The other day (three weeks ago) [Thomas] Macnamara said in the Commons with a smile at me that the unregenerate man loves fighting and I replied that the unregenerate man does not love taxes.

Last week I wrote to [J. A.] Spender of the 'W[estminster] G[azette]' pointing out that none of this year's taxes are...yet voted anywhere in the world, that the whole world is beastly hard up and that there was a chance, if only somebody had the pluck to give the diplomatists the go-by, of giving a favourable turn to the situation.

'Punch' makes me out a sentimental fool. I am not thinking of heart speaking to heart, but of pocket crying out to pocket.

The Junker hates death-duties, or the prospect of them to the full, as much as our Cavendishes and Percys did in '94. (The latter, by the way, patriotically evaded them.)

Then I have written to Asquith, reminding him of my speech from the chair at the Reform Club...I warned him that if [we] do nothing and offer to do nothing to help trade, the trading community will succumb to the temptations of the Tariff Reformers.

I know my business in trade.

Three years gone and with the exception of Lloyd George's Patent Act, long overdue, nothing has been done, nothing has been offered.

The situation is exceedingly serious and if not courageously dealt with, we shall be landed in the midst of all the corrupt horrors of Protectionism... after the next General Election.

I have encouraged Asquith to go in for Railway Nationalisation, [which]... would in my opinion go like wild-fire. I know all the risks—they jump to the eyes—but what I have seen and heard of the results in Germany during my visits there as a member of the Royal Commission on Canals have convinced me. And the risks are as nothing compared to the risks of Protection.

How I long to be able to persuade you, but good luck to you anyhow, my kind friend.[1]

[1] Brunner to Crewe, April 12, 1909 (copy), BP. Spender replied to Brunner's letter with a catalogue of his attempts to ease Anglo-German tensions: The hostility toward Britain of Germany's 'governing class, if not their public generally, is an ugly fact which, I'm afraid, we can't overlook. Though I agree with you in hoping that both countries may be brought to a more reasonable frame of mind when they come to count the cost.' Spender to Brunner, April 13, 1909. BP.

From afar, Brunner also kept watch upon political developments in his constituency, where a Unionist speaker had recently denounced him as 'the greatest Protectionist that ever was', notwithstanding his public espousals of Free Trade. He was by now used to such slanders, more the subject of amusement than annoyance: 'It has been the habit of my political opponents for nearly a quarter of a century to attack my methods in trade, and they have always made a mess of it.' Again he affirmed that he was 'a Free Trader, convinced and inveterate'. The introduction of tariffs would admittedly benefit his company by raising the price of alkali, but he was convinced that such a step would be 'very unwise' for the nation, which 'as a whole is best served when everybody is left free to buy and to sell as he or she pleases, no matter what duties other nations gather in at their customhouses'.[1]

Substantially more than an affirmation of faith in Free Trade was needed to revive Liberal spirits and to restore party unity. At his interview with Asquith early the previous December, Brunner had urged him to take up cudgels against the House of Lords, more than ever the sanctuary of reactionary and obscurantist elements. He guaranteed the Prime Minister that 'his followers would back him with enthusiasm and that the stronger he showed himself the greater would be that enthusiasm'. With his son's assistance, he drafted and circulated a petition calling upon the Government to fulfill the historic mission bequeathed to it by Bright, Gladstone, and Campbell-Bannerman. Ramsay MacDonald, committed as Labour leader to a policy of abolishing the upper house, declined to sign, though he promised full support for 'any attempt that may be made to deal effectively with the present impossible position of constitutional authority enjoyed by the Peers'. Asquith, smarting from the blow the Government's licensing bill had suffered on November 27 at the hands of the second chamber, was receptive and on December 11 emitted a menacing growl that left Brunner 'heartily contented'.[2]

---

[1] Brunner to ?, April 14, 1909 (copy), BP.
[2] Brunner to 'Mr Hoyle', December 13, 1908 (copy), BP; MacDonald to Brunner, December 10, 1908, BP.

Refreshed, Brunner returned from holiday in time to hear
Lloyd George introduce his 'People's Budget' to the Commons
on April 29. Though a number of prominent ministerialists were
known to have serious reservations, if not about the financial provisions of the bill then certainly about the bloodthirstiness with
which the chancellor plied his taunts, Brunner could not have
been more pleased on either score. All the better, so far as he was
concerned, if their lordships were tempted to take the fatal mis-
step of defying constitutional canons. He ardently defended the
budget on May 3 and again, when it received a third reading, the
following November. A genuinely Radical measure, it also
seemed to him—as it had to Lloyd George at Limehouse—just
retribution upon the well heeled gentlemen who had cried most
loudly for heavier expenditure on armaments: 'I have said over
and over again in this House and out that I deplore from the
bottom of my heart the need for "Dreadnoughts",' he proclaimed;

but when this House has once decided that 'Dreadnoughts' should be built,
I take it to be my duty to pay my share towards them. Whilst I have no
pity or sympathy for those who first cried for them and then refused to pay
for them, I am delighted to offer them some consolation, namely, that I do
not believe that the need for 'Dreadnoughts' on the present scale will last
very long. Sir, the Germans have learnt better.[1]

If Lloyd George won Brunner's unbounded enthusiasm, Asquith
commanded his deep respect. He found the Prime Minister's
speech at Birmingham on September 17 'admirable throughout',
and credited his forceful oratory as a key factor in 'the securing
of the greatest reform of all, the reform which includes all reforms, the increase of our powers and the decrease of the powers
of the Lords'.[2] He doubted neither the inevitability of the
upper house's destruction nor the consequent benefits, chief
among them the legislation of Home Rule, to which the House
of Lords was a permanent obstacle. T. P. O'Connor, a partner
in past ventures, heard of his activities through John Redmond
and wrote in joyful anticipation of their belated victory:

[1] *Parliamentary Debates* (*Commons*), 5th ser., XII, cols. 1710 ff. (November 2, 1909).
[2] Brunner to Asquith, September 18, 1909 (copy), BP.

I trust . . . that the policy of self-Government to Ireland to which you and I have devoted so much of our lives, is nearing realisation, and that you and I will live to see the two people as fully reconciled as the two races in South Africa have been by this wise policy of self-Government within the Empire.[1]

The final session of the great 1906 Parliament provided a fitting climax to Sir John Brunner's career. He was sufficiently distracted from his infirmities to entertain second thoughts about his decision to retire; these passed, however, as soon as he realized how long and steep the road ahead would be. Aware of all that remained to be done and of the limited time left to him, he abstained from his customary holiday during the recess. Instead he attended frequent meetings of the Reduction of Armaments Committee, whose members refused to be deterred by recurrent defeat.[2] He supported a variety of projects to encourage understanding among the peoples of different countries, attending on the same day a luncheon in honor of visiting German workmen and a dinner for Anglo-French amity. He paid a hurried visit to Dublin, where he consulted with old friends whose disapproval of the budget threatened to disrupt the Home Rule alliance. He held periodic discussions with Asquith and the Webbs, and kept up a vigorous defense of Free Trade. Finally, he plunged himself into the budget controversy and the constitutional crisis to which it gave rise. His crusade barely underway, he was relegated to the sidelines. On November 30 the Tory majority in the House of Lords, persuaded by Lord Milner to 'damn the consequences', rejected the disputed finance bill and precipitated a dissolution of Parliament, after which Brunner, who did not defend his seat, was more a spectator than a participant; his interventions were

[1] O'Connor to Brunner, May 23, 1910, BP.

[2] J. E. Ellis wrote to Joshua Rowntree late on July 26, 1909, after his amendment for naval reductions was defeated by a vote of 280 to 98: '. . . The papers will tell you of the result before this reaches you. The minority was about ten less than I hoped. But the Labour men were by no means united, and as for our Liberals—!

'The usual reports were diligently set afloat by the Liberal Whips—"that the Tories would vote with us and the Government [would] be out",'—'that the Tories would abstain and it would be a narrow thing', &c, &c.

'. . . But I am at the bottom well satisfied with having taken this action. No one, except one who has been at the House, can form any conception of what the effect is at the end of a Parliament, with a lot of men quaking in their shoes for fear of their seats.' Cited in Bassett, *Life of Ellis*, pp. 262–3.

henceforth limited to letters he wrote to the press and speeches he delivered to advance the candidacies of selected Liberals in the two general elections that rapidly followed. Yet, however much he might occasionally have regretted his enforced leisure, it was all to the good, for it allowed him to concentrate his energies where they were more imperatively needed.

CHAPTER II

KEEPER OF THE FAITH

Failing health, made worse by the death of his wife on April 4, forced Sir John Brunner to cancel engagements: he 'did not go to town' for King Edward's funeral on May 20, nor 'to my great regret' could he summon sufficient strength to attend the privy council the following afternoon. Feeling older than his years, he spent the remainder of 1910 and the early months of 1911 wearily surveying the political scene and travelling abroad in the company of one or another of his daughters.

Yet even had he the inclination to cut himself adrift, his reputation and his following would have made it difficult. Liberals whose seats survived the two general elections of 1910 continued to seek him out for encouragement and advice; those not so fortunate, as well as many Irish and Labour members, frequently consulted him on matters of common concern. The most inexorable of his critics on the Tory right, incensed by his stout resistance to Tariff Reform and the 'pro-German' campaign he had waged against rising navy estimates, refused to believe that out of Parliament he had ceased to be a national menace. Leo Maxse, proprietor of the rabidly partisan *National Review*, in fact stepped up his attacks after Brunner had stepped down.[1] And when Brunner died in 1919, the *Financial Times* unforgivingly recalled him as one who, during prewar years, had not been 'far short of being the most powerful man in the country', a wirepuller whose vast fortune enabled him to infect the body politic with the pernicious doctrines of 'passifism'. Such a view not only exaggerates his influence but also mistakes its source. No longer bound

---

[1] See especially the September 1911 number. Brunner had previously clashed with Maxse when he replied on March 9, 1909, to aspersions cast upon his patriotism in the *National Review*: 'I, whose fortune has been made in Cheshire, and is rooted in Cheshire, cannot be indifferent to the fate of the English community.' His letter was subsequently published (May 11) in the *Westminster Gazette*. Maxse, delighted that his taunts had hit home, told Brunner that 'the infamous campaign of yourself and your friends' was 'simply paving the way for a German invasion of your adopted country'. Maxse to Brunner, March 12, 1909, BP.

by obligations to constituents or to the party whips, he could speak more freely and with a moral authority that owed little to his wealth.

Brunner was too much a man of his times not to share the prevailing preoccupation with foreign affairs. A full-scale international crisis flared in July 1911 with the arrival of the German gunboat *Panther* at the Moroccan port of Agadir, where it had been sent to protect German interests which were difficult to discern. The Royal Navy was alerted for unspecified action, and Lloyd George, in a speech at the Mansion House on the 21st, took a strong stand—some thought a provocative one—against Germany. Popular passions on both sides of the North Sea continued to run high long after a diplomatic settlement was concluded in October, and the suspicion lingered in Berlin that Britain had 'meditated an unprovoked attack on Germany, even if she herself took no warlike step'.[1] Germany, denied her vague aspirations and yearning for recognition of her greatness, contemplated proposals for an expanded shipbuilding program to which Britain, equally shaken by the events of the preceding summer, prepared to respond in kind.

The Agadir crisis had a cataclysmic effect upon British politicians and public opinion. A Cabinet reconstruction that followed in its wake brought Churchill, no longer an advocate of retrenchment, to the Admiralty. Under the circumstances, Brunner did not feel that he could afford the luxury of continued leisure. Those within the Cabinet upon whom he had depended to hold the line had suffered a change of heart or, in successive reshufflings, were either dropped or shunted aside. Like many, he feared the possibility that the Government, now dominated by Liberal Imperialists and Navy Leaguers, might overreact to a threat more apparent than real. Lord Loreburn, isolated among his Cabinet colleagues and soon to resign the lord chancellorship, spoke 'gravely and warningly' to C. P. Scott 'of the *immediate danger of a quarrel with Germany*... Take care', he implored,

we don't get into a war with Germany. Always remember that this is a Liberal League Government. The Government of France is a tinpot

---

[1] Hugh O'Beirne, British ambassador to Russia, to Grey, July 10, 1912, Cabinet memorandum (printed), Harcourt Papers.

Government. Germany has but to stamp her foot and they will give way. They are capable of leaving us in the lurch. It would suit them admirably that we should be involved in a war with Germany.[1]

Scott and Herbert Sidebotham, in successive *Guardian* leaders, urged their countrymen to take a calm and unprejudiced view. As head of the Manchester Liberal Federation, historically one of the most important in the country, Scott wrote to Asquith, strenuously denying the existence of any

feeling among Liberals here against Germany—it is generally recognised that her policy of the open-door in Morocco has been of material assistance to us...I can imagine no more foolish war and none more fatal alike to party and to national interests than one with Germany on this matter.[2]

Other influential Liberal journalists—Massingham, Gardiner, Hirst, and H. N. Brailsford—wrote in the same vein, and the correspondence columns of the *Nation* were crowded, week after week, with letters endorsing that journal's appeal for 'an amelioration of our relations with Germany'.

It is noteworthy that among the prominent critics of British diplomacy in the summer and autumn of 1911, all were veterans of the anti-armaments campaign and several were subsequently founders of the Union of Democratic Control. It was the Agadir crisis and not the outbreak of war three years later that convinced these individuals of the need for a foreign policy more responsible, though not necessarily more responsive, to public opinion. Arthur Ponsonby, who had served as private secretary to Campbell-Bannerman, spoke eloquently on the subject of open diplomacy at a November 14 meeting of the New Reform Club. Lord Courtney of Penwith presided, and those in attendance included L. T. Hobhouse, W. T. Stead, J. A. Hobson, and Noel Buxton. The *Manchester Guardian* echoed Ponsonby's condemnation of 'the cult of secrecy' that surrounded Britain's dealings with other nations, and especially called upon Sir Edward Grey to justify the double standard by which the Foreign Office had reacted to the appearance of a German gunboat at Agadir and not to the appearance of a French expeditionary force at Fez.

[1] Scott Papers, British Museum Add. MSS. 50901, fol. 21.
[2] Scott to Asquith, July 20, 1911 (copy courtesy of D. G. O. Ayerst).

What exactly was contained in the unpublished articles that accompanied the 1904 Anglo-French agreement, and what commitments had since been made? The *Guardian* enviously noted that both the German Reichstag and the French Chamber possessed standing committees on foreign affairs to which their respective chancelleries were supposedly fully accountable. Why should officials at Whitehall be permitted to escape comparable surveillance by the elected representatives of the British people?

On November 23, meeting in the octagonal cardroom of the Assembly Rooms at Bath immortalized by Dickens in *Pickwick Papers*, the thirty-third annual session of the National Liberal Federation elected Brunner its president. Grateful for the confidence reposed in him, but never one content with empty honors, he immediately set to work to revive the Federation's influence upon the party, the party's influence upon the Government, and the Government's influence in international councils of peace.

The Federation's new president had regularly attended its meetings ever since its creation in 1877. Before then he had been active in the National Education League, its precursor. Intended to provide an antidote to 'club government', the Federation was designed by its founder and first president, Joseph Chamberlain, to be 'a real Liberal parliament outside the Imperial Legislature, and unlike it, elected by universal suffrage, and with some regard to a fair distribution of political power'. From the start, it was hoped that this agency would provide a link between Liberals in the country and the party organization in London, too often oblivious of their concerns. Unfortunately, the breach between the Federation and the official party leadership was evident as early as 1879, when Lord Hartington, then party leader, declined to cooperate with the Federation's executive council. With the Home Rule split of 1886 and Chamberlain's defection, the Federation moved its headquarters from Birmingham to London and was no longer—to quote Augustine Birrell, a later president —'Joe's caucus'. The secretary of the Federation, whose functions often eclipsed those of the president, doubled as secretary to the Liberal Central Association; through him, the chief whip obtained an indirect control over Federation affairs. By various means, it remained possible for the Federation to bring pressure on the party: this was the case at the time of the Parnell scandal in 1890 and, more formally, in the adoption of the Newcastle Programme two years later. But increasingly the Federation came to place the party's interests above its own, assisting in the election of candidates selected by the central office, contributing its revenues to the chief whip's election fund, and passing automatic resolutions in favor of official party policy. The party's electoral victory in 1906 further diminished the Federation's relevance, leaving it dominated by the whips and discounted by Liberal leaders. Its existence was not ignored, but its compliance was taken for granted.

Brunner's election provided him with weapons that had rusted with disuse over the preceding decade. To a large extent, this inactivity reflected upon the quality of his predecessors. By tradition, presidents of the Federation could not be members of Parliament, but were private individuals annually re-elected until they tendered their resignations. Since the retirement in 1902 of Dr Robert Spence Watson, the office had not carried nearly the weight that was attached to it. J. A. Spender justly described Spence Watson as 'the leading Liberal outside Parliament' who, in his time, exerted an 'influence with the rank and file...only matched by that of the most influential men' on the front bench.[1] Augustine Birrell, Spence Watson's successor, was a genial politician who was more concerned with business in the House, from which he had been evicted in the 1900 general election and to which he returned in 1906. Arthur Acland thereupon served for two years and Sir William Angus for three; both were earnest and well intentioned, but neither was particularly forceful or imaginative. In background, Brunner resembled his predecessors, who were as a rule strong nonconformists and north country businessmen. But he brought to the office a greater sense of purpose and, in strategy and disposition, he was a man of another stamp.

Under his stewardship, the National Liberal Federation received what was to prove its last lease on life. Yet this period

[1] Spender, *Sir Robert Hudson, A Memoir*, pp. 122–5.

in its history, the most vital since at least the turn of the century, has been all but ignored by scholars. The reasons are not difficult to appreciate. For one thing, the Federation's records, always informally and sometimes haphazardly kept, have been the victim of the Liberal Central Association's nomadic existence. Most of the regional associations have long since ceased operation, and the few still extant, forced by necessity to impose upon themselves the retrenchment that they had vainly urged upon the Government in happier days, have emptied their files; miscellaneous minute books have survived, but no correspondence. The private papers of key figures have been destroyed, most lamentably those of Sir Robert Hudson, who from 1893 occupied the pivotal secretaryship of the Federation. After the war, many Liberals were loath to recall the Federation's prewar activities, a subject of personal embarrassment and electoral inconvenience. Spender, for example, preferred in his biography of Hudson to focus upon his subject's wartime attempts 'to rally the public and aid recruiting' to the absolute exclusion of Hudson's intimate participation in the crusade to promote disarmament.[1]

This is not to say that the National Liberal Federation, during Brunner's tenure as president, neglected its customary duties: resolutions were passed and pamphlets were issued on behalf of Home Rule, Welsh disestablishment, Free Trade, franchise reform, and in support of the Government in its fracas with the House of Lords. But from the day of Brunner's election the international situation became a dominant concern. Surely his views were well known beforehand to the members of the Federation council who, weeks before the Bath meeting, persuaded him to accept nomination. And he was a familiar figure to the assembled delegates, who returned him unopposed. On behalf of the general committee, his name was placed before the Federation by Sir John Barlow, who described him as 'a man of peace . . . [who] had been a man of war from his youth in a political sense'. Charles Morley, president of the Bath Liberal association and another old friend, seconded the nomination with a tribute to the

---

[1] *Ibid.* p. 127; there is literally no mention of Federation opposition to the Liberal Government's foreign and defense policies in this otherwise sound work.

candidate's devotion to such causes as education, Free Trade, land reform, and industrial relations: ' . . . Sir John Brunner never believed that as between employer and employed the mere payment of wages ended the contract, and relieved the employer of all further responsibility for the welfare of those who worked for him.'[1]

In accepting, Brunner delivered 'one of his buoyant and cheerful speeches' that dwelled upon the necessity of 'Home Rule for Ireland and a pacific spirit in foreign politics'. He invited his audience to consider all that could be done with the anticipated revenues from Lloyd George's taxation scheme if only Great Britain might reduce her naval expenditures:

> What an amount of refined pleasure we could bring into thousands and thousands of homes, how we could train our young people to be sufficiently efficient to please Lord Rosebery, how we could bring up our girls to be as graceful as countesses. . ., how much money we should have to buy for the small holders of today the land that was robbed from their grandfathers, what joy and what benefit we could bring to the people of England. . .

On the whole it was a typical N.L.F. session, a bit boisterous, but never unruly. With courtesy and 'cordial sympathy', the new president ruled out of order a motion to amend the resolution on franchise reform to include a plea for women's suffrage. Other resolutions were passed without incident, including one on Free Trade appropriately moved by Sir Alfred Mond, the son of Brunner's deceased partner and a rising politician.[2]

The occasion was not allowed to pass, nor did the majority of those present wish it to, without specific mention of the previous summer's international crisis and the mutual resentment between Britain and Germany that was its legacy. Brunner, in his presi-

---

[1] Detailed reports of the 1911 N.L.F. proceedings appeared in the *Manchester Guardian* and *The Times* (November 24), and in the *Liberal Magazine* for December 1911.

[2] Mond's speech was published in *Questions of Today and To-morrow*, pp. 52 ff. Inspired by his boyhood conversations with Brunner to enter politics, Mond (later the first Baron Melchett) was a man of less tact, less patience, and infinitely greater ambition. He proposed himself at this time to become Lloyd George's 'right hand man as Financial Secretary to the Treasury', adding a blunt reminder 'that if I don't get ahead in the political fighting line there is little attraction to me in being merely one of those rich men who are called on to supply funds for the party and then forgotten'. Mond to Lloyd George [December 1911], Lloyd George Papers, Beaverbrook Library C/9/2/6. After the war, Mond converted first to protectionism and eventually to Conservatism.

dential address, expressed 'great comfort' to hear that the German chancellor had recently 'rebuked the angry expressions which had been used [against Britain] in the Reichstag'. It was clear to him that Bethmann-Hollweg had so acted at the behest of 'his mighty master whose mind he spoke', and Brunner invited the Federation to join him in voting a formal resolution of thanks to the Kaiser, who 'had used his influence in the direction of peace'. He proudly observed that the chorus of 'ayes' that greeted his motion was 'more unanimous than he had ever known in the House of Commons', and he trusted that the British Government would be moved to take reciprocal steps to mute anti-German sentiments.

There are indications that Brunner accepted the presidency on an interim basis and to oblige his friends. The editors of the *Liberal Magazine*, who might be expected to know, were gratified to report that 'although Sir John Brunner has found that Parliamentary duties are too exacting at his time of life, he is still able to continue his usefulness to the Party in another sphere... if only for a year'. Yet whatever his original intention, he remained president until 1918, serving longer than any of his predecessors with the exception of Spence Watson. As the Federation did not meet during wartime, his powers for half his term were largely titular. But in the preceding half he provided leadership more vigorous than probably he himself had anticipated.

The Radical press was glad to welcome a veteran ally back to the fold and the National Liberal Federation to the fray. Massingham, reviewing the week's events in the *Nation*, interpreted the Bath proceedings as 'a powerful and enthusiastic demonstration in favor of an understanding with Germany' that, in effect, gave 'direct marching orders to the Government'. He recalled with particular satisfaction the applause that had greeted one delegate's remark: 'We do not want any treaties that will draw us into Continental trouble. We do not want to have to go to war over a few miles of African desert.' Though J. A. Spender did not share Massingham's suspicions of the Foreign Office, he was forced to agree in the *Westminster Gazette* that the spirit of the session had provided 'a message to Germany' and, unmistakably, 'an instruction to the Cabinet and Parliament'. Brunner, too, inferred this message from the response he had received at Bath. His only regret was that he had not consulted the Bible so that he could have confounded his enemies, who dissipated upon Dreadnoughts money that might pay for social reforms, with a quotation from Isaiah: 'It is ye who have eaten up the vineyard. The spoil of the poor is in your houses. What mean ye that ye crush My people and grind the face of the poor?'[1] Here was further testimony to the religious conviction, less pronounced in his case than in others, that provided the peace campaign with both an impulse and a justification.

Brunner's presidential duties brought him into close association with F. W. Hirst, a kindred soul, who was then editor of the *Economist*. A devoted disciple of Lord Morley, whom he had assisted in the preparation of his three-volume life of Gladstone, Hirst fancied himself the heir, once removed, to the Gladstonian tradition. He was a curious figure, a link between a living past and a future for which he waited in vain. Despite the disappointments he suffered, his Cobdenite principles remained intact and his spirit indomitable. 'Mr Hirst was a true fanatic,' his friend A. F. Thompson affectionately recalled, 'and his faith that men would eventually see the light was inexhaustible. Meanwhile, his zest in observing their folly was unbounded.'[2] As the self-appointed custodian of the Liberal pantheon, Hirst stubbornly refused to recognize the fact that his countrymen now worshipped at other shrines.

Hirst possessed a willing pen, a profound sense of moral indignation, and, most important, affiliations with the various, often disparate groups that comprised the anti-armaments movement. 'It would not be difficult to smash Grey if there were a Cobden or a Bright in the House of Commons,' he wrote to Brunner on December 5, betraying his ambivalence in the next breath; 'I'm not sure we want to.' Grey's position, he was convinced, had been seriously weakened by disclosures of concessions to Russia in Persia, 'and I think that if pressure is steadily applied we may get what we want'. Recalling the strict neutrality that Gladstone had

---

[1] Brunner to Hammond, December 3, 1911, Hammond Papers.
[2] *F. W. Hirst By His Friends* (London, 1958), p. 37.

observed at the time of the Franco-Prussian war—a factor to which he ascribed the containment of that struggle—he saw no reason for Britain to take sides in Continental disputes, still less to pledge her support in advance. As Morley had professed to Gladstone in 1889: 'All I care for is that English Liberals should not be called anti-German, or anti-French, or anti-anybody, and should give no excuse to German Liberals for being anti-English.'[1] An attentive pupil, Hirst had learned lessons that would last him a lifetime.

In Hirst's opinion, prevailing tensions were the deliberate work of the scaremongers along Fleet Street, who, like their counterparts in Berlin, sold newspapers by playing upon popular fears of the nation in danger. These yellow journalists therefore exaggerated Anglo-German conflicts and ignored the wide realms of cooperation and inter-dependence between the two empires. It did not escape his notice that these same sources—he called them 'the Armour plate press'—led the agitation for higher and higher naval estimates. As the first step to counteract this mischief, Hirst proposed to send to Berlin a correspondent who could be depended upon to remit more objective, less incendiary reports of German events and opinion. He settled upon Dudley Ward, 'an honest journalist' and 'a real lover of peace', who agreed to take up residence in the German capital for a year. Ernest Schuster, a Liberal financier like his brother, Sir Felix, agreed to provide half of Ward's salary, and Brunner the remainder. Brunner was host at a lunch at the National Liberal Club, at which Lord Courtney was present, to introduce Ward to the editors of various Liberal newspapers for which he would 'act as press-correspondent with the object of promoting friendly relations between Germany and England'.[2]

<hr>

[1] Morley to Gladstone, January 15, 1889, Gladstone Papers, British Museum Add. MSS. 44256, fol. 3.

[2] Hirst to Brunner, December 5 and 19, 1911, BP. Among the newspapers represented were the *Liverpool Post*, the *Yorkshire Observer*, the *Sheffield Independent*, the *Darlington Echo*, the *South Wales Daily News*, the *Aberdeen Free Press*, and the *Dundee Advertiser*. Hirst considered it 'likely' that the *Western Daily Mercury*, the *Eastern Morning News*, the *Manchester Guardian*, the *Daily News*, and the *Daily Chronicle* 'may also join in the service'. An undated note from Hirst, written in pencil on the back of an envelope, dates the lunch as December 10, but Brunner's appointment diary—usually a reliable source—lists it for the 18th.

It was also Hirst who first suggested to Brunner the idea of bringing pressure to bear upon the Government through the component organizations of the National Liberal Federation. This would, it was hoped, provide a means to sustain throughout the year the Federation's influence upon Liberal policy and policy-makers. Would it be possible, he asked Brunner, to 'procure, without giving the reason, a list of chairmen and secretaries of Liberal associations for England, Wales, and Scotland'? He knew better than to request such a list himself, for the whips might suspect his purpose and 'would be afraid I might be getting up trouble for them!' Brunner fared no better. 'How amazingly cool these officials are!' Hirst exclaimed. 'Fancy refusing the request of the President. It is a regular caucus for the pulling of wires and not for the translation of principles into practice...What is the use of electing a President if he cannot even know the names and addresses of the persons over whom he presides...?' The only solution, Hirst concluded, was to summon 'a special meeting for the purpose of laying before the leading Liberals of the N.L.F. the actual facts of the armament situation in connection with Anglo-German friction...Such a meeting, if successful, would practically compel the Government both to approach Germany and to economise in armaments.' Massingham, with whom he collaborated, had accorded warm approval to such a strategy, and Hirst reported a few days later that others he had 'confidentially' consulted 'all agree[d] it would be a splendid move'. For his own part, he confessed he 'often wondered why the President of the National Liberal Federation has never attempted to make use of his enormous influence on behalf of principles which the party once in office is so apt to violate'. Nor could he understand why the president of the Federation should go into hibernation after adjourning the November meeting.[1]

On December 30 a letter to the editor of the *Nation*, signed 'Public Economy' and unmistakably Hirst's work, instructed 'each Chairman of a Liberal Association, from Dundee to Camberwell, [to] do his duty and do it promptly... The Liberal Press and the opinion of the rank and file are powerful agencies.' Among

[1] Hirst to Brunner, December 29, 1911, and January 1, 1912, BP.

those to heed the call was the Manchester Liberal Federation, which sent Grey an expression of 'deep concern...at recent developments of the foreign policy of the Government', and urged him 'to make it absolutely clear' that the terms of the Anglo-French entente did not preclude a similar agreement with Germany.[1] The *Manchester Guardian*, linked to the local Federation through its editor, devoted its January 13 leader to this theme. Four days later the executive committee of the National Liberal Federation met in London at its president's invitation and declared itself in favor of 'an earnest effort after a friendly understanding with Germany, a country with which we have no real ground of quarrel, but, on the contrary, many powerful ties of race, commerce, and historic association'. This resolution, moved by Brunner, 'was carried with perfect unanimity'. Two of the committee members who left before the matter was put to a vote soon wrote to say 'that they had discussed the resolution on their way home together and had decided...that they were entirely in sympathy with me'.[2]

Events appeared to be moving swiftly in the right direction. Francis William Fox, a self-commissioned lieutenant in the peace brigade, had a 'satisfactory interview' at the Foreign Office on the 8th at which he 'endeavoured to impress upon Sir E. Grey the importance of doing something to strike the imagination of the German people', particularly at this 'psychological moment' when the *Novelle*, the new navy law, was about to be presented to the Reichstag. Grey, Fox reported to Lord Courtney, offered assurances that he had given the problem 'considerable thought during the Xmas season' and 'seemed favourably disposed to the suggestion that Lord Haldane should be sent to Berlin...on a Special Mission to open up negotiations...'[3] The proposal for such a mission had already come from other quarters, and, for personal as well as political reasons, Haldane was considered the likely candidate for such an assignment. His Cabinet colleagues

[1] Letter of January 12, 1912, cited in J. L. Hammond, *C. P. Scott* (London, 1934), p. 164.
[2] Brunner's circular letter to presidents of Liberal associations, February 8, 1912, BP; also the *Manchester Guardian*, January 19, 1912; the *Nation*, January 20, 1912.
[3] Fox to Courtney, January 9, 1912, Courtney Papers (British Library of Political and Economic Science, London), x.

had everything to gain and nothing to lose in allowing him to try his hand at preliminary discussions on a naval accommodation. As the military correspondent of *The Times*, an astute observer of the political scene, informed his editor, 'the inner circle of the Cabinet' was anxious 'to humour their followers', and sending Haldane to Berlin seemed to them 'as good a way' as any. 'Personally,' he concluded, 'I do not anticipate any result from the mission except possibly some increased reasonableness among the Radical Left, whom Haldane will purr to sleep when he returns.'[1]

There can be no doubt that the Liberal Government, driven to distraction by Irish difficulties, social disorders, and the composition of its parliamentary majority, could ill afford to lose the confidence of its Radical tail. Nor could it ignore the fact that the Labour Party, upon whose votes it often depended, convened at Birmingham on January 26 and, encouraged by the socialist showing in the recent Reichstag elections, affirmed its dedication to friendship between the British and German peoples. The *Nation* was moved to 'admit that on issues of peace and militarism, of foreign and Imperial policy, Labour members and the Labour Party...have shown a more consistent and enlightened Liberalism than some official representatives of the Liberal Party'. On the 29th a town meeting at Glasgow passed strong resolutions in favor of 'better official relations between this country and Germany'. The *Manchester Guardian* urged other cities to follow suit 'so that the capitals of the industrial North may speak to the Foreign Office with a single voice'.

As pressures mounted in Parliament, in the party, and in the country, the Government lost not only its complacency but also the unanimity it had projected during the previous summer's diplomatic crisis. Lord Loreburn 'spoke in high terms' to Hirst about Brunner's resolution, and indicated 'that with the help of

---

[1] Colonel Charles à Court Repington to G. E. Buckle, February 8, 1912 (copy courtesy of Sir Geoffrey Harmsworth). Churchill, the first sea lord, calculated that his position would be 'all the stronger in asking the Cabinet and the House of Commons for the necessary monies, if I could go hand in hand with the Chancellor of the Exchequer and testify that we had tried our best to secure a mitigation of the naval rivalry and failed'. *The World Crisis* (New York, 1923), I, 95.

support from outside, the change we desire can be accomplished'.[1] Further encouragement came from Lloyd George, who in a speech on February 3 sounded agreeably like his old self, with none of the belligerence of his Mansion House foray. His remarks were sufficient to persuade Brunner 'that the Government would be glad to have [his] resolution carried by many meetings of Liberals' and he obligingly circulated copies among party leaders throughout the country, requesting them to return their endorsement 'at as early a date as possible'.[2]

It is impossible to ascertain exactly what effect Brunner's strategy achieved. Before his letter could have reached most of those to whom it was addressed, news was received that Lord Haldane had arrived in Berlin. Presumably many Liberals who supported Brunner's resolution no longer saw the urgency, even the necessity, of complying with his request. It seemed imperative to do nothing that might embarrass the Government and thereby prejudice Haldane's chances for success. Brunner, too, adopted a wait-and-see policy. He was mollified partly by the Haldane mission and partly because Asquith at last 'consented to the appointment of an Estimates Committee' to look into spending on armaments. He took the occasion to propose to the Prime Minister the creation of what he called a 'Departmental Cabinet' at which 'the permanent heads of the spending Departments' would regularly gather to exchange information about their projects and procedures: 'Our great national Departments are watertight compartments practically knowing nothing about each other, the Treasury alone knowing something about all of them.'[3] A reform along these lines awaited Lloyd George's wartime premiership.

He did not have to wait nearly so long for Lloyd George to effect another proposal he had long advocated: national insurance on the Bismarckian model against sickness, disability, and, at least in certain cases, unemployment. Like many pieces of progressive legislation, it incurred the disapprobation of those whom it was

[1] Hirst to Brunner, January 18, 1912, BP.
[2] Circular letter, February 8, 1912, BP.
[3] Brunner to Asquith, February 5, 1912 (copy), BP.

intended primarily to benefit: the workers, who took strong exception to its contributory provisions. But national insurance had other opponents, equally vehement. Tory matrons resented the indignity of licking health insurance stamps, and incited their domestic servants to protest. Far more damaging, at least in the short run, was the criticism of the British Medical Association, which resisted any intrusion by the state into the relationship between patient and physician. On February 12 the National Liberal Federation sponsored a meeting at the London Opera House, where Lloyd George replied to his respected critics in the medical profession. 'We are suffering from a plague of misrepresentation,' he declared. 'It has been let loose on Tory platforms, in Tory leaflets, and in the Tory Press.' 'And in Tory drawing-rooms,' Brunner interjected. Lloyd George won affectionate laughter from his audience by professing, with mock solemnity, that he dared not 'suggest for a moment' that his old friend was an authority on what transpired in such infamous places. Brunner later brought the meeting to a close with 'warmest thanks' to the chancellor and 'congratulations on his efforts'.[1]

While furtive negotiations for an Anglo-German naval formula continued in London, Brunner slipped away to Cannes for his spring holiday. Prepared, if necessary, to return at a moment's notice—he was back for four days in early April—he was away from February 14 until April 22. Without a seat in the House, there was little that kept him in London, where the anti-armaments campaign was temporarily at a standstill. Until March 18, when Churchill presented the naval estimates for 1912–13, debate was more or less confined to the pages of political journals—the *Economist*, the *Nation*, and the *Contemporary Review*.

Even in his absence from Parliament and the country, Brunner continued to suffer personal attacks in the right-wing Tory press. The *National Review*, which derided the Liberal ministry as 'our Brunner–Mond Government', identified him as a member of the 'Potsdam Party', a

miscellaneous assortment...of ex-Ambassadors on the stump, Cocoa Quakers, Hebrew journalists at the beck and call of German diplomats,

[1] The *Daily Telegraph* and *The Times*, February 13, 1912.

soft-headed Sentimentalists, snobs hypnotised by Hohenzollern blandishments, cranks convinced that their own country is always in the wrong, cosmopolitan financiers domiciled in London in order to do 'good work' for the Fatherland.

Others protested less offensively, but no less vigorously, about Brunner's misplaced confidence in Germany's intentions. Sir Henry Angst, British consul in Zurich for a quarter century and an old friend, wrote him letter after letter warning of Anglophobia and ambitions for conquest among the well-placed Germans he met.[1] Brunner refused to listen, for he could not accept as inevitable a war too terrible to contemplate.

It was Churchill, and the menacing tone with which he announced his estimates, that brought the Radicals back into action. By this time Anglo-German talks had virtually broken down over Germany's demand for a guarantee of unqualified British neutrality in the event of a European war. It was already known to the Cabinet, if not yet outside, that Germany was determined to persevere with the full shipbuilding program outlined in the *Novelle*. To an equal extent, the Cabinet was influenced by strategic considerations in the Mediterranean, where, should war break out, the lifeline to India and the east would be inadequately defended. The alternatives, equally odious to Radical critics, were either increased estimates or greater reliance upon the French ('an absurdly disproportionate remedy', in the *Manchester Guardian*'s opinion) and, some suggested, the Russians.

Churchill presented the Admiralty position on the Mediterranean situation to the Committee of Imperial Defence on July 4, to the Cabinet on the 15th and 16th, and to the Commons on the 22nd. Arguing the case for three ships more than he had requested in March, he persuaded the Opposition more easily than his own side. To the consternation of the *Nation*, British naval and foreign policy—the two wedded in unholy alliance—appeared to have reached the point of no return: 'a virtual naval alliance

---

[1] Among Angst's informants was F. A. Bebel, the German socialist leader, who frequently visited Zurich where his wife was hospitalized and who was 'convinced that the Kaiser and his Junkers will declare war against England the moment they feel strong enough'. On February 23, 1908, Angst predicted that Germany would 'strike ...in 1914, when their huge naval programme will be carried out'. BP.

between France and ourselves with Russia as a third (and slippery) partner. It seems to make an Anglo-German *rapprochement* impossible, and to open up a fresh and indefinite war of building programmes and counter-programmes.' More incensed than dismayed, Brunner met on July 5 with Lord Courtney and repeatedly in the weeks that followed with Sir Robert Hudson. Massingham told Hirst, who promptly relayed word to Brunner, that 'Ll. George is almost on the point of resignation, and a break up of the Cabinet is threatened on Churchill's proposal'. Taking for granted that the Cabinet would be deadlocked for a matter of weeks, Massingham recommended 'a special meeting of the N.L.F.', and Hirst urged Brunner to threaten Asquith to call one. Meanwhile, Hirst set off like a latter-day Paul Revere to awaken Scottish chambers of commerce to the peril.[1]

The question of supplementary estimates came before the Cabinet sooner than Massingham and Hirst had anticipated. And Brunner, who was briefly out of town, did not receive their appeal until it was too late. Still, Hirst was convinced,

a letter to Asquith from you would be of the greatest service. I think you might say you heard privately on an authority which you can hardly doubt that Churchill (not content with his huge spring programme) is now asking for six millions more, chiefly for new Dreadnoughts, in spite of the strong resolution passed by the Committee of the National Liberal Federation at your instance. You might add that, if the Government endorses this policy and proposes it to the House of Commons, you would feel conscientiously bound to summon a meeting of the National Liberal Federation in the hope of bringing Liberal opinion to bear upon this fatal and provocative policy.

I do not think it will be at all wise to use my name or Massingham's in your letter to A. . . . I had a very long talk with Morley chiefly about this, and Harold Spender [the Liberal journalist] has had two talks with Ll. G. on the same subject. You may like to know for your own information how opinion is divided at the moment. George, Harcourt, Morley, McKenna sharply against. Grey, Haldane, Asquith mildly for Winston.

Whatever decision is arrived at, I am certain that a firm letter on the subject from you would produce a very good impression, for A. is a party man par excellence.[2]

[1] Hirst to Brunner, July 12, 1912, BP. The next day, Massingham called prominently in the *Nation* for 'an emergency meeting of the Federation. . .[to] act for the menaced cause of peace and Liberalism'.
[2] Hirst to Brunner, July 15, 1912, BP.

One cannot be certain whether Brunner went along with Hirst's suggestion: no letter from him on this matter survives among the Asquith papers, nor is there a copy among his own correspondence. Yet the Prime Minister could not have doubted for a moment where the Federation and its president stood, and this knowledge must have contributed to the Government's decision to rely upon Canada for the three additional ships.

Not the least pleased with the compromise that was effected, the Little Navyites henceforth concentrated their energies upon the approaching thirty-fourth session of the Federation. Hirst, after further deliberation with Massingham, revived the proposal 'of preparing for signature an appeal to be forwarded to the Chairman of every Liberal Association'. Such a move, he calculated, would impart extra force to the resolutions that would be passed at Nottingham in November. 'Unless something is done we may expect another increase of several millions in the Navy next year, and very possibly a great war.'[1] Morley promised Hirst that he would 'communicate with Grey on the subject of an understanding with Germany' and he was hopeful that 'an effort now might succeed'. It was especially important to press the issue of private property at sea. Hirst regarded the coming 'meeting of the Federation...[as] a golden opportunity, which should not on any account be lost. The ground has been prepared and sown by your letter,' he reminded Brunner, 'and we really ought not to fail to water the ground and get in the crop.'[2] He also reported that 'Massingham, [L. T.] Hobhouse, and others are very keen about the Federation meeting. They think that a change of foreign policy is the only way to save the credit of the Government and of the party.'[3]

Brunner proceeded cautiously, preferring to speak with the Federation's voice rather than his own. He was in close consultation with Lord Loreburn, who had recently left the Cabinet

---

[1] Hirst to Brunner, September 15, 1912, BP.
[2] Hirst to Brunner, September 23, 1912, BP.
[3] Hirst to Brunner, September 24, 1912, BP. According to the September 28th *Nation*: 'It is...for the National Liberal Federation, at its coming meetings, to consider well, not merely how a Liberal Ministry can be sustained, but how Liberalism itself can be kept alive.'

ostensibly on grounds of poor health, and with Hirst, whom he delegated to collect from prominent Liberals resolutions that could be brought before the general membership at Nottingham. The decision to publish a letter on foreign policy prefaced with suitable quotations from Liberal statesmen, past and present, brought a protest from Sir John Simon, whose appointment as solicitor-general had made him sensitive to Cabinet feeling and reluctant to recall his earlier pronouncements against the Admiralty and Foreign Office. Attempting to reconcile Liberal principle and personal ambition, Simon wrote to Brunner 'privately for your own eye alone' to emphasize the need for a foreign policy resolution 'so framed as not to be capable of being represented as a hostile criticism of the Government'. In particular, he hoped that the Federation would not bind itself 'on so technical a matter as the Abolition of the right of Capture of Private Property at sea', a subject on which he had expressed 'strong views' before his transfer to the front bench.[1]

Older hands did not share Simon's fears about embarrassing the Government. Arthur Chamberlain, the venerable temperance reformer, 'was much relieved to hear' of Brunner's stand: 'I feel that they will take such a warning better from you, and regard it more seriously, than if it came from any other man now in public life...'[2] Massingham, in a postscript to a reader's letter to the October 12 *Nation*, urged the application of strong pressure through the Federation. Brunner's actions made clear his agreement that the time had long passed for pious platitudes and gracious formalities.

With Hirst's ready assistance, he drafted a lengthy letter which he sent on October 15, over his own signature, to the chairman of every Liberal association (see Appendix II). Arguing that the Government had listened more attentively to the 'Jingo press' than to its own supporters, he called for the passage of two resolutions, the first in favor of extending the entente to include Germany, and the second for an international agreement that would exempt commerce from capture or destruction at sea in

1 Simon to Brunner, October 10, 1912, BP.
2 Chamberlain to Brunner, October 10, 1912, BP.

time of war. The letter was printed at his expense on the *Econo-mist*'s presses, and he bore out of pocket the charges for postage (£2. 8s. 4d.) and addressing (15s.).[1] His friends responded with predictable enthusiasm: Francis William Fox sent 'thanks for the powerful and most excellent manifesto'; Loreburn thought it, on the whole, 'an admirable appeal'; and Hammond read it with 'delight, sympathy, and admiration'.[2] Hirst, who expected 'at least two millions of people' to read it and agree, was most concerned at this juncture with press coverage. The *Liverpool Post* disappointed him by its silence, leaving a clear field to the local 'Tory rag', which wrote in abusive terms. The *Yorkshire Post* featured 'a curious article', the *Nottingham Express* 'a splendid little' one, and the *Scotsman* a cynical attack, which, Hirst reasoned, 'is about the highest praise that a public man can receive'. Most gratifying was the *Manchester Guardian*, which gave prominent display to the letter and defended Brunner's right to speak plainly in the name of traditional Liberalism: the resolutions he submitted for the consideration of 'local Liberal executives' represented 'the irreducible minimum if we are to abate the danger which threatens to submerge our civilisation'. Other Liberal organs were more guarded, indicating to Hirst that 'the official policy is to lie low and say nothing. . .'[3]

A fortnight later some twenty Liberal associations had responded with resolutions. The number was far fewer than Brunner had hoped for, but Hirst found it 'quite good and encouraging'. Regardless of how many groups reacted, Hirst was confident that Brunner's 'letter had given a great impulse to the movement for an Anglo-German understanding (everyone says so)', and he lifted its author's spirits with a reminder 'that in 1877 or 1878 the National Liberal Federation or the Birmingham Caucus (as it was then called) brought round the Liberal Party to Gladstone's side. (See Morley's Life of Mr G. and Wemyss Reid's Life of Mr G.)'[4]

[1] Hirst to Brunner, October 14, 1912, BP.
[2] Fox to Brunner, October 15, 1912, BP; Loreburn to Brunner, October 16, 1912, BP; Hammond to Brunner, October 20, 1912, BP.
[3] Hirst to Brunner, October 16, 1912, BP. On the 19th, the *Nation* gave unqualified praise to Brunner's efforts and to the sense of party loyalty that motivated him.
[4] Hirst to Brunner, October 29, 1912, BP.

SIR JOHN BRUNNER

But history was not to repeat itself, and it became evident that Brunner's letter was best received by those whose minds were predisposed to its plea: the Skipton Liberal Association and the Manchester Liberal Federation both passed appropriate resolutions even before they had heard formally from the national president. On the other hand, the Lancashire, Cheshire, and North Western Liberal Federation, which boasted Brunner as its head, 'took note' of his request without acting upon it.[1]

Although Brunner had spoken exclusively on his own authority, his letter, before its release, 'was submitted to prominent Liberals peculiarly qualified to be considered representative of the views of the party...'[2] Still, many sympathetic Liberals held back out of fear that they might betray the Government they had helped to elect. In a communication to the press on the 19th, Brunner attempted to allay such apprehensions and, incidentally, to defend his party loyalty:

My own opinion is that the Government would be immensely strengthened by a frank acceptance of the two resolutions as the expression of the strongly felt wish of the most devoted of their followers... Such a demonstration would, I believe, induce them to... overcome the efforts of the Tory party in Germany, backed by the powerful makers of war material, to keep the two nations asunder. The Social Democratic Party, who represent more than one-third of the German voters, are with us already, as all the world knows.[3]

Nor did he or Hirst think it in the least inconceivable that Sir Edward Grey might welcome these resolutions as fortification against the 'anti-German reactionaries' who surrounded him at the Foreign Office.[4]

Brunner did not wait for the Federation to convene at Nottingham to press his views. With A. G. C. Harvey and others, he sponsored an Anglo-German conference that opened at the London Guildhall on October 30 and closed with a royal reception at Windsor three days later. At a dinner he gave for German industrialists, financiers, and journalists, he made it a point to

[1] Minutes, executive committee meeting, October 11, 1912.
[2] *Manchester Guardian*, October 16, 1912.
[3] Letter of October 19, the *Manchester Guardian*, October 21, 1912.
[4] Hirst to Brunner, October 21 and 23, 1912, BP.

broach the topic of abolishing the right of capture at sea. He also struck an active alliance at this time with the Foreign Policy Committee, the most distinguished of the parliamentary groups that agitated for the assertion of democratic control over diplomacy. Philip Morrell, who praised Brunner's 'remarkable letter' in the November *Contemporary Review*, conveyed to him the Committee's unanimous wish that he join Arthur Chamberlain, Thomas Burt, and C. P. Scott as an honorary vice-president. It was a reciprocal arrangement: the Committee claimed the president of the National Liberal Federation among its officers, for which it agreed to add to its list of 'objects', enumerated in the previous April's *Contemporary Review*, a call for the protection of private property at sea.[1]

L. T. Hobhouse, the chairman of the Committee, greeted Brunner's appeal to party leaders as 'a good opening for reasoning amicably with the Government' and a means to 'get many with us who wd. not join in a regular attack'. He acquainted Lord Courtney, the Committee's president, with plans 'to organise a small conference, about 200 people', at the Caxton Hall in late November. 'We hope to get Brunner, Norman Angell, Arthur Chamberlain..., W. H. Dickinson, Gilbert Murray, besides our ordinary friends, to take part.'[2] The conference, which took place on the 26th, heard remarks from Brunner, Morrell, Ramsay MacDonald, and Arthur Ponsonby, and approved a resolution calling for the inviolability of private property at sea and an end to 'the increasing competitive expenditure on armaments'.

Brunner came to the Caxton Hall on November 26 fresh from

---

[1] Morrell to Brunner, November 7, 1912, BP. The Committee defined its 'objects' as follows:

(1) To oppose the extension of friendly understandings with foreign countries into working alliances...and thereby to vindicate for this country a free hand in dealing with international questions in accordance with its own interests and sympathies.

(2) To reassert the traditional sympathy of this country with the causes of national freedom and constitutional government abroad...

(3) To advocate practical measures of policy which may serve as a basis of friendly relations with Germany.

(4) To advocate greater publicity as to foreign affairs, and fuller Parliamentary control of the main lines of policy and of all important agreements concluded with other Governments.

[2] Hobhouse to Courtney, October 21, 1912, Courtney Papers, x.

the performance of his presidential duties at the Albert Hall, Nottingham, on the 21st and 22nd. In his Nottingham address to more than ten times as many delegates, he had called anew for Anglo-German understanding. 'Racially, intellectually, and morally, we are much nearer Germany than France,' he declared. 'The Germans [are] a strong and manly people like the English,' and deserved as much consideration as the French and certainly more than the Russians, who were engaged in 'destroying the liberties of Finland'. As a man of business, he knew first hand 'that an Anglo-German war would spell loss of profit, and even ruin and unemployment on a ghastly scale'. On the same score, he renewed his appeal to exempt merchant shipping from the risk of capture during wartime: 'Good trade in England could hardly coexist at any time with bad trade in Germany, and most certainly it could not coexist in a war of commerce destruction in the North Sea.'[1]

The *Nation* was proud to report that Sir John had put his case before the Federation 'with great power, and apparently with the entire assent of his audience'. The *Manchester Guardian*'s special correspondent at Nottingham gave Brunner credit for making relations with Germany 'the main preoccupation' of the meeting, and for 'travel[ling] the same ground up and down with the authority of one who did much some years ago to bring about happier relations with France'. It was Brunner's impression, however, that the Federation knew its own mind on the subject, and that the turnout at Nottingham was 'so large because the party values the opportunity of... sending out a call which cannot fail to get behind the closed curtains of diplomacy'.

The second day of the Nottingham meeting brought appearances by John Redmond, to whom many of the delegates looked with greater sympathy and affection than to their own leader, and by the Prime Minister, who sought to clarify the intentions of his Government. Asquith, whose address was the climax of the session, was respectfully received, except by a suffragette who had to be forcibly removed from the hall. The *Manchester Guardian*

[1] Accounts of the Federation's proceedings and the text of Brunner's presidential address appear in *The Times* and the *Manchester Guardian* (November 22 and 23, 1912), and in the next month's *Liberal Magazine*.

found his speech satisfactory, but least convincing with regard to international affairs, where policy did not necessarily follow from 'sentiment'. Before rising, the Federation passed its customary declarations of allegiance to Home Rule, Welsh disestablishment, Free Trade, and franchise reform. The last touched off unexpected fireworks. Advocates of women's suffrage were annoyed that Brunner had allowed the franchise resolution to be moved by Dr John Massie, an avowed opponent of their cause, and they were further irritated when he ruled out of order an amendment to Massie's resolution that demanded the enfranchisement of women. The Federation was thrown into an uproar, and Brunner did not help matters by his patronizing appeal to a lady heckler in the side gallery. Representatives of the Women's Liberal Federation stalked from the platform in protest, and Brunner was henceforth forced to defend himself against charges that he showed more concern for the betrayal of liberty in Persia and Finland than for the grievances of his countrywomen.[1]

However embarrassing, this matter was but a momentary distraction from the larger controversy in which he was more deeply engaged. He was denounced by the Duke of Rutland, to whom he replied in the *Westminster Gazette*, as 'the greatest [of] the enormously rich men who run the Radical Party [and who] are foreigners down to the soles of their boots'. And the *National Review*, which took the Duke's part, pilloried Brunner month after month as 'one of the most active friends of every enemy of Great Britain' who, given the chance, would impose a 'grotesque Swiss foreign policy' upon the proud British nation. Needless to say, others regarded his activities in a more favorable light. The National Peace Council voted him a resolution of thanks, while the secretary of the International Arbitration League applauded the work of the Federation and its president: 'One hears on all hands how timely your action was.'[2]

---

[1] Brunner replied to his critics in letters to the *Manchester Guardian* on November 26 and 28, 1912. One might note that his own lack of enthusiasm for female suffrage did not prevent his youngest daughter, a widow who lived with him at Silverlands in his later years, from being an ardent—though non-militant—supporter of the suffragettes.
[2] F. Maddison to Brunner, December 6, 1912, BP.

Worn out by his labors, Brunner left early in the new year on a three-month voyage to the West Indies and America. An enthusiast for canal construction, he could not resist a visit to the new locks at Panama, about which he promised the Prime Minister full information. His 'old and valued friend', James (now Viscount) Bryce, entertained him at the embassy in Washington, and provided him with letters of introduction to the leaders of the American peace movement. He boarded ship at New York and disembarked at Liverpool on April 26. Aside from a brief attack of ptomaine at sea, his health had been no difficulty. Yet the journey proved less therapeutic than his friends and family had hoped. Weeks after his return, he was confined to bed, where he remained for most of June. His condition caused considerable alarm, and *The Times* was 'invited to say' on the 19th 'that Sir John Brunner is in no sense an invalid and has gone into the country for a rest'. By July 5 he was well enough to give a garden party at Silverlands for the delegates to the fifth annual congress for the suppression of the white slave traffic.

Although his public appearances were fewer, Brunner lost no opportunity to disseminate his message. Presiding at a meeting of company shareholders, he decried the millions spent upon armaments 'not only as wasted money, but as mischievous money'. He made the same point when he unveiled a statue of Mond at Winnington Hall on September 13, and when, as pro-chancellor of Liverpool University, he lamented the inadequacy of its chemistry facilities. There is no indication in the press that he participated, as planned, in the conference on national expenditure at the Westminster Palace Hotel, London, on November 18; probably his doctor advised him to save his strength for the National Liberal Federation the following week.

The Federation met at Leeds on the 26th and 27th under the threat of further naval increases. Earlier that month Brunner had written in protest to Churchill, advocating the abolition of capture at sea as a means to economize upon shipbuilding. Churchill had replied politely with assurances, hardly satisfactory,

that the subject...is constantly in my mind. It is however one on wh. I am not able at present to add anything to the official statements of Government policy wh. have been made by my predecessors and by Sir Edward Grey with the deliberate concurrence of the present Cabinet.[1]

Always regarded with suspicion by the rank and file of the party to which he had been converted, Churchill tended to be looked upon, no doubt unfairly, as the least Liberal of ministers, a compulsive adventurer, and the agent of doom within the Cabinet. His rhetoric, no less than his antecedents, invited mistrust.

By this time opponents of increased estimates had come to despair of their chances of exerting influence through the Federation. The *Nation* had no doubt that Churchill's latest 'challenge' to the cardinal tenets of Liberalism would be met, 'as it always is met—with words, with speeches, with articles', but to what avail? The National Liberal Federation could be depended upon to pass 'strong resolutions', and the Liberal press to write 'strong articles', but to what effect? The Federation had become an empty ritual, an 'annual protest which goes unheeded made in the full knowledge that it would pass unheeded'. It was time to borrow Tory techniques: obstruction in the Commons and, if that failed, carrying the 'protest to the country'. On the eve of the Federation meeting, Hirst spoke to the Leeds chamber of commerce in similar terms.

Nevertheless, the delegates assembled at Leeds—some 1200 strong—their hopes undimmed, their enthusiasm unabated, and their leaders outwardly confident. Re-elected for a third term, Brunner reviewed the Government's legislative record and concluded with a condemnation of 'this gross, growing, mad expenditure' upon armaments, inimical to the spirit of Liberalism and a fatal drain upon funds for social reform. J. Allen Baker, 'the fighting Quaker', moved the resolution against the 'continued growth of armaments' and implored the Government to reconvene the Hague Conference, which was adjourned until 1914. Henry Vivian and A. G. C. Harvey also addressed themselves to the subject, the latter threatening to resign from the House if his constituents failed to back up his stand. Asquith, again the principal speaker, passionately affirmed the Government's commitment to Home Rule, but 'gave no substantial offer of relief'

[1] Churchill to Brunner, November 5, 1913, BP.

on the matter of naval estimates. Indeed, as the *Nation* uneasily observed, he 'virtually accepted . . . the fatalistic formula . . . that, while other Powers do nothing, we can do nothing either'.[1]

The efficacy as well as the good name of Liberalism was at stake. With greater appropriations for the navy, how was the Government to finance national insurance, the new land program, and an increased educational endowment? Hirst, among those aghast at the prospect that the Government might be forced to starve its own children, infuriated Sir Robert Hudson by proclaiming that the Federation, however 'great' its spirit, was 'of no account'.[2] Yet Hirst's sense of desperation becomes all too comprehensible in retrospect, with the knowledge that war was eight months away.

Determined not to allow their party leaders to discount the resolutions they had passed at Leeds, the opponents of naval armaments kept up their pressure. Various chambers of commerce, Liberal associations, and Free Church councils formally declared themselves to the Government, while several members followed Harvey's lead and vowed that they would rather resign than vote for the forthcoming naval estimates. 'The question is now becoming one of conscience,' Massingham wrote in the *Nation* on December 6, 'as well as a feeling that if a Liberal Government merely commits itself to the uncritical Imperialist view on the question of armaments, its estimates are bound to be higher (because of the absence of all hostile pressure both on its foreign policy and its war services) than those of a Tory Government, on which pressure is constant.' On December 17 a deputation of Radical critics—led by P. A. Molteno, Arthur Ponsonby, Leif Jones, and J. Annan Bryce—informed the Prime Minister of determined backbench opposition to Churchill's proposals.

Never far in the background, Brunner emerged on New Year's Day with an appeal, widely published, for 'every Liberal Association which believes in the good old Liberal doctrine of peace, retrenchment, and reform to pass resolutions before the end of

---

[1] On the 1913 N.L.F., see the *Nation*, November 29, 1913; also the *Manchester Guardian* and *The Times*, November 27 and 28, 1913; also Elizabeth and P. J. Noel Baker, *J. Allen Baker* (London, 1927), pp. 166–7.

[2] Hudson to Brunner, December 1, 1913, BP.

January in favour of reductions in our armament expenditure so that the Government may have fresh evidence of the wishes of the party before the Military and Naval Estimates for next year are finally settled'. He was convinced that the Prime Minister would welcome such expressions, which, to be effective, would have to be received while the matter was before the Cabinet and before Parliament met in February. There were unmistakable signs that both the business community and the working classes had had enough of 'unproductive expenditure' financed out of increased taxation. 'I, for my part, trust that in the next session of Parliament we may see a fruitful change of policy, which will send a message of relief to British taxpayers and of our goodwill to all the nations of the world.'

More than any of his previous open letters, Brunner's greeting to 1914 won prominent attention and warm commendation from Liberal editors. 'It is certainly time', the *Daily News* agreed, 'that the Liberal Party took a definite and final stand against the sacrifice of its deepest convictions.' Support from the *Nation* and the *Manchester Guardian* was to be expected, but that of the *Daily Chronicle* came as a bonus. On the same day that the *Chronicle* published Brunner's letter, it featured an interview with Lloyd George, who delivered a forthright attack upon the 'organised insanity' of renewed naval competition, and who warned that 'unless Liberalism seizes the opportunity, those who have its conscience in their charge will be written down as having grossly betrayed their trust'. *The Times* noted these stirrings in the Liberal camp, citing them as 'abundant confirmation' of its recent prediction 'that the coming Naval Estimates will mark a critical stage in the history of the Liberal Party'.

There is every indication that Brunner's appeal was coordinated with moves within the Cabinet. F. E. Smith, speaking at Liverpool on January 8, blandly asserted that 'it did not matter so long' as his friend, Winston Churchill, was criticized 'by people like Sir John Brunner and the old whining brigade of the same class, but I confess it was surprising and unexpected to me that the Chancellor of the Exchequer . . . should have . . . expressed the view that the psychological moment had come for us to reduce our naval armaments'. The previous evening, in an address to his constituents at East Bristol, Charles Hobhouse, the chancellor of the Duchy of Lancaster, revealed an unsuspected devotion to principles of economy and Anglo-German conciliation. He proceeded to rally support among his Cabinet colleagues, writing on the 15th to 'Loulou' Harcourt, the colonial secretary:

...Last Sunday I gathered from Sydney [Buxton] that he regarded the navy estimates...as accepted...I did not so understand the attitude of the Cabinet...If we go to them [the public] with demands for more money and new taxes in order to meet naval bills, we shall alienate completely that section of the artisan class which is wavering between Liberalism and Socialism. To lose Churchill might be a parliamentary blow. To lose the electorate I refer to would be to permanently cripple, if not destroy progressive but sane Liberalism. If you think as I do, can you not intervene to stop this unnecessary expansion of destructive expenditure...? The party, or shall I say the friends of economy, have procured delay. We have brought the Ch. of Ex. out of his tent, and we have...procured the hesitation of the P.M. So much depends on the issue that I venture...to appeal for action in words next week.[1]

Liberals throughout the country and from many sectors of public life made clear their sympathies. The Bishop of Lincoln wrote to the *Manchester Guardian* as president of the Church of England Peace League ('Our numbers are increasing daily and include a number of bishops'), and the national executive of the League of Young Liberals implored the Government to 'take practical steps toward arresting an increase...in this unproductive and menacing competition'. The Bradford Chamber of Commerce applauded Prince Lichnowsky, the German ambassador, who described Anglo-German cooperation as 'a mutual necessity', while the Manchester Chamber of Commerce unanimously passed a resolution, declaring it 'not only just but expedient that private property, other than contraband, should be exempt from capture or confiscation at sea in time of war'. The *Guardian* was quick to point out that 'quite half the membership of the various Chambers of Commerce which have passed resolutions...must be Conservative', thereby demonstrating 'that the views of

[1] Hobhouse to Harcourt, January 15, 1914, Harcourt Papers.

Liberal economists are not those of a clique, but have a currency wider even than the Liberal Party'.

At the same time that debate within the Cabinet intensified, popular pressures grew. The lord provost of Glasgow refused the Navy League's request for a town meeting with the argument that national security depended not upon further armament, but upon a lessening of tensions. At Newcastle, another center of the shipbuilding industry, the local Liberal association met on the 12th and carried unanimously Sir Walter Runciman's resolution against increased expenditure on armaments. On the same day, Molteno, who contributed a rousing piece to the following month's *Contemporary Review* ('There is no cloud on the horizon which could possibly grow, so far as we can see, to bring about the storm of war'), addressed an overflow meeting at the Manchester Reform Club. *Ad hoc* bodies blossomed in the heat of controversy and quickly faded. The Committee for the Reduction of Expenditure on Armaments, no more durable than dozens of groups similarly named and inspired, was distinguished chiefly by the quality of its leadership. It met at the Cannon Street Hotel, London, on the 16th under the chairmanship of Hirst, who likened Churchill to Dryden's Zimri:

> A man so various that he seem'd to be
> Not one, but all mankind's epitome:
> Stiff in opinions, always in the wrong;
> Was everything by starts and nothing long.

Brunner joined him on the platform and professed a greater fear 'of the armament firms,...who conspired all over the world to induce people to spend money against each other in armaments, than...of Germany'. He was frequently a participant in events of this nature, and kept close contact with his allies, including the members of the Federation executive committee, which he called into special session on the 21st.

Yet however vocal party and popular opinion, the decisive battle could only be waged in the Cabinet and, most people realized, by Lloyd George. Alone among the ministerial opponents of increased estimates, the Chancellor of the Exchequer commanded strong reserves of power, a personal dynamism, and proved fighting skills. Nor can there be any doubt of the sincerity of his convictions. T. P. O'Connor, whose holiday with Lloyd George in Algiers was cut short by the publication of the *Daily Chronicle* interview, wrote to John Dillon of his friend's determination 'to break with Churchill on the Navy Estimates' and his belief that most ministers would be relieved to see Churchill resign on the issue.[1] C. P. Scott, Lloyd George's friend and faithful supporter, urged him to leave the Government sooner than acquiesce 'in the face of the enormous liabilities incurred by Churchill without authority...'[2] Yet Lloyd George's very strength as a politician was in large measure responsible for his weakness in this situation. He was torn by ties of friendship to Churchill, who in happier days had been his alter ego, by a justifiable reluctance to embarrass (even destroy) the Government at a time of grave crisis over Ulster, and, not least of all, by his overweening ambition, which would not be served by pushing matters too far. 'Winston has sent in revised figures,' he sheepishly informed Scott on the 23rd. 'A swelling expenditure without any prospect or hope of reduction would have justified such a course [resignation]; so would a mere nominal or colourable reduction. But what about this offer?'[3]

The economists within the Cabinet and without could only lose ground with the passing of time. Little had been settled by the end of the month, and on February 2 John Redmond found the Prime Minister 'greatly harrassed' (*sic*) by the naval problem: 'tho' he speaks hopefully of averting a split in the Cabinet, he seriously fears a dry rot in the House which might easily lead to accidents'.[4] Not until March 1, weeks later than anticipated, did Churchill introduce his supplementary estimates in the Commons. The *Nation* angrily reckoned that 'this year's total Parliamentary expenditure on the Navy' had been brought 'to

[1] O'Connor to Dillon, January 13, 1914, cited in Lyons, *John Dillon*, pp. 344–5.
[2] Scott to Lloyd George, January 18, 1914 (copy courtesy of D. G. O. Ayerst).
[3] Lloyd George to Scott, January 23, 1914 (copy courtesy of D. G. O. Ayerst).
[4] Redmond to Dillon, February 2, 1914, cited in Lyons, *John Dillon*, p. 345. The controversy in the Cabinet and Parliament surrounding the 1914–15 estimates is skilfully reconstructed in Marder, *From the Dreadnought to Scapa Flow*, I, 323–7.

over £48,800,000,' and that this sum constituted, 'at least in part,...a new Navy Estimate, involving a fresh policy which was never submitted or made clear to Parliament'. On the 17th, Churchill presented record estimates for 1914–15, made slightly more palatable by a promise of reductions in the year to follow. During these weeks one Liberal member after another rose to dispute the first lord's statistics, deplore the probable effects of his actions upon international relations, or impugn the quality of his Liberalism. But it was a Labour member, Philip Snowden, who most moved the House and the Liberal press with his fiery condemnation of Churchill and the 'armaments trusts'.

What could Brunner have possibly expected when he departed for Cannes on February 10? Surely he was aware that Cabinet resistance had failed and that the party was powerless to avert the increases against which it had spoken so emphatically. He remained abroad without interruption until April 15, and although Hudson and other associates took advantage of his hospitality, he appears to have been politically quiescent. When he returned, his primary concern was scientific education, a subject about which he wrote at length to the *Morning Post* on June 11. He presided at a routine meeting of the Federation's executive committee on July 24 and, two days later, left with his daughter on an ambitious journey that was to have taken him through Switzerland to Vienna and Stockholm before November, when he was due at Manchester for the annual session of the Federation. He travelled only as far as Neuchâtel, where, on August 1, he heard 'rumours of war' and noted apprehensively that the last through train to England left early the next morning. Reversing his itinerary, he proceeded 'through Paris to Amiens' on the 4th, recording in his pocket diary that Parisian hotels now 'closed at 8 p.m.', and that the Elysée Palace, where he stayed, 'had no milk for café au lait' at breakfast. He returned to London on August 5, the day and the war only a few hours old. The remaining appointments in his diary were struck out, including the National Liberal Federation, which did not hold its thirty-sixth session until 1919, when it elected a new president.

CHAPTER 12

THE DEATH OF A LIBERAL

After a spate of Balkan wars, all fought with relative dispatch and without the direct intervention of the major powers, the assassination of a Hapsburg archduke at Sarajevo was hardly an incident, however deplorable, that contemporaries expected to ignite a full-scale European conflagration. Even the convicted culprit recognized no link between his act of political terrorism and the dire events that flowed belatedly from it. Only in retrospect, if indeed then, did men come to understand the forces that had overtaken them in those fateful weeks. To Sir John Brunner and those who shared his sensibilities, the immediate situation was particularly distressing: having long dreaded the prospect of an Anglo-German confrontation, they found it impossible to believe that it had come at last from so remote a source. The outbreak of hostilities registered less a shock than 'a defeat for those in all the belligerent countries who believed in the application of reason to the settlement of disputes, who believed that all problems have solutions, and that international goodwill and cooperation would suffice to prevent war'.[1]

Events moved more swiftly and, so it seemed, more deliberately than statesmen. Within the British Government, opposition again depended largely upon Lloyd George and, for this reason above all others, again failed. Only two ministers, Lord Morley and John Burns, made good their threats to resign. Despite the lack of support from party leaders, the champions of peace did not submit without a struggle. Feverishly active, they were, however, hopelessly divided on strategy and, as usual, poor judges of popular sentiment. On July 29 Arthur Ponsonby served Grey with a petition, signed by twenty-two backbenchers, that called for Britain to hold aloof from Continental entanglements. '...In my opinion nine-tenths of the party are behind us', Ponsonby wrote the next day to the Prime Minister, 'and

---

[1] James Joll, *1914: The Unspoken Assumptions* (London, 1968), p. 22.

before long we may see fit to ask them all to express their opinion openly.'[1] C. P. Scott reported to Lloyd George on August 3 a 'feeling of intense exasperation' on the part of Manchester Liberals, who were aghast at the 'prospect of [the] Government embarking on War' and fiercely determined that 'no man who is responsible can lead us again'.[2] A group of distinguished Cambridge academics declared their abiding respect for German culture, while socialists and trade unionists assembled at Trafalgar Square to demonstrate their solidarity with their German brethren. Financiers and businessmen made clear their consternation; and, in the final hours of peace, Mrs Fawcett and her 'constitutional suffragists' gathered mournfully at the Kingsway Hall to condemn this latest example of 'man's work'.[3]

It was, of course, tempting for Liberal critics of the Government's foreign policy to overestimate the support they commanded within the party and the country. They were abetted in their delusion by Tory spokesmen, anxious to help their opponents incriminate themselves as defeatists and isolationists. Yet the *Nation* grievously erred in its supposition that there existed a vast 'public opinion...definitely opposed to war'. On the contrary, one finds that those who advocated caution, let alone pacifism, had a difficult time making themselves heard above the jingoistic din. In part, they had only themselves to blame. Some, like the irascible Lord Loreburn, were rendered ineffective by the fact that they had spoken prematurely; others, because they waited in vain for the appropriate time. Morley flattered himself that, if he maintained a strict silence, the combatants would eventually call upon him to arrange a negotiated settlement. Lord Courtney, perhaps recalling the frustrations he had suffered as a pro-Boer, gratefully declined A. G. Gardiner's invitation to employ the columns of the *Daily News*: '...Many things have to be taken into account. I have been moving among men saying a word here and there;...but I must choose the moment for speech or writing even at the risk of being too late.'[4] As it was, war had

[1] Ponsonby to Asquith, July 30, 1914 (copy), Ponsonby Papers.
[2] Scott to Lloyd George, August 3, 1914 (telegram; copy courtesy of D. G. O. Ayerst).
[3] For a detailed catalogue of this activity, see the *Nation*, August 1 and 8, 1914.
[4] Courtney to Gardiner, July 30, 1914, Gardiner Papers.

already been declared when he broke his silence to join Lords Loreburn and Bryce in a plea for further negotiations on the dubious ground that Belgian neutrality was not technically violated. Massingham, citing the murky precedent of the 1864 Schleswig–Holstein affair, took the same line in a letter to *The Times*, while the *Daily News* enumerated the reasons 'why we must not fight'. By this time moral as well as strategic considerations insured the fact that such appeals would fall upon deaf ears.

How could politicians who had failed in their previous exertions against rising naval estimates now hope to keep a jittery nation out of war? Steeped in the doctrines that Norman Angell had popularized, they remained convinced until the last moment that enlightened self-interest would prevail. Some, reluctant to trust exclusively to human reason, put their faith in the mercy of God. Others drew their confidence from history, believing that at the critical moment they would raise the country against Grey's foreign policy as their forebears had against Disraeli's. Their misfortune was to lack not only a Gladstone, but also an understanding of popular anxieties and an accurate assessment of the Government's intentions. The most highly placed among them were largely ignorant (though perhaps not to the extent that they later insisted) of the commitments the Foreign Office had made, of the tacit assurances that the Admiralty had given to France, and of the deliberations of the Committee of Imperial Defence, the body which they held responsible for the worst of their troubles.

Discounted by their countrymen and betrayed by Germany's defiance of international law, the peace men—to call them as they often called themselves—had few options left open to them. Those most advanced in age and most despondent withdrew from public life. But the vast majority were sustained by their visions of a better world to rise from the ashes of the old. Several of the most intellectually prominent among them founded the Union of Democratic Control in the hope of providing an effective means to subordinate diplomacy to representative institutions. They, along with many of their prewar allies, drifted into the Labour Party, from which they expected greater fidelity to principles of internationalism. But the overwhelming number remained Liberals, of one type or another, at least for the duration of the war. Regardless of their political labels, they tended to give ardent support to the war effort. George Cadbury, according to his biographer, was typical of 'those who, while preserving their abstract hostility to war, found in the circumstances of the war with Germany so clear an issue between right and wrong as made a departure from the strict letter of the doctrine justifiable and necessary'.[1]

Brunner, too, was resolute in the belief that war, once it came, had to be fought and won. He suffered neither regret nor shame for his earlier stand, which, under the circumstances, had been the only one morally defensible and consistent with his principles. His error, a noble one, had been to suppose that all men acted according to the same rational criteria. War, he could console himself, had come from a direction which no one had anticipated, least of all those who warned of a German naval invasion. More in sorrow than in anger, he continued to believe that had the British Government done more to strengthen the hands of the German moderates it might have been possible to avert the catastrophe. But now there was no choice but to destroy the insatiable militarists who dictated policy at Berlin.

Placing his London house at the disposal of the Serbian Red Cross, he retired to Silverlands, where he helped to settle Belgian refugees. The cooperation he received from his neighbors seemed to him the only blessing of the war, which 'had brought the whole Empire together as brothers', and the classes of English society 'together as friends'.[2] Otherwise, there was little satisfaction to be taken. Aside from Hirst and Hudson, whom he entertained occasionally, he saw few of his old colleagues. But he

---

[1] Gardiner, *Cadbury*, pp. 273–4. 'We have no need to be ashamed,' Cadbury wrote to Gardiner on November 27, 1914, 'but to rejoice in the fact that we did what we could to prevent war,...which we still believe might have been avoided if England had maintained her old position as a friend of Germany. Now that we have entered into the war it is as impossible to stop it as to stop a raging torrent.'

[2] Speech at Lyne, *Surrey Advertiser*, July 24, 1915.

remained an active correspondent, exchanging frequent letters with Lloyd George, Asquith, Grey (about fishing), and even Balfour. He took solitary exercise walking through the woods, armed with a longhandled saw that he used to prune dead limbs from the pine trees. Devoted as ever to his family, he mourned two nephews who fell in combat, and read every letter that his grandson, Felix, sent from the western front. '...The wearing anxiety about the war', he reflected to his own son, 'is not at your dear boy's end of the journey, but with father and mother at home.'[1] Another grandson, Sidney Buckley, escaped from a German prisoner-of-war camp.

As an industrialist, Brunner was proud to contribute all he could to an allied victory. On June 4, 1915, he revealed to a meeting of shareholders at Liverpool that the company had begun the manufacture of 'two chemical substances with which to fill the shells Mr Lloyd George', recently appointed minister for munitions, 'had asked for. It was a serious responsibility to undertake, but it has been undertaken willingly.' With enthusiastic support from its workers, the firm accelerated production 'on an extensive scale without profit'. To compensate for the loss of manpower to the armed services, the working week was extended to fifty-eight hours. Brunner explained the technical aspects of these changes to Professor Henry E. Armstrong, the noted chemist:

Lord Moulton, as the chairman of the High Explosives Committee..., consulted Brunner, Mond & Co. a good many weeks ago... We have been making Ammonium Nitrate for some time to the tune of 10 tons a day, and now, I believe, 20 tons a day by the Ammonia Soda Process, and we are doing our best with synthetic Phenol. He sent us more recently some impure T.N.T. and asked if we could purify it. After careful enquiry we decided to undertake this at our Silvertown works..., where it cannot be done on any great scale, but we are specially building a new works in Cheshire at which we shall be able to deal with all the impure T.N.T. in the country.

The new plant was completed and put into operation in the autumn of 1916; but, at the urgent request of the authorities,

[1] Brunner to J. F. L. Brunner, November 3, 1917, BP.

maximum production continued simultaneously at Silvertown until early the following year, when a violent explosion put it out of commission.[1]

Despite the political truce to which the parties were officially committed by their leaders, fierce antagonisms persisted. If any thing, hatreds were intensified by wartime restraints upon Parliament and the press. Some, who saw the nation's struggle as proof that they had been right about Germany all along, seethed when they recalled Brunner's earlier pronouncements and detested him all the more for his failure to ask their pardon. The most insidious of his critics wrote letters to the Tory press, particularly the *Globe*, alleging that he shamelessly reaped huge profits by providing munitions for an army and navy he had tried his best to weaken. Brunner strenuously denied that his company profited from war production—'Not a penny of our published profits has been made out of dealing with the Government'—and, borrowing the words of John Bright, he took his accusers to task for 'climbing through dirt to dignity'.[2]

But Brunner was less distressed by such foolish attacks, to which he could rarely resist a reply, than by the merciless persecution suffered by those in prominent places with German antecedents or who were identified, like Lord Haldane, with German culture. J. A. Pease, writing to him about developments at the Board of Education, joined him in deploring the unscrupulous press campaign that drove Prince Louis of Battenberg from his place at the Admiralty. Brunner, appalled by the hysteria that gripped wartime society, wrote to *The Times* in defense of foreign-born subjects ('...If we have at hand trustworthy evidence of their good will towards us we ought to secure their friendship'), citing as an example the case of his late partner,

[1] *The Times*, June 5, 1915; *Manchester Guardian*, June 5, 1915; Brunner to Armstrong, June 21, 1915, Armstrong Papers; A. W. Tangye's diary, 'war years', ICI Archives. Tangye recalled that the name 'Silvertown' for this high explosive had been decided by Lord Moulton, Sir John Jarmay, and himself, at 'The Savoy', London. 'I have always felt responsible when looking at the Memorial Column at Winnington.'

[2] See Brunner's letter in the *Westminster Gazette*, October 11, 1915, in reply to Donald Norman Reid's letter to the *Globe* three days earlier; also a leader in the *Globe* on the 19th.

Prussian by birth, but nonetheless one who, above all else, 'desired to be one of a free people'.[1]

Brunner was in most respects the perfect victim for Tory propagandists, who were eager to cast aspersions upon the Liberal Party without appearing unpatriotic by outright attacks upon the Government. In their eyes, he personified all the worst in Liberalism: its preoccupation with legality; its aversion to military and imperial glory; its refusal, even in a time of peril, to wield commerce as a national weapon; and its respect for the rights of the individual, including those of neutrals and resident aliens. As one who loved a good fight, particularly in defense of the old cause, he could be depended upon to attract attention to himself: what other millionaire would go to court—as Brunner did on August 29, 1915—before he paid a two-penny charge that a cabman had added to his fare? Better known for his immense wealth than for his political service, he was easily caricatured by his enemies, skilled in the arts of vituperation, as a sinister figure who misled British opinion in order to protect his friends and investments abroad. And, finally, his name was linked inextricably to that of Sir Alfred Mond, whose attempts at self-vindication only added insult to injury. Despite his previous rebukes to 'scaremongers', Mond insisted that he had always supported a strong navy, that he had secretly sympathized with Lord Roberts's agitation for conscription, and that he had known all along about Germany's aggressive designs. The *National Review*, to whom these statements smacked of conscious opportunism, wondered why Mond had 'sedulously concealed this priceless knowledge from his political clientele in Wales, in the Press, and in Parliament', and especially from Brunner, whom he ungallantly allowed 'to make a perpetual and consummate ass of himself'.

During the first winter of the war, when popular frenzy reached lunatic proportions, Brunner suffered unremitting attacks in the

[1] *The Times*, November 9, 1914. Brunner's reference to Mond was perhaps disingenuous. On September 13, 1913, he recalled his partner, whose statue he dedicated at Winnington Hall, as 'an enthusiastic Englishman', but cautioned those present: 'Dismiss it from your minds, if the idea be there, that he thought little of his native country. He showed great appreciation of his native Germany and of his native town of Cassel, by giving huge sums in his lifetime, and by leaving not only money but pictures to Germany.'

right-wing Tory press. Month, after month, the *National Review* hammered at him:

Sir John Brunner's political activity has been conspicuous in one channel, namely the disarmament of the British Empire which must necessarily have involved its dismemberment. He was not merely a Little Navy man, who in his ignorance might conceivably have misjudged the relative strength of German and British sea-power...He was a No Navy man.

Impressionable readers, inflamed by such rhetoric, resorted to more crude libels. With Mond, Brunner brought suit against a Leicester paper merchant, who had sent them a letter—formally addressed to 'Those German Swine, Rt Hon Sir John Brunner, M.P., and Sir Alfred Mond, M.P.'—that read: 'Hope you are satisfied with devastation and misery caused by your fellow-Hogs in Belgium and France.' The defendant was ordered to apologize and pay costs, but the action was hardly as effective a deterrent as the plaintiffs had wished. Brunner also instituted proceedings against the incomparable Horatio Bottomley, editor of *John Bull*, who promised 'not to make or publish any statement at any future time suggesting that you are a German subject or of German birth, nor will I at any time suggest that you have any anti-British sympathies'.[1]

Attacks upon his loyalty rankled, especially in wartime, but Brunner tried his best to see the humor of them. Early in 1915 he met Robert Gladstone at Liverpool and mentioned that during the last few months he 'had been accused of being a German... traitor, a German spy, and a man of German origin having German sympathies'. So far as he could recall, he related, his first contact with Germans had been 'when my dear old mother-in-law implored me to keep German beggars from her doorstep'.[2] He consoled himself that he suffered in good company and that his friends stood by him. 'I am very much distressed to see that you have been put to annoyance and trouble by the outrageous manner of some very contemptible people,' J. L. Hammond wrote to him. '...Everyone knows that if there were many

---

[1] George Lewis, solicitor, to Brunner, January 30, 1915, BP.
[2] Note dated January 26, 1915, BP.

Englishmen who did half as much or worked half as hard for
their country as you do, England would be in a very different
condition today.' On a smaller scale, Hammond was experiencing
similar treatment from his neighbors at Hemel Hempstead, who
presumed him to be a German spy: 'The evidence is apparently
1) that I don't go to Church & 2) that I have a beard...'[1]

Brunner undeniably possessed a reputation that those who
sought to discredit Liberalism and embarrass Liberal leaders found
convenient to recall. On January 5, 1915, the *Morning Post* re-
printed and commented at length upon the letter he had addressed
a year earlier to the chairmen of Liberal associations whom he
implored to speak out against proposed naval increases. 'To
revive such a document at the present juncture may seem a little
cruel,' the editor conceded, disclaiming any intention to 'bring
confusion' on its unfortunate author, whose 'perversity...is a
small thing'. Rather, the object was 'to remind the country, at a
moment when its perceptions have been made clear by the logic
of facts, how dangerously mistaken were those counsellors and
guides', Lloyd George first and foremost, 'who but a twelvemonth
ago...did their best to hamper those defensive precautions
which we have now seen to have been so abundantly necessary'.
The *National Review*, which that month identified Brunner as the
'ringleader' of the 'Little Navyites', featured his letter of New
Year's Day 1914 in its February number as 'an interesting
historical document'.

By the end of the year Brunner, who had had all he could bear,
wrote to the *Morning Post* to defend himself against the mis-
representations that had appeared persistently in its pages. First
of all, he flatly denied an account that he had toasted the Kaiser's
health at a public dinner during a period of 'sharp crisis with
Germany': 'The only occasion on which I proposed his health
was when I was in the chair at a dinner in Homburg, where I
had the honour of representing the English visitors. This was
surely a proper thing for me to do under the circumstances.' His
letter, which appeared on November 16, went on politely to
suggest that the *Morning Post* had confused this occasion with

[1] Hammond to Brunner, December 13, 1914, BP.

278

the 1911 meeting of the National Liberal Federation at which he had moved a resolution of thanks to the Kaiser for putting an end to 'offensive remarks about England' in the Reichstag: 'I look back upon this incident without any feeling of shame, and I remember with pleasure the unanimous fervour of my audience in approval of my suggestion.'

At the same time he struck back at an assailant in the *Globe*, who, boasting 'the blood of Edward the First of England in his veins', denounced the presence in the Privy Council of 'pro-Germans' to whom 'England is a money-making machine for the enrichment of patentees'. Brunner was obliged to admit that his 'Swiss ancestors [had] never had any relation with Kings (I include Dukes) except when they went to fight against them'. But, he pointed out in a letter to the *Westminster Gazette* on November 6, there existed 'in Switzerland, carved in stone,...records of the names of men who have fought for their liberty,...and the names of my ancestors appear...as far back as July 9, 1386'. Inspired by 'the example of my ancestors', and as one who had 'lived happily for nearly seventy-four years under the Union Jack', he was as loyal to King and Country as any man.[1] Brunner's many friends were agreed that he had had the best of the exchange. 'These boobies think that everyone who is not an Englishman must be a German', G. W. E. Russell wrote in response to his 'excellent letter'. 'A Scottish baker called *Strahan* had his shop wrecked, and a French chef has just been run in as a spy.'[2] And R. B. Cunninghame Graham, in the days of his militant socialism a relentless critic of Brunner, congratulated him notwithstanding the fact that the author of the attack was a fellow Scotsman: 'You fairly wipe the floor with my unlucky compatriot, and he deserves the well merited castigation you give him.'[3] This was high praise indeed from one who, when Brunner

[1] Despite his contempt for those who claimed deference on the basis of birth or inheritance, Brunner was as self-conscious about his antecedents as any late-Victorian. With the connivance of Sir Henry Angst, he prepared for *Burke's Peerage* a 'pedigree' that listed a long line of Brunners, not all of whom were related to him.

[2] Russell to Brunner, November 6, 1915, BP. Russell, a privy councillor and former Liberal M.P., was a veteran journalist, political biographer, and chairman of the Churchmen's Liberation League.

[3] Cunninghame Graham to Brunner, November 6, 1915, BP.

was proprietor of the *Star*, had resentfully christened him the 'Star-spangled Brunner'.[1]

As one might have predicted, he was less successful in bringing around opponents of more recent vintage. J. S. Sandars, who served as Balfour's private secretary, was amused to hear Brunner express second thoughts about the German character. 'But isn't that just an instance', he told Maxse of the *National Review*, 'of what you so happily designate as "patriotism overnight"—Haldane talking blandly of compulsory service after his anti-Roberts record. But they are all alike.'[2] Brunner was not, however, attempting to ingratiate himself with his critics, but rather was expressing a disillusionment common among Liberals of his generation. For decades, he had stood in awe of German education, urging the importation of its methods to England. Yet what respect could he have for a system that inculcated a spirit of uncritical obedience? Military training began in Germany 'when the child first came to school, and continued with some of them even to the age of twenty-five, when they were at college'. The technical skills they had acquired were no substitute for principles of liberty, and he came to the unhappy conclusion that the Germans were 'a poor, cowardly lot to submit to the infamous Government which they had over them to-day'.[3]

Much to the displeasure of some of his prewar allies, Brunner was adamant that there could be no lasting peace so long as there continued at Berlin 'a Government which is symbolized by the mailed fist and shining armour and the sword rattling in its scabbard'. Invited by the secretary of the International Arbitration League to contribute his thoughts to the League's journal, the *Arbitrator*, for July 1916, he rejected the notion of a negotiated settlement and declared: 'We are fighting for freedom of the human intellect and for good faith between the nations, and we ought to wait until the Germans have not only given up the cry of "Deutschland über alles" and "Gott strafe England", but

[1] The *Nation*, July 5, 1919.
[2] Sandars to Maxse, January 31, 1915, Maxse Papers (County Record Office, Chichester, Sussex).
[3] *Westminster Gazette*, September 24, 1915; *The Times*, September 24, 1915; also the *Morning Post*, September 22, 1915.

also have begun to try to rid themselves of the Berlin military spirit.' Ponsonby, a pacifist, grieved to hear such strong words from his old comrade, to whom he explained that 'Deutschland über alles' does not mean as commonly supposed 'Germany everywhere' or 'over everyone', but 'Germany above everything', 'a perfectly legitimate patriotic expression, far less offensive than "Britannia rules the waves"'. He denied that he held a 'brief for the Germans', but he considered it 'important that we should find fault with them for what is wrong and not for what is harmless'. Along with the slaughter and sacrifice of war, he regretted the disruption of the Liberal alliance for progress and consequently the fact that he and Brunner no longer 'see eye to eye'.[1]

Yet it would be mistaken to label Brunner, as some of his former associates did, a belated convert to jingoism. His primary concern was to obtain conditions in which a new domestic and world order could be built. To this end, he retained his faith in education, encouraging the members of a Liberal luncheon club at Leeds 'to look forward to a future of bold and wise reconstruction' in which 'intellectual training and scientific preparation' would play a vital part. In a letter to the *Westminster Gazette* on July 10, 1916, he applauded 'Lord Haldane's great speech in the House of Lords' on the subject of university expansion. A few months later he upbraided the members of the Surrey Education Committee for suspending prize-giving in local evening schools for the duration of the war. 'The most pitiful piece of economy I have ever heard in my life,' he exclaimed, announcing that he would give the customary prizes out of his own pocket until such time as the Committee 'return[ed] to their senses' and recognized national priorities.[2]

Like most Liberals, Brunner preferred to fix his mind not upon the trials of war, but upon the opportunities that peace would eventually bring. He subscribed generously to Bryce's efforts 'to bring an enlightened public opinion to bear upon the settlement . . . and on the future foreign policy of the country' by collecting

---

[1] Ponsonby to Brunner, July 3, 1916, BP.
[2] M. E. (?) Sadler to Brunner, May 4, 1915, BP; also the *Evening Standard*, September 21, 1916.

information to assist 'in formulating the details of a peace settlement' when the time arrived.[1] To insure the achievement of a just and lasting peace, it was imperative to keep the reins of British government secure in Liberal hands and, at the same time, to keep Liberal statesmen secure in their heritage. A victory won by methods borrowed from the Prussians would be a hollow one; a treaty that imposed crushing penalties upon the defeated parties would destroy the chances for economic recovery for victors and vanquished alike. The consequences were far too great, Brunner was convinced, to entrust affairs to self-seeking, small-minded Tories, implacable in their cries for revenge, and insatiable in their greed for the spoils of war.

On this score, he experienced a series of severe disappointments. In May 1915 Asquith suddenly exchanged his Liberal ministry for a wartime coalition, designed to accommodate a number of prominent Unionists and a lone Labourite. The Liberal rank and file, to whom the Prime Minister offered only a hasty explanation *ex post facto*, could only surmise that the way was being paved for the introduction of compulsion, that most illiberal of measures. F. W. Hirst was not alone in suspecting collusion between 'the Liberal imperialists and the Tory imperialists, [who] together are quite capable of working up a panic and rushing the country into military slavery'. With Morley's approval, he prepared 'a good strong well argued pamphlet' against the conscription of men for either the army or industry, and Brunner sent him fifty pounds to help defray the cost of publication.[2]

Despite Asquith's confidence that, as head of an all-party government, he could retain mastery of the situation, Liberals were soon confronted with the prospect they found most distasteful. They would either have to betray their principles or face repudiation by their coalition colleagues and certain defeat at the polls. By no means was the struggle waged along strict party

[1] Bryce to Brunner, September 21, 1915, BP.
[2] Hirst to Brunner, May 31, 1915, BP. On May 28, Hirst wrote to Scott: 'The present outcry for conscription is clearly manufactured—the object being to discipline and enslave the working classes and to keep down Ireland.' Scott Papers, Add. MSS. 50908, fol. 197.

lines, for a minority of influential Liberals—chief among them Lloyd George—had thrown in their lot with the conscriptionists, while Balfour and several other ranking Tories were temporarily defenders of the voluntary principle. Dissension within the Cabinet between the advocates of *laissez-faire* and those of tighter governmental regulation and control was well known to the supporters of both sides outside. 'Will the Government or the war come to an end first?' Hirst asked Brunner with malicious satisfaction in the summer of 1916.[1]

Pained to see Liberals compromise themselves and their tradition, even in the professed cause of a national emergency, Brunner nursed vain hopes that party honor and the electoral situation might somehow be salvaged. He offered Lloyd George suggestions regarding the recruitment of men, and, incidentally, stressed the need for Liberals to stand together: 'I believe with Asquith that if he resigns, or if you resign, the Allies will be enormously weakened, and that is certainly not the way to win the war.'[2] To his horror, internecine warfare within the Liberal camp broke into the open at year's end. Lloyd George formed another coalition, this one more dependent than its predecessor upon Unionist backing, and supplanted Asquith in the premiership.

In the light of the humiliation he suffered, Asquith appeared to many of his followers, including some who had been least enthusiastic about him, as another Grand Old Man, a repository of the lost virtues of public life. Lloyd George, on the other hand, was widely regarded as another Chamberlain, underprincipled, over-ambitious, too impatient to allow the succession to take its normal course. Brunner, thoroughly incensed by the rumors carried to him by Hirst and others, lost no time in calling a special meeting of the National Liberal Federation's executive committee, which met on the afternoon of December 12 to vote Asquith a resolution of warm appreciation and to assure him of 'unflinching support in the difficult days to come'.[3] Their fallen

---

[1] Hirst to Brunner, July 10, 1916, BP.
[2] Brunner to Lloyd George, April 22, 1916, Lloyd George Papers, D/20/2/87.
[3] Brunner to Asquith, December 13, 1916, Asquith Papers, XVII, fols. 259–60.

chief took 'profound satisfaction' in Brunner's report 'that I retain the confidence and (as you are good enough to add) the affection of my old political comrades'.[1] Yet he had discounted the Federation too often in the past to have expected the support of its executive committee to count for much.

Again, as in May 1915, Liberal loyalties were put to the test and consciences disquieted. How many crises of this sort could even the healthiest party weather? Hirst baited Brunner for failing to seize the opportunity for a vigorous reassertion of Liberal principles: '"I believe in Asquith" is not a sufficient creed...It sounds like: "I believe in the Archbishop of Canterbury" instead of "I believe in Original Sin". Now if you had *both* a leader and a faith, we should all feel better.'[2] Brunner, however, was reluctant to force a showdown, as much for the sake of the party as for that of the war effort. In his opinion, there was no choice but to support Asquith, who promised a better chance than Lloyd George of restoring Liberal cohesion. Meanwhile, the political scene was brightened only by the presence of H. A. L. Fisher at the education office. Brunner had met Fisher, then vice-chancellor of Sheffield University, on the eve of war, and, with great expectations, went with C. P. Scott to hear him present his education bill to the Commons on April 19, 1917. He was spotted in the gallery by the clerk, Sir Courtenay Ilbert, who confidentially agreed that the appointment of Fisher, his son-in-law, was 'the one redeeming feature of a not very satisfactory government'.[3]

His associates on the executive committee prevailed upon Brunner to retain the presidency of the Federation, a burden more moral than physical which he yearned to relinquish. They cited the difficulty of choosing and installing a successor at a time when annual meetings were suspended. Asquith joined in their supplications: 'It is quite right that you should continue to be President of the N.L.F. and the Executive show their wisdom in insisting that you should remain at their head.' Reluctant to see

[1] Asquith to Brunner, December 15, 1916, BP.
[2] Hirst to Brunner, January 13, and 22, 1917, BP.
[3] Ilbert to Brunner, March 17 and April 20, 1917, BP.

the office left vacant in such critical times, Asquith did not wish to see it the object of a tug-of-war between the feuding Liberal factions. 'I was interested and gratified by what you say as to the reports of the local Secretaries,' he told Brunner on October 3.

Nothing has touched me more in my political life than the signs of loyalty and affection which have come to me, during the last 9 months, from our old party throughout Great Britain. I hope more than ever that it will keep its organisation solid and alert, and its powder dry.

I am delighted to find that you and I are in such complete agreement as to the *post bellum* future.

Physically I was never better: the relaxation of the strain, which for 11 years had been constant and ceaseless, has done me a world of good.[1]

Brunner, in his seventy-fifth year, was not nearly so sanguine about either the party's condition or his own. His appointment diaries for the later wartime years provide a depressing catalogue of his illnesses and convalescences, including a throat operation in February 1917 at which he was attended by '2 of the nicest nurses that ever was'. Friends urged him to ignore the advancing years: 'Palmerston', Hirst reminded him, 'was just beginning to think of his long Premiership' at that age, 'and Gladstone was stumping the country for Home Rule'.[2] His seventy-sixth birthday, which found him frail, brought tributes and fond wishes from his friends. 'As Johnson said of someone,' Hudson, a past president of the Johnson Club, wrote to him, 'you have "a genius for friendship", and the longer we know you, the more we love you...May this awful War come to a rightful end before you celebrate your next birthday.'[3] Proud of the age he had attained, Brunner sent greetings of his own to Ernest Solvay, four years his senior: 'I hope I live to come to Brussels again to greet you once more as a free man in a free country and to see you surrounded by your family and friends, and I hope also to be full of joy because England shall have succeeded in keeping her solemn promise to Belgium.'[4]

In the months remaining to him, Brunner distributed among

[1] Asquith to Brunner, October 3, 1917, BP.
[2] Hirst to Brunner, January 22, 1917, BP.
[3] Hudson to Brunner, February 7, 1918, BP.
[4] Brunner to Solvay, March 1918 (copy), BP.

his children the numerous portraits for which he had sat. In addition, he divested himself of a variety of formal obligations, the duties of which he had already delegated to others. In April 1918 he resigned the chairmanship of Brunner, Mond and Company, to which he was first elected in 1891. He was succeeded by his son, Roscoe, who often in recent years had presided in his place at board meetings. It was an arrangement that gave him enormous satisfaction. One son had replaced him as member for Northwich, the other as company chairman. Both strove earnestly, in the face of mounting difficulties, to carry on in their father's tradition; but the first lost his seat in the 'khaki' election of 1918 (he made a brief reappearance in the House five years later as member for Stockport), and the second committed suicide in 1926.

In a printed letter dated September 16 and addressed to Hudson, Brunner announced that his formal resignation as president of the National Liberal Federation 'has been in the hands of the Executive for some weeks past, and that my decision to retire is final'. The time had come, he proclaimed, to 'make way for someone younger', who would bring greater energy to 'the vast problems, political, industrial, and social, which will confront us at the conclusion of this World's War'. It did not, however, suit his purpose to disguise the reasons that underlay his move. He was outraged by Lloyd George's intention 'to plunge the country into the strife and turmoil of a General Election' the moment that victory was won. Like many Liberals, among whom Scott and Gardiner were perhaps most fiercely vocal, he feared that an early renewal of partisan activity would destroy 'national unity' and subvert efforts at reconstruction. 'As a means of eliciting the considered opinions of the voters', many of whom remained stationed on foreign soil, 'a General Election at this juncture would be a mere mockery'. Not least of all, he dreaded the effects of a premature polling upon the Liberal Party, which, he continued to believe, 'never had a more essential task to perform than awaits it on the declaration of Peace'.[1]

On October 13 Brunner heard news that the Germans had

[1] Brunner to Hudson, September 16, 1918 (printed), BP; also *The Times*, September 27, 1918.

telegraphed their acceptance of Woodrow Wilson's Fourteen Points and had sued for an armistice. Jubilantly, he wrote to Balfour that he had hoisted the Union Jack over Silverlands: 'I am now out of the hands of the doctor and am a constant student of national affairs.'[1] One wonders whether he, at this time, suspected the direction in which his studies would lead him. The more closely he examined the electoral situation, the more firmly he was convinced that Liberals owed their misfortune to the fact that they had too long defaulted on their moral obligations. Before 1914, the party had taken too lightly the slogans with which it came into office. In the stress of wartime, Liberal ministers had dealt violent blows to freedom of speech, Free Trade, and, by introducing conscription, to the most essential of individual liberties. However much he railed against Lloyd George, he could not forgive the part played by Asquith, who, in 1915, had first admitted the enemy to the Liberal citadel.

Early in December Brunner declared his intention to cast his vote in the imminent general election for the Labour candidate at Chertsey, who stood with little hope of success against a 'couponed' Unionist. It was not at this juncture the least unusual for independent Liberals to make common cause with right-minded Labourites, particularly in constituencies where they did not themselves take the field. But Brunner's announcement, which took the form of an open letter to his neighbors whom he represented in the Surrey County Council, was unusually blunt and all the more surprising in view of the fact that his son was standing in the Asquithian interest at Northwich. He intended his action specifically as a protest against the 'unworthy and unpatriotic trick of the Coalition Government' of rushing the country to the polls, an opportunistic move that imperilled national unity and precluded a thoughtful assessment of the issues at stake.[2] Others, who shared his indignation, did not—at least

[1] Brunner to Balfour, October 15, 1918, Balfour Papers (British Museum).
[2] *The Times*, December 7, 1918. 'Down here', Gilbert Murray reported to A. G. Gardiner from the Westbury division, where he was speaking for the independent Liberal candidate, 'the strongest feeling we meet with is indignation at the Election being held now, before the soldiers can vote or the home electors learn what it is all about.' Murray to Gardiner, December 6, 1918, Gardiner Papers.

for the time being—carry their protest to such lengths. Like the majority of them, Brunner might have continued to support Asquith, who, after all, was not a party to the Government's strategy; but he found the former premier distressingly vague on social issues, and rightly counted him as an impediment to a meaningful Lib-Lab alliance. Besides, Brunner was never one to deal in half measures.

To the consternation of many former colleagues, Brunner took the chair at meetings of the Labour Party, whose campaign in the Chertsey division he financed. 'Were I back in the House of Commons,' he professed to a local audience, 'I would cheerfully vote for every part of the Labour Party programme.'[1] His enthusiasm was not always reciprocated, and one of the 'out-and-out Labourites' from party headquarters let it be known that he 'would much have preferred such a wealthy man among the audience, instead of being on the platform'.[2] Brunner, who knew better than to take seriously the rhetoric of class warfare, was not perturbed. He had enjoyed excellent relations with his employees, and many of his closest political friends had been workingmen, Liberals and Labourites alike. True, it was significantly easier for him to affiliate with Labour at this stage, when the party was not yet wedded to socialist doctrine. Even so, he had often found certain socialists dependable allies in his various battles against privilege at home and jingoism abroad. If he did not always agree with them, he nonetheless perceived that they were a force more to respect than to fear.

In supporting Labour, Brunner sincerely believed that he was best serving the interests and ideals of an abused Liberalism. The progressive alliance that he had vainly expected first from Chamberlain and then from Lloyd George, he now hoped—as did so many—that Labour might forge. Despite his eleventh-hour conversion, he remained faithful to the values and attitudes of the age that had created him, losing neither hope for the future nor confidence that men could be educated to serve society in their own interest. 'While the memories of the late war are fresh and

[1] *The Times*, December 5, 1918; also the *Evening Standard*, July 1, 1919.
[2] *Surrey Herald*, July 4, 1919.

its economic results are still a burden', he called upon the nations of the world to dedicate themselves to the timeless principles of peace, retrenchment, and reform.[1]

He died on July 1, 1919, and his ashes were buried beside his second wife's in the parish churchyard at Lyne, adjoining Silverlands. A Unitarian minister came from London to deliver a brief service. The chemical Croesus left an estate of over £906,000, exclusive of the amounts he had settled upon his five married daughters (reportedly about £100,000 each), the investments he had transferred to his sons, and the huge sums he had lavished upon political and philanthropic causes. The attainment of his worldly success was, however, not nearly so notable as the uses to which it had been put. Surely he deserved a more generous memorial tribute than the perfunctory one he was paid the following November, when the National Liberal Federation met for the first time in six years and elected his successor. But the 'parliament of Liberalism', its ranks depleted, had more to mourn on that occasion than a politician who belonged, like his tradition, to a bygone age.

[1] Fragmentary notes for a postwar speech, BP.

PRINTED LETTER TO THE RT HON.
SIR HENRY CAMPBELL-BANNERMAN,
G.C.B., M.P.[1]

Sir: We venture to make a respectful but earnest appeal to you in favour of a reduction of expenditure on the Army and the Navy.

For many years before the late Government resigned office, the Liberal party had made constant protests against the extravagance of their military and naval policy; and when the present Government came into office there was a widespread expectation that its advent to power would be followed by a large reduction in expenditure.

Last year, when the question was raised, the Government pleaded the short time they had had, since taking office, for considering the grave questions of policy involved in reduction; and the justice of the plea was generally admitted. With the exception of a few minor adjustments, the estimates that they then presented to the House were the estimates that had come into their hands from their predecessors.

This year reductions have taken place amounting, in the case of the Navy, to £1,427,000, and in the case of the Army to £2,036,000. In neither case, however, can we regard these reductions as due to any change of policy initiated by the Government, nor as a fulfillment of the expectation that reductions would be made. They are due almost entirely to considerations that were not, and could not, have been foreseen when the Government took office. In the case of the Navy the reduction is in the Shipbuilding Vote, and is due to the fact that foreign Powers have not advanced with their ship-building programmes as rapidly as had been anticipated. In the case of the Army the reduction is due mainly to the fact that Mr Haldane put a stop to a custom, that he discovered existed in the War Office, of habitually over-loading the estimates for that Department.

While recognising the necessity of being well-armed, we maintain that our present expenditure is excessive and injurious; and we do so on three grounds.

The first is the international situation. It is admitted that the strength of our Army and Navy ought to be determined by the state of our relations with foreign Powers. The enormous increase in our peace establishments since 1895–96 is represented, according to the estimates, by an increased expenditure of £21,517,609 or more than 58 per cent. Is there anything in

---

[1] Undated [November 1907], Campbell-Bannerman Papers, Add. MSS. 41240, fols. 140–1.

the present situation to justify the continued maintenance of so large an increase? So far from this being the case, it is our belief that, on a review of the state of the world, we stand in less danger at the present moment from any Power in it than we have done at any time during the last quarter of a century; that our relations with all the great Powers are friendly in their character; and that there is no great outstanding question between us and any one of them that need prevent these relations from becoming even more friendly than they are. Outstanding difficulties between us and Russia are in process of settlement, as the result, we gratefully acknowledge, of the policy being pursued by the Government... The political and military balance of Europe has also, it seems to us, been completely altered in the last few years to the advantage of this country. There is no longer any cause for alarm in the possible combination of France and Russia for aggressive purposes. We have most happily come to an amicable agreement with France as regards all the many serious questions which affected our relationships, and which for so many years were the threatening cause of war. Our relations with Germany are improving, and the two peoples are coming to realise that the community of interest that unites them far outweighs any possible differences. Finally, the grant of self-government in the Transvaal and Orange River Colonies makes unnecessary the continued maintenance of large military forces in South Africa... The second ground on which we plead for reduction is that the maintenance of our present enormous peace establishments destroys the financial elasticity of the country's resources and depletes those financial reserves upon which success in wars so largely depends.

And the third is that every penny we apply to the maintenance of our excessive armaments is taken from the resources at our disposal for promoting the well-being of our people. But that well-being is at least as essential a factor of success in a great war as is a great Army or a great Navy... The strength of a people and its position among the nations of the world is in the last resort determined by its intelligence and its character. But in recent years there has been a marked tendency to forget this. We have spent our resources too freely, without sufficient care and forethought, on the factors that tell least, and that have the least permanent influence in preparing us to play our part among the nations of the world. The same tendency showed itself repeatedly during the course of last century. But it was the constant and not unsuccessful effort of two great men to curb and restrain it. We refer to Peel and Gladstone. When fears were entertained and expressed that our forces were too weak to meet the forces of foreign Powers, these two men were untiring in the energy with which they pressed the consideration that though the great military Powers of the Continent might be proud of their strength, and might cherish the belief that by means of their vast armaments they secured themselves against attack, yet the cost of these armaments was exhausting their resources and enfeebling their capacity of sustained exertions. They were never weary of holding up the action of these

Powers to us, not as an example of what we should do, but as a warning of what we should avoid.

It is in humble imitation of their spirit and their policy that we approach you at a time when the estimates for next year are being prepared, and respectfully ask that they should be materially reduced, and the people be allowed to reap the natural fruits of peace. We are Sir your obedient servants.

Percy Alden	G. P. Gooch	R. Pearce
T. G. Ashton	Corrie Grant	R. W. Perks
J. Allen Baker	George Greenwood	G. H. Pollard
John Barker	John W. Gulland	C. E. Price
John E. Barlow	Brampton Gurdon	A. Priestley
W. P. Beale	G. A. Hardy	Robert Pullar
Hubert Beaumont	T. Hart-Davies	Geo. H. Radford
T. H. D. Berridge	A. G. C. Harvey	A. Rendall
T. R. Bethell	W. E. Harvey	Thomas Richards
Wm. Brace	Jas. Haslam	Arthur Richardson
James Branch	A. E. W. Hazel	Charles Roberts
John Brigg	Norval W. Helme	J. M. Robertson
J. A. Bright	Ivor Herbert	Sidney Robinson
Stopford W. Brooke	John S. Higham	T. Roe
John Brunner	Richard D. Holt	James Rowlands
J. F. L. Brunner	Arthur G. Hooper	V. H. Rutherford
S. O. Buckmaster	John D. Hope	Duncan Schwann
Thos. Burt	W. B. H. Hope	A. H. Scott
W. P. Byles	T. H. W. Idris	Arthur Sherwell
Robert Cameron	R. S. Jackson	J. G. Shipman
Francis A. Channing	John Jardine	T. B. Silcock
Goddard Clarke	John Johnson	J. A. Simon
William Clough	Wm. Johnson	W. C. Steadman
Felix T. Cobbold	Alfred J. King	Halley Stewart
Stephen Collins	H. C. Lea	B. S. Straus
George Cooper	R. C. Lehmann	Franklin Thomasson
C. H. Corbett	A. Levy Lever	J. W. H. Thompson
Henry Cotton	Maurice Levy	Geo. Toulmin
W. Randal Cremer	Arnold Lupton	Frederick Verney
W. J. Crossley	Hugh Fownes Luttrell	Henry Vivian
Ellis W. Davies	John M. McCallum	John Wadsworth
Timothy Davies	J. A. Murray Macdonald	H. de R. Walker
W. Howell Davies	F. C. Mackarness	John Ward
W. H. Dickinson	F. Maddison	H. A. Watt
James Duckworth	H. R. Mansfield	Josiah C. Wedgwood
J. Hastings Duncan	John Massie	J. Galloway Weir
John E. Ellis	Walter Menzies	George White
Geo. R. Esslemont	N. Micklem	T. Wiles
R. L. Everett	P. A. Molteno	A. W. Wills
Geo. Hy. Faber	L. Lapper Morse	Henry J. Wilson
C. Fenwick	Alpheus C. Morton	John Wilson
Thos. R. Ferens	Horatio Myer	John W. Wilson
Alexander Findlay	George Nicholls	P. W. Wilson
Hugh Fullerton	C. N. Nicholson	R. Winfrey
J. Gibb	Harry Nuttall	
D. Ford Goddard	Herbert Paul	

A LETTER ON LIBERAL POLICY[1]

With Sir John Brunner's Compliments

Silverlands, Chertsey

12th October, 1912

DEAR SIR,

I am impelled to write this letter to you by a strong feeling of responsibility. The Liberal party has been engaged during six years of office in an arduous struggle with the mighty forces of privilege, monopoly and protection. In this short period three great General Elections have been fought and won. The Budget, the Parliament Bill, Old Age Pensions, National Insurance, Home Rule and Welsh Disestablishment have absorbed all our energies. Foreign politics have not received the attention they deserve. But the Morocco crisis of last year, and the warlike concentration of fleets in the North Sea which has excited so much apprehension, have opened the eyes of the sleepiest politicians to a new and pressing danger. Everyone now sees that prosperity and progress at home are bound up with the cause of International peace. Armaments and war spell poverty and ruin.

The great Liberal victory of 1906 was won on a programme of peace, retrenchment and reform. Conciliation in South Africa seemed to usher in a policy of friendliness and goodwill which would be followed by a wide extension of International Arbitration, large improvements of International Law, and a general happy reduction in the burden of armaments. We can still say with thankfulness that Great Britain has remained at peace during the whole period of Liberal rule—a happy contrast with the previous ten years of Unionist administration, which promoted a dozen wars in different parts of the Empire. Moreover, while Sir Henry Campbell-Bannerman lived, there was some relaxation in the growth of military and naval expenditure, though by no means in proportion to the legitimate expectations of the party. Mr Asquith as Chancellor of the Exchequer put a severe check on the wasteful system of borrowing for naval and military works. But the false and shameful naval panic of 1909 swept away the spirit of prudence and economy. Since then no less than 13 millions have been added to the Navy Estimates, while the cost of the German navy has increased by only four. Our Foreign Office and Admiralty have yielded to the clamour of the Jingo press in its campaign of mendacity and provocation. Parliament has been misled, and estimates have been founded upon false forecasts of German expenditure.

---

[1] Addressed 'to the Hon. Secs. of the Liberal associations of England and Wales, through the favour of Sir Robert Hudson, Secretary to the N.L.F.' (printed copy), BP.

No heed has been paid to the protests of the National Liberal Federation, or to the constant criticisms of Liberal economists in Parliament and the Press. The invention and advertisement of the Dreadnought by our Admiralty have proved a curse to mankind, and not least to our own people and our German neighbours, for both sorely need the money thus wasted, to remove slums, to improve housing in town and country, and to multiply gardens. If this destructive rivalry in naval armaments goes on unchecked it threatens to submerge civilisation and to destroy society. There is no limit to the taxation which armaments can impose on rich and poor alike, as we see by the case of Japan, which now has a high tariff and an income tax rising to five shillings in the pound in order to pay for a conscript army and a large fleet.

To my mind it is the plain duty of the British Government, which forced modern battleships upon the world, to make amends. It is the plain duty of the Liberal party, the inheritor of Gladstone's teachings, to express itself now in language which the Prime Minister and his colleagues cannot mistake. There has been a lamentable failure to devise remedies for a situation, the misery, folly, and wickedness of which has been emphasised over and over again by Mr Asquith and Sir Edward Grey. Perhaps the central mischief is that diplomacy by secret treaties and dubious understandings has twisted and perverted the welcome friendship with France into a dangerous entanglement which has spoiled our relations with Germany. The result is that the military party in France has been encouraged to hope for British aid in an attack on Germany, while the Russian Government has used the moral prestige of our support for a policy of aggression and oppression in Finland and Persia. And worst of all for purely British interests the North Sea has become the scene of mutual suspicion and of warlike preparations unparalleled in cost and magnitude. Over the North Sea one half of our shipping and commerce passes daily. Our chief European customer and our best commercial friend among the great Powers is arming nervously and rapidly in order to protect her own mercantile marine from the menace of our greatly superior fleet. With equal nervousness and greater rapidity our own fleet is being enlarged regardless of cost. The awful warning of the Morocco crisis has gone by, but the sore is unhealed. Lord Haldane's mission to Berlin was ruined by Mr Churchill's warlike speeches. There have been faults on both sides; but who can doubt that the coldness and pessimism of our own Foreign Office has been a persistent obstacle to that Anglo-German entente which the peoples on both sides of the North Sea clearly desire?

We have been told over and over again that armaments depend upon policy. If this be true there must be something wrong in a policy which has increased the cost of armaments by 13 millions in four years. Our National Liberal Federation is the accredited organ of Liberalism. It has now a duty to perform to the Government and to the country. It has to ask for a change of policy which will remove the friction and suspicions by which war is generated, and thus lead to a reduction in armaments. Let us, at any rate of the National Liberal Federation, make known that we wish to live on terms of friendship and mutual confidence with our German neighbours.

We ask that the British Government shall frankly adopt the policy of exempting from capture all peaceful shipping and all peaceful property on sea in time of war. This is the American proposal, which was supported at the last Hague Conference by Germany and a majority of the Powers. If this policy is adopted, the main reason—the reason which has been accepted and endorsed by the German people—for the expansion of the German fleet will be removed, and the one great danger to our food supply in time of war will disappear.

Let it go forth from the National Liberal Federation that we demand and require a clear understanding—that English Liberalism at any rate shall have no part or lot in military and naval projects for an attack on Germany. This is a sane and a simple policy. In pressing it forward we are advocating an enlightened patriotism, and we are merely asking that the best traditions of Liberal policy should be maintained abroad as well as at home.

This is a personal and not an official letter, but I take this opportunity of strongly recommending to you the adoption by your Association of the two appended resolutions. They should be sent up to the N.L.F. not later than the *twenty-fifth* of this month.

Believe me,
Yours faithfully,

JOHN BRUNNER

RESOLUTION I

That this meeting, while heartily desiring a continuance of the friendly relations which have been established with France, urges the Government to make it clear that no understanding or intention is thereby implied as to military or naval action against any other Power, and further expresses a strong opinion that equally friendly relations upon a similar footing ought to be established with Germany.

RESOLUTION 2

That this meeting urges His Majesty's Government to enter into international treaties with the United States and other Powers for the purpose of securing all peaceful shipping and merchandise from capture or destruction in time of war.

SELECTED BIBLIOGRAPHY

MANUSCRIPTS AND RECORDS

The single most important source for the present study was the collection of correspondence, letterbooks, and family memorabilia in the possession of Sir Felix Brunner, Sir John's grandson at Grey's Court, near Henley-on-Thames, Oxfordshire. Among the other archives, public and private, that were consulted, those that yielded pertinent materials include:

Prof. Henry E. Armstrong Papers, Imperial College of Science and Technology, London.

H. H. Asquith [Earl of Oxford and Asquith] Papers, Bodleian Library, Oxford.

A. J. Balfour [Earl of Balfour] Papers, the British Museum, London.

Henry Broadhurst Papers, the British Library of Political and Economic Science, London.

Viscount Bryce Papers, Bodleian Library, Oxford.

John Burns Papers, the British Museum, London.

Sir Henry Campbell-Bannerman Papers, the British Museum, London.

Baron Courtney of Penwith Papers, the British Library of Political and Economic Science, London.

D. R. Daniel Papers, the National Library of Wales, Aberystwyth.

Sir Charles Dilke Papers, the British Museum, London.

T. E. Ellis Papers, the National Library of Wales, Aberystwyth.

R. C. K. Ensor Papers, Corpus Christi College, Oxford.

A. G. Gardiner Papers, courtesy of Mr Patrick Gardiner, Wytham, Oxfordshire.

Herbert [Viscount] Gladstone Papers, the British Museum, London.

W. E. Gladstone Papers, the British Museum, London.

Sir Edward Hamilton Papers, the British Museum, London.

J. L. Hammond Papers, Bodleian Library, Oxford.

Lewis [Viscount] Harcourt Papers, courtesy of Viscount Harcourt, Stanton Harcourt, Oxfordshire.

Imperial Chemical Industries, London and Winnington Hall, Cheshire.

Lancashire, Cheshire and North Western Liberal Federation, Manchester.

David Lloyd George [Earl Lloyd George of Dwyfor] Papers, Beaverbrook Library, London.

Reginald McKenna Papers, the Library, Churchill College, Cambridge.

Manchester Liberal Federation.

Leo J. Maxse Papers, County Record Office, Chichester, Sussex.

A. J. Mundella Papers, the University Library, Sheffield.

Arthur Ponsonby [Baron Ponsonby of Shulbrede] Papers, courtesy of Baron Ponsonby, Shulbrede Priory, Haslemere, Surrey.

C. P. Scott Papers, the British Museum, London; also copies of additional items, courtesy of D. G. O. Ayerst, official historian, the *Manchester Guardian*.

J. A. Spender Papers, the British Museum, London.

University of Liverpool archives.

OFFICIAL PAPERS AND DOCUMENTS

Parliamentary Debates (Hansard)

Parliamentary Papers

PRINTED SOURCES

Addison, Christopher: *Politics from Within*. 2 vols. London, 1924.

Albert Spicer, 1847–1934. London, 1938.

Albertini, Luigi: *The Origins of the War of 1914*. 3 vols. London, 1957.

Allen, J. Fenwick: *Some Founders of the Chemical Industry*. London, 1906.

Armytage, W. H. G.: *A. J. Mundella 1825–1897: The Liberal Background to the Labour Movement*. London, 1951.

Ashworth, William: *An Economic History of England, 1870–1939*. London, 1960.

Asquith, Earl of Oxford and: *Fifty Years of Parliament*. 2 vols. London, 1926.

The Genesis of the War. London, 1923.

Memories and Reflections. 2 vols. London, 1926.

Baker, Elizabeth B. and P. J. Noel: *J. Allen Baker, M.P., A Memoir*. London, 1927.

Bassett, Arthur T.: *The Life of the Rt. Hon. John Edward Ellis, M.P.* London, 1914.

Beer, Samuel H.: *British Politics in the Collectivist Age*, New York, 1965.

Birrell, Augustine: *Things Past Redress*. London, 1937.

Blunt, Wilfrid Scawen: *My Diaries*. 2 vols. London, 1919, 1920.

Bolitho, Hector: *Alfred Mond, first Lord Melchett*. New York, 1933.

Bonham Carter, Violet: *Winston Churchill as I Knew Him*. London, 1965.

Bottomley, J. K.: 'The Chemical Industry's Participation in Industrial Relations', in *Chemistry and Industry*, October 26, 1968.

Brebner, J. Bartlet: 'Laissez Faire and State Intervention in Nineteenth-Century Britain', in R. L. Schuyler and H. Ausubel, eds., *The Making of English History*. New York, 1966.

Brett, M. V., ed.: *Journals and Letters of Reginald, Viscount Esher*. Vols. II and III. London, 1934, 1938.

British Documents on the Origins of the War, 1898–1914. Vol. XI. London, 1926.

Broadhurst, Henry: *Henry Broadhurst, M.P., the story of his life from a stonemason's bench to the Treasury bench told by himself*. London, 1901.

Brown, E. H. Phelps: *The Growth of British Industrial Relations*. London, 1965.

Brunner, Sir John: *Copy Conveyance of Land and Buildings to be used as a Village Hall and School...at Barnton..., 8th January, 1898*. Liverpool, 1898.

Unveiling of the Statue of the late Dr. Ludwig Mond, F.R.S., at Winnington...13 September 1913. Liverpool, 1913?

A Scheme for the redistribution of Cheshire, with remarks on the proposals of the Boundary Commissioners. Liverpool, 1885? [Bodleian Gough Adds. Ches. 8° 54ᵉ/5].

Brunner, Sir John, and T. E. Ellis: *Public Education in Cheshire*. Manchester, 1890.

Brunner, Sir John, and J. Lawrence Hammond: *Public Education in Cheshire in 1896*. Manchester, 1896.

Brunner, J. F. L.: 'Industrial Politics', in *The Policy of Social Reform in England*. Brussels, 1913.

Butler, Jeffrey: *The Liberal Party and the Jameson Raid*. Oxford, 1968.

Calvert, Albert F.: *Salt in Cheshire*. London, 1915.

Checkland, S. G.: *The Rise of Industrial Society in England, 1815–1885*. New York, 1966.

Churchill, Winston S.: *The World Crisis*. 3 vols. New York, 1923–31.

Clapham, Sir John: *An Economic History of Modern Britain*. Vol. III. Cambridge, 1938.

Clark, G. Kitson: *The Making of Victorian England*. London, 1962.

Cline, Catherine Ann: *Recruits to Labour*. Syracuse, N.Y., 1963.

Cocks, H. F. L.: *The Nonconformist Conscience*. London, 1943.

Cohen, J. M.: *The Life of Ludwig Mond*. London, 1956.

Cole, G. D. H.: 'British Trade Unions in the Third Quarter of the Nineteenth Century', in E. M. Carus-Wilson, ed.: *Essays in Economic History*. Vol. III. New York, 1962.

Colman, Helen Caroline: *Jeremiah James Colman, a Memoir*. London, 1905.

Cooke, J. H.: *The Diamond Jubilee in Cheshire*. Warrington, 1899.

Corder, Percy: *The Life of Robert Spence Watson*. London, 1914.

Cruickshank, Marjorie: *Church and State in English Education, 1870 to the Present Day*. London, 1963.

Curtis, L. P., Jr: *Coercion and Conciliation in Ireland, 1880–1892*. Princeton, 1963.

Curtis, S. J. and M. E. A. Boultwood: *A Short History of Educational Ideas*. London, 1961.

Dangerfield, George: *The Strange Death of Liberal England*. London, 1935.

Dean, Joseph: *Hatred, Ridicule or Contempt*. New York, 1954.

de Guimps, Roger: *Pestalozzi, His Life and Work*. New York, 1890.

Derry, John W.: *The Radical Tradition*. London, 1967.

Diggle, George E.: *A History of Widnes*. Widnes, 1961.

SELECTED BIBLIOGRAPHY

Ensor, R. C. K.: *England, 1870–1914.* Oxford, 1963.

F. W. Hirst By His Friends. London, 1958.

Fischer, Fritz: *Germany's Aims in the First World War.* New York, 1967.

Fitzroy, Sir Almeric: *Memoirs.* 2 vols. London, 1927?

Forster, E. M.: *Goldsworthy Lowes Dickinson.* London, 1934.

Forwood, Sir W. B.: *Recollections of a Busy Life.* Liverpool, 1911.

Fyfe, Hamilton: *T. P. O'Connor.* London, 1934.

Gardiner, A. G.: *Life of George Cadbury.* London, 1923.

Life of Sir William Harcourt. 2 vols. London, 1923.

Glaser, J. F.: 'English Nonconformity and the Decline of Liberalism', *American Historical Review*, LXIII (1957–8), 352–63.

'Parnell's Fall and the Nonconformist Conscience', *Irish Historical Studies*, XII (1960), 119–38.

Gollin, Alfred M.: *The Observer and J. L. Garvin.* London, 1960.

Gooch, G. P.: *Under Six Reigns.* London, 1959.

Life of Lord Courtney. London, 1920.

Grey of Fallodon, Viscount: *Twenty-Five Years.* 2 vols. New York, 1925.

Gulley, Elsie E.: *Joseph Chamberlain and English Social Politics.* New York, 1926.

Hale, James Oron: *Publicity and Diplomacy.* Gloucester, Mass., 1964.

Halévy, Elie: *Imperialism and the Rise of Labour (1895–1905).* New York, 1961.

The Rule of Democracy (1905–1914). New York, 1961.

Hamer, D. A.: *John Morley: Liberal Intellectual in Politics.* London, 1968.

Hammond, J. L.: *C. P. Scott of the Manchester Guardian.* London, 1934.

Hanes, David G.: *The First British Workmen's Compensation Act, 1897.* New Haven, 1968.

Hanham, H. J.: *Elections and Party Management.* London, 1959.

Herrick, F. H.: 'The Origins of the National Liberal Federation', *Journal of Modern History*, XVII (1945), 116–29.

Healy, T. M.: *Letters and Leaders of My Day.* Vol. I. New York, 1929.

Hirst, F. W.: *In the Golden Days.* London, 1947.

The Political Economy of War. London, 1915.

See also *F. W. Hirst By His Friends.*

Holt, Raymond V.: *The Unitarian Contribution to Social Progress in England.* London, 1938.

Hughes, K. M.: 'A Political Party and Education: Reflections on the Liberal Party's Educational Policy, 1867–1902', *British Journal of Educational Studies*, VIII (1959–60), 111–26.

Hurst, Michael: *Joseph Chamberlain and Liberal Reunion.* London, 1967.

Hynes, Samuel: *The Edwardian Turn of Mind.* Princeton, 1968.

Inglis, K. S.: 'English Nonconformity and Social Reform, 1880–1900', *Past and Present*, XIII (1958), 73–88.

Irvine, A. S.: *A History of Winnington Hall.* Runcorn, 1966.

Jenkins, Roy: *Asquith.* London, 1964.

Jenkins, Roy: *Mr. Balfour's Poodle*. London, 1954.

Joll, James: *1914: The Unspoken Assumptions*. London, 1968.

Kent, William: *John Burns: Labour's Lost Leader*. London, 1950.

Koss, Stephen E.: 'The Destruction of Britain's Last Liberal Government',
 Journal of Modern History, XL (1968), 257–77.

 John Morley at the India Office, 1905–1910. New Haven, 1969.

 Lord Haldane: Scapegoat for Liberalism. New York, 1969.

 'Morley in the Middle', *English Historical Review*, LXXXII (1967), 553–62.

Lee, J. M.: *Social Leaders and Public Persons*. Oxford, 1963.

Lloyd George, David: *War Memoirs*. 2 vols. London, 1934?

Luke, W. B.: *Sir Wilfrid Lawson*. London, 1900.

Lyons, F. S. L.: *The Fall of Parnell, 1890–91*. London, 1960.

 John Dillon. London, 1968.

McCaffrey, L. J.: *The Irish Question, 1800–1922*. Lexington, Ky., 1968.

Maccoby, Simon: *English Radicalism, 1853–1886*. London, 1938.

 English Radicalism, 1886–1914. London, 1953.

 The English Radical Tradition, 1763–1914. New York, 1957.

McGill, Barry: 'Francis Schnadhorst and Liberal Party Organization',
 Journal of Modern History, XXXIV (1962), 19–39.

McKenna, Stephen: *Reginald McKenna*. London, 1948.

McLachlan, Herbert: *Records of a Family, 1800–1933*. Manchester, 1935.

Marder, A. J., ed.: *Fear God and Dread Nought*. 2 vols. London, 1956.

 From the Dreadnought to Scapa Flow. Vol. I. London, 1961.

Masterman, Lucy: *C. F. G. Masterman*. London, 1935.

Mond, Sir Alfred: *Questions of To-day and To-morrow*. London, 1912.

Monger, George: *The End of Isolation*. London, 1963.

Morley, John, Viscount: *The Life of William Ewart Gladstone*. Vol. III.
 London, 1903.

 Memorandum on Resignation. London, 1928.

 Recollections. 2 vols. New York, 1917.

Musson, A. E.: *Enterprise in Soap and Chemicals: Joseph Crosfield and Sons,
 Limited, 1815–1965*. Manchester, 1965.

Neilson, Francis: *My Life in Two Worlds*. 2 vols. Appleton, Wisc., 1952,
 1953.

Newton, David: *Sir Halley Stewart*. London, 1968.

O'Connor, T. P.: *Memoirs of an Old Parliamentarian*. 2 vols. London, 1929.

 'Men, Women, and Memories', *Sunday Times*, May 6, 1928.

 Sketches in the House. London, 1893.

Orchard, B. G.: *The Clerks of Liverpool*. Liverpool, 1871.

 Liverpool's Legion of Honour. Birkenhead, 1893.

Pelling, Henry: *A History of British Trade Unionism*. London (Pelican ed.),
 1963.

 The Origins of the Labour Party. Oxford, 1965.

 Popular Politics and Society in Late Victorian Britain. New York, 1968.

Poirier, Philip P.: *The Advent of the British Labour Party*. New York, 1958.

Pope, Wilson, and others: *The Story of the Star, 1888–1938*. London, 1938.

Porter, Bernard: *Critics of Empire*. London, 1968.

Pound, Reginald and Geoffrey Harmsworth: *Northcliffe*. London, 1959.

Rathbone, Eleanor F.: *William Rathbone, a Memoir*. London, 1908.

Reader, W. J.: *Life in Victorian England*. London, 1964.

Richardson, H. W.: 'Chemicals', in Derek H. Aldcroft, ed., *The Development of British Industry and Foreign Competition, 1875–1914*. London, 1968.

Richter, Louise M.: *Recollections of Dr. Ludwig Mond*. London, 1910?

Robson, Robert, ed.: *Ideas and Institutions of Victorian Britain*. London, 1967.

Rover, Constance: *Women's Suffrage and Party Politics in Britain, 1866–1914*. London, 1967.

Rowland, Peter: *The Last Liberal Governments*. New York, 1969.

Russell, G. W. E., ed.: *Sir Wilfrid Lawson, a Memoir*. London, 1909.

Shannon, R. T.: *Gladstone and the Bulgarian Agitation, 1876*. London, 1963.

Simey, Margaret B.: *Charitable Effort in Liverpool in the Nineteenth Century*. Liverpool, 1951.

Spender, J. A.: *Sir Robert Hudson, a Memoir*. London, 1930.

Spender, J. A. and Cyril Asquith: *Life of Lord Oxford and Asquith*. 2 vols. London, 1932.

Stansky, Peter: *Ambitions and Strategies*. Oxford, 1964.

Taylor, A. J. P.: *English History, 1914–1945*. Oxford, 1965.
  The Struggle for Mastery in Europe, 1848–1918. Oxford, 1957.
  The Troublemakers. London, 1964.

Thompson, Paul: *Socialists, Liberals and Labour: The Struggle for London, 1885–1914*. London, 1967.

Thornton, A. P.: *The Imperial Idea and its Enemies*. London, 1959.

Thorold, A.: *The Life of Henry Labouchere*. London, 1913.

Trevelyan, G. M.: *Grey of Fallodon*. London, 1937.

Vernon, Anne: *A Quaker Business Man: The Life of Joseph Rowntree, 1836–1925*. London, 1958.

Vincent, John: *The Formation of the Liberal Party*. London, 1966.
  Pollbooks: How Victorians Voted. Cambridge, 1967.

Watson, Robert Spence: *The National Liberal Federation from its Commencement to the General Election of 1906*. London, 1907.

Watts, John I.: *The First Fifty Years of Brunner, Mond and Company*. Derby, 1923.

Webb, Beatrice: *My Apprenticeship*. London, 1926.
  Our Partnership. London, 1948.

West, Sir Algernon: *Private Diaries*. London, 1922.

[Wilcox, Lucy, and others]: *Alexander Gordon Cummins Harvey, a Memoir*. London, 1925?

SELECTED BIBLIOGRAPHY

Wilson, Charles: *The History of Unilever*. 2 vols. London, 1954.
Wilson, Trevor: *The Downfall of the Liberal Party*. London, 1966.

SERIAL PUBLICATIONS

A wide range of newspapers and journals has been consulted, of which the most important include the *Contemporary Review*, the *Daily News*, the *Freeman's Journal*, the *Liberal Magazine*, the *Liberal and Radical*, the *Liverpool Courier*, the *Liverpool Daily Post and Mercury*, the *Manchester Guardian*, the *Nation*, the *National Review*, the *Northwich and Winsford Chronicle*, the *Observer*, the *Pall Mall Gazette*, the *Speaker*, the *Star*, *The Times*, *Truth*, and the *Westminster Gazette*.

INDEX

INDEX

Hague Conference, 233, 263
Haldane, R. B. (Viscount Haldane),
    Brunner's relations with, 190, 196, 214,
    281; joins 1905 Government, 201;
    War Office reforms, 214–15; goes to
    Berlin, 249–50, 251; wartime attacks
    upon, 275, 280; mentioned, 160, 218,
    254
Hallé, Sir Charles, 28
Hamilton, Sir Edward, 101, 112
Hammond, J. L., 11, 160, 167–8, 184,
    185, 257, 277, 278
Hampstead Garden Suburb, 211
Handley, James, 105
Harcourt, Lewis (1st Viscount Harcourt),
    78, 219, 254
Harcourt, Sir William, 61, 78, 105, 123,
    137, 142, 175, 178, 180, 182, 183
Hardie, Keir, 142, 146, 147
Harland, Edward, 31
Harmer family, 33
Harrington, Timothy, 127
Harrison, Frederic, 160
Hartington, Marquess of (8th Duke of
    Devonshire), 75, 77, 97, 98, 99, 103 n.,
    112, 113, 160, 241
Harvey, A. G. C., 230, 258, 263, 264
Healy, T. M., 157
Herkomer, Sir Hubert von, 224
Herschell, 1st Baron, 74
Herz, Henriette, 32
Hewitt, David B., 34
Hicks, Edward Lee, Bishop of Lincoln,
    266
Hicks-Beach, Sir Michael (1st Earl
    St Aldwyn), 124
Hill, Edward, 63
Himmelfarb, Gertrude, 141 n.
Hirst, F. W., personality of, 246; on
    Grey, 258; despairs of NLF, 263, 264;
    on Churchill, 267; on wartime politics,
    283, 284; counsels Brunner, 257, 285;
    mentioned, 231, 240, 254, 255, 273
Hobhouse, Charles, 266
Hobhouse, L. T., 232 n., 240, 255, 259
Hobson, J. A., 240
Holland, Charles M., 27, 32
Holland, Sir W. H., 198 n.
Holt, Richard, 230
Holt, Robert, 177
Home Rule, splits Liberal party, 1, 75 ff.,
    113, 241; Brunner on, 7, 54, 62, 72,
    75–7, 80, 82, 91, 96, 100, 132–3, 141,

162, 171, 173, 178, 190, 235, 236, 244;
    Chamberlain on, 76; and Gladstone,
    69, 88; spotlighted at Northwich,
    103–4, 107, 114; and Parnell, 134,
    138; NLF on, 243, 261; Asquith on,
    263; Mond rejects, 58–9; mentioned,
    172, 177, 229
Home Rule Bills, (1886), 75 ff., 100;
    (1893), 174
Home Rule Union, 132
House of Lords, reform of, 70, 71, 92,
    175, 177, 178, 208, 221, 234, 243;
    rejects Liberal legislation, 205, 207,
    236
Hudson, Sir Robert A., 52, 204, 243,
    254, 264, 269, 273, 285, 286
Hughes, Rev. Hugh Price, 136
Hutchinson, John, 13, 14, 19
Hutchinson and Sons, Widnes, 13, 21, 23 n.

Iddesleigh, 1st Earl of, see Sir Stafford
    Northcote
Ilbert, Sir Courtenay, 284
Ilkeston, by-election at (1887), 99
Illustrated London News, 113
Imperial Chemical Industries, 23, 26, 149
industrial relations, at BM & Co., 144 ff.,
    152–7, 274–5
International Arbitration League, 261,
    280
Inter-Parliamentary Union, 212
Ireland, see Home Rule
Irish National League, 63, 115, 126, 127,
    129
Irish Press Agency, 126
Irish Protestant Home Rule Association,
    127
Irvine, A. S., 29 n.
Irving, Sir Henry, 177

Jarmay, Gustave (Sir John Jarmay), 151,
    152, 155, 156, 275
Jayne, Francis John, Bishop of Chester,
    168
John Bull, 277
Joll, James, 270
Jones, Sir Alfred, 195
Jones, Leif (1st Baron Rhayader), 264
Jones-Griffith, Ellis, 137
Justice, 146

Kenrick family, 33
Khartoum, 182

308